Migration, Minorities and Citizenship

General Editors: **Zig Layton-Henry**, Professor of Politics, University of Warwick; and **Danièle Joly**, Director, Centre for Research in Ethnic Relations, University of Warwick

Titles include:

Muhammad Anwar, Patrick Roach and Ranjit Sondhi (*editors*)
FROM LEGISLATION TO INTEGRATION?
Race Relations in Britain

Naomi Carmon (*editor*)
IMMIGRATION AND INTEGRATION IN POST-INDUSTRIAL SOCIETIES
Theoretical Analysis and Policy-Related Research

Adrian Favell
PHILOSOPHIES OF INTEGRATION
Immigration and the Idea of Citizenship in France and Britain

Sophie Body-Gendrot and Marco Martiniello (*editors*)
MINORITIES IN EUROPEAN CITIES
The Dynamics of Social Integration and Social Exclusion at the Neighbourhood Level

Simon Holdaway and Anne-Marie Barron
RESIGNERS? THE EXPERIENCE OF BLACK AND ASIAN POLICE OFFICERS

Danièle Joly
HAVEN OR HELL?
Asylum Policies and Refugees in Europe
SCAPEGOATS AND SOCIAL ACTORS
The Exclusion and Integration of Minorities in Western and Eastern Europe

Jørgen S. Nielsen
TOWARDS A EUROPEAN ISLAM

John Rex
ETHNIC MINORITIES IN THE MODERN NATION STATE
Working Papers in the Theory of Multiculturalism and Political Integration

Carl-Ulrik Schierup (*editor*)
SCRAMBLE FOR THE BALKANS
Nationalism, Globalism and the Political Economy of Reconstruction

Steven Vertovec and Ceri Peach (*editors*)
ISLAM IN EUROPE
The Politics of Religion and Community

Östen Wahlbeck
KURDISH DIASPORAS
A Comparative Study of Kurdish Refugee Communities

Migration, Minorities and Citizenship
Series Standing Order ISBN 0-333-71047-9
(*outside North America only*)

You can receive future titles in this series as they are published by placing a standing order.
Please contact your bookseller or, in case of difficulty, write to us at the address below with
your name and address, the title of the series and the ISBN quoted above.

Customer Services Department, Macmillan Distribution Ltd, Houndmills, Basingstoke,
Hampshire RG21 6XS, England

Minorities in European Cities

The Dynamics of Social Integration and Social Exclusion at the Neighbourhood Level

Edited by

Sophie Body-Gendrot
Professor, University of the Sorbonne
Paris

and

Marco Martiniello
Senior Research Fellow
National Fund for Scientific Research
and
Director of CEDEM
University of Liège
Liège

in association with
CENTRE FOR RESEARCH IN ETHNIC RELATIONS
UNIVERSITY OF WARWICK

First published in Great Britain 2000 by
MACMILLAN PRESS LTD
Houndmills, Basingstoke, Hampshire RG21 6XS and London
Companies and representatives throughout the world

A catalogue record for this book is available from the British Library.

ISBN 0–333–75418–2

First published in the United States of America 2000 by
ST. MARTIN'S PRESS, INC.,
Scholarly and Reference Division,
175 Fifth Avenue, New York, N.Y. 10010

ISBN 0–312–23132–6

Library of Congress Cataloging-in-Publication Data
Minorities in European cities : the dynamics of social integration and social exclusion at the neighborhood level / edited by Sophie Body-Gendrot, Marco Martiniello.
p. cm. — (Migration, minorities, and citizenship)
Includes bibliographical references and index.
ISBN 0–312–23132–6 (cloth)
1. Minorities—Europe—Social conditions. 2. Social integration. 3. Cities and towns—Europe. 4. Europe—Emigration and immigration. I. Body-Gendrot, Sophie. II. Martiniello, Marco. III. Series.
HN377 .M56   2000
305.5'6'094—dc21

99–054922

This book is printed on paper suitable for recycling and made from fully managed and sustained forest sources.

10   9   8   7   6   5   4   3   2   1
09   08   07   06   05   04   03   02   01   00

Printed and bound in Great Britain by Antony Rowe Ltd, Chippenham, Wiltshire

Contents

v

PART III   POLITICAL INCLUSION/EXCLUSION AT THE NEIGHBOURHOOD LEVEL

PART IV   LAW AND ORDER, SECURITY AND JUSTICE

Acronyms and Abbreviations

ADR	alternative dispute resolution
ADRI	Agence pour le Développement des Relations intellectuelles
AMMU	Associatie Marokkaanse Migranten Utrecht (Association of Moroccan Migrants in Utrecht)
ASLK	Algemene Spaar en Lijfrentekas (a Belgian bank)
ATD	Aide à Toute Détresse (help for all distress)
ATMF	Association des Travailleurs Marocains en France
BBR	*bleu blanc rouge* (red, white and blue)
Caritas	Catholic welfare organization
CCILg	Conseil consultatif des Immigrés de la ville de Liège
CCPD	Conseil communal de Prévention de la Délinquance
CCPOE	Conseil consultatif pour les Populations d'origine étrangère
CGT	Confédération générale du Travail
FAJQ	Fédération des Associations des Jeunes de Quartier
IMES	Institute for Migration and Ethnic Studies
INED	National Demographic Institute, Paris
InIIS	Institute for Intercultural and International Studies
IREMAM	Institute for Studies and Research on the Arabic and Muslim World
ISEO	Institute for Socio-Economic Research, University of Rotterdam
ISHA	Institute of Applied Human Sciences, University of Paris IV
KMAN	Komitee Marokkaanse Arbeiders in Nederland (Association of Moroccan Workers in the Netherlands)
KMANU	Komitee Marokkaanse Arbeiders in Nederland sectie Utrecht (Association of Moroccan Workers in the Netherlands section of Utrecht)
MERCI	European Movement for the Recognition of Citizens
NYC	New York City

OECD	Organization for Economic Cooperation and Development
PKK	*Partiya Karkarên Kurdistan* (Kurdistan Workers' Party)
PMJU	Platform Marokkaanse Jongeren Utrecht (Platform of Moroccan Youth in Utrecht)
SOS	Save our Cities/SOS-Racisme
SUN	Socialistische Uitgeverij Nijmegen
TGV	très grande vitesse (high-speed train)
TRT	Turkish state television channel
UCL	University College of London
UMMON	Union of Moroccan Mosques in the Netherlands
UNEM	National Union of Moroccan Students
VVD	Volkspartij voor Vrijheid en Democratie (Popular Party for Freedom and Democracy)

Biographical Notes

Les Back is a lecturer in the Department of Sociology at Goldsmiths College, University of London. Among his recent publications are *New Ethnicities and Urban Culture* (London: UCL Press, 1996) and *Racism and Society* (with John Solomos, Basingstoke: Macmillan, 1996).

Sigrid Baringhorst is lecturer in politics and sociology in the School of Economic and Social Studies at the University of East Anglia (UK). Her books include *Politik als Kampagne: Zur symbolischen Konstruktion von Solidaritaet in Medienkampagnen* (Opladen: Westdeutscher Verlag, 1998) and, jointly edited with Mechtild M. Jansen and Martina Ritter, *Frauen in der Defensive? Zur backlash-Debatte in Deutschland* (Muenster: Lit, 1995).

Sophie Body-Gendrot, a political scientist, is a professor at the Sorbonne and at the Institute of Political Science. Her latest books are *Les Villes américaines: Les politiques urbaines* (Paris: Hachette, 1998) and *Ville et Violence* (Paris: Presses Universtaires de France, 1995).

Jean-Pierre Bonafe-Schmitt is a researcher in sociology of law at the GLYSI (CNRS-University Lyon II). He is the author of *La médiation une justice douce* (Syros-alternative, 1992).

Hassan Bousetta is a political scientist currently working at the Katholieke Universiteit in Brussels.

Jocelyne Cesari is a French political scientist. She is a principal research fellow at the National Centre for Scientific Research (CNRS) working in Aix-en-Provence at the Institute for Studies and Research on the Arabic and Muslim World (IREMAM). Her latest books include *Etre Musulman en France Aujourd'hui* (Paris: Hachette, 1997), *Géopolitique des Islams* (Paris: Economica, 1997) and *Faut-il avoir Peur de l'Islam?* (Paris: Presses de Science Politique, 1997).

Thomas Faist is Assistant Professor of Political Science at the Institute for Intercultural and International Studies (InIIS), University of Bremen, Germany. He is the author of *Social Citizenship for Whom? Young Turks in Germany and Mexican Americans in the United States* (1995); and co-editor and co-author of *International Migration, Immobility and Development: A Multi-Disciplinary Perspective* (1997).

Simon Holdaway is Professor of Sociology at Sheffield University. He is currently writing a book about visible minority officers' experience of employment in the Metropolitan Toronto Police.

Jef Huysmans is a lecturer at the London Centre of International Relations of the University of Kent at Canterbury. He has published in *Millennium, Cooperation and Conflict*, and *The European Journal of International Relations* and has contributed several chapters to edited volumes.

Christian Kesteloot is Research Director at the Belgian National Fund for Scientific Research, an associate professor at the Institute for Social and Economic Geography of the Catholic University of Leuven and a lecturer at the (French-speaking) Free University of Brussels.

Marco Martiniello, a sociologist and political scientist, is a senior research fellow at the National Fund for Scientific Research and director of the Centre d'Études de l'Ethnicité et des Migrations at the University of Liège, Belgium. He has recently published *Sortir des ghettos culturels* (Paris: Presses de Science Politique, 1997) and edited *Multicultural Policies and the State* (Utrecht: ERCOMER, 1998).

Henk Meert is a postdoctoral fellow of the Fund for Scientific Research in Flanders. He is affiliated to the Institute of Social and Economic Geography at the Catholic University in Leuven. He was the editor of *Vlaams-Brabant: wonen en werken in de schaduw van Brussel* (Flemish-Brabant: Living and Working in the Shadow of Brussels) (1993).

Michel Péraldi is a sociologist working at the CNRS's Laboratoire Méditerranéen de Sociologie. For the last three years, he has been engaged in a research project on the informal economy in the Euro-Mediterranean metropolis.

Fabio Quassoli is a postdoctoral fellow at the Universty of Pavia. Among his recent publications are *La formazione linguistica per lavoratori stranieri: dare voce ai diritti e alle risorse* (Milan: Franco Angeli, 1997, with Cristina Venzo), and *La comunicazione degli immigrati a Milano, Quaderni ISMU* (Milan: Franco Angeli, 1997 with Paolo Barbesino).

Jan Rath coordinates a programme on immigrant businesses, comprising an international comparative study of the clothing contract industry, with special reference to Amsterdam. He is the editor of *Immigrant Businesses in the Urban Economic Fringe* (Basingstoke: Macmillan, 1998), and co-editor of *Immigrant Entrepreneurship in the Netherlands* (1998).

Patrick Simon is a senior researcher at the National Demographic Institute in Paris (INED) and a lecturer in demography at the Institute of Applied Human Sciences, University of Paris IV (ISHA).

John Solomos is Professor of Sociology and Social Policy at the University of South Bank. Among his publications are *Race, Politics and Social Change* (with Les Back, 1995) and *Racism and Society* (with Les Back, 1996).

Aristide R. Zolberg is university-in-exile professor at the graduate faculty of the New School for Social Research in New York City. He is also director of the International Center for Migration, Ethnicity and Citizenship. He has written extensively in the fields of comparative politics and historical sociology, on ethnic conflict and immigration and refugee issues, in both English and French.

Preface
Aristide R. Zolberg

Thanks to the original initiative of the editors, the contributions assembled in this volume provide an unprecedented opportunity to gain an intimate glimpse of the dynamics of social integration and social exclusion that govern the lives of minorities in European cities. Although most of the chapters focus on particularistic interactions at the level of the neighbourhood, each of them also reveals explicitly or implicitly how the 'local' is indelibly marked by the 'global'. Hence it is appropriate in this preface to briefly reflect on the larger structural forces that are at the root of the processes under examination, while also locating the present moment in an historical context.

In short, we appear to be caught up in a *film noir* whose *auteur* is none other than Karl Marx. European cities as presently constituted – much like their transatlantic counterparts – are largely the product of imperatives generated by the world capitalist economy in the course of earlier phases of its development. However, as Daniel Bell observed as far back as a quarter of a century ago, we are now at the dawn of 'post-industrial society' (Bell, 1973: 165–265). Driven by an unprecedented avalanche of technological innovations, and extending their domain to encompass the world as a whole – the multifaceted phenomenon commonly termed 'globalization' – contemporary changes amount to an evolutionary step in the development of the 'productive forces' to which Marx attributed explanatory primacy. Whether or not one subscribes to Marx's theory of history, there is every reason to expect that such a profound transformation will bring about fundamental changes in every sphere of every society throughout the globe.

With regard to Europe and the other affluent democracies, one thing is quite certain: much as the advent of industrial capitalism brought about conditions that fostered the distinctive social formation we term 'working class', the waning of these conditions undermines its continued existence. Industrial workers, whose struggles brought about the welfare state, are rapidly disappearing as a constituted class, leaving the vast urban expanses that were their historical home bereft of purpose. Whereas most of the descendants of earlier working-class generations have moved out, both socially and spatially, the latest to join their ranks live on as beleaguered human beings who, in the brutal perspective of short-term economic rationality, constitute a burdensome and unmanageable 'surplus'.

The industrial world's cities were brought to life by the need for gigantic quantities of muscular labour, spatially concentrated where the requirements of mechanical production powered by coal and water dictated. Where there were only 23 European towns of more than 100,000 in 1800, there were 135 a century later (Moch, 1992: 126). The phase of speeded-up growth to unprecedented size was inaugurated in Britain, where the first factory towns like Manchester mushroomed at the end of the eighteenth century; on the Continent, capitals began to expand after the Napoleonic wars, and new factory towns began to appear as well. Although Europe had entered into a phase of rapid population growth induced by a drop in the death rate, initially the cities themselves remained death traps, whose rate of natural reproduction fell below the replacement level; hence, most of this spectacular transformation was attributable to migration.

The monstrous agglomerations fed on the desperate masses uprooted in neighbouring rural regions by the modernization of agriculture and the extinction of local crafts and proto-industrial establishments. The remaining rural industries were wiped out by the crises of the late 1840s, propelling the structurally unemployed to relocate permanently. However, the European economies revived, and the boom years that followed through the 1870s fostered an unprecedented expansion of the urban markets for labour. In the more advanced countries, many of the remaining peasants were uprooted in the 1880s, when agricultural prices collapsed under the impact of massive imports from overseas, where, thanks to the lower costs of land and the advances of mechanization, the costs of production were much lower. Concurrently, the 'second industrial revolution' – powered by electricity and eventually petroleum – stimulated the further expansion of the industrial cities. Eventually, these became less deadly, and more of their growth was due to natural increase rather than migration. Again, England was the pioneer: London had a self-maintaining population as of 1800 and, in the second half of the century, only 16 per cent of its growth was attributable to in-migration. The turning point in Sweden occurred between 1850 and 1860. However, Italian and French cities remained immigrant worlds: for example, 64 per cent of the net expansion of the Paris population was due to immigration.

Although the majority of urban migrants came from within the region, these movements included some sizeable international migrations, such as the Flemings who crossed the border from Belgium into French Flanders, the Italians who moved to France along the Mediterranean littoral, and the Poles who carried out seasonal labour in east Prussia. However, long distance movements arose remarkably early on as well, and with greater distance came also, in many cases, greater difference. By 1840, when Engels carried out his detailed study of Manchester as the preview of things to come, some 40 per cent of its workers were Irish. With the advent of the railroad, which revolutionized migrations within Europe much as the steamship did with respect to overseas movement, labour markets vastly expanded their domain: by Bismarck's time, Poles were no longer confined to east Prussian agriculture, but surfaced also in the burgeoning industry of the Ruhr. While considerable attention has been given to the movement of east European Jews to North America, one should remember also that concurrently, this population also flowed toward western Europe and gave rise to the formation of distinct proletariats in Berlin, Paris, London, Vienna, and Amsterdam.

Wherever historical research has been carried out, it reveals that immigrant groups from near and far colonized distinct neighbourhoods, imparting to working-class neighbourhoods a mosaic character similar to the one observed today, governed by proximity to places of employment, the real estate market, and social exclusion. A case in point are the occupational and geographical niches carved out in mid-nineteenth century Paris by French provincials from the Auvergne, Brittany, and Limousin, soon followed by Italian construction workers as well as Jewish garment workers from Poland and Russia (Green, 1986). Within Belgium, the Dutch-speaking Flemings who migrated to the country's industrial cities, located only a few dozen kilometres away in the French-speaking Walloon south, were as 'strange' to the local population as they would be had they come from a different country altogether. It is noteworthy that in every case, the 'strangers' were perceived by the 'natives' as an unfair instrument manipulated by the bosses to break solidarity and resistance, and hence regarded as a source of their misery. The presence of a substantial Irish minority in the ranks of England's industrial workforce was identified by Marx early on as a major source of tension and division within the British working class as a whole, and one remembers also the hatred of the intruding Belgians expressed by the French miners in Zola's *Germinal*.

In summary, in the early phases of the industrial age, the cities were conflictual arenas where uprooted members of disparate peasant societies were brutally transformed into a national working class. By the same token, cultural groups hitherto separated by space were brought into sudden confrontation. Although contemporary social scientific and political discourse is founded on a categoric difference between internal 'migrants' and foreign 'immigrants', with regard to interactions between groups and in the perspective of the dynamics of social integration and exclusion, the distinction is quite artificial and irrelevant. This is applicable also to the notion of 'minorities': whereas in Europe today the term evokes people of colour whose presence is attributable to relatively recent immigration, it acquires greater heuristic value when used more analytically, referring to a particular type of *structured social relationship*. It then becomes evident that the formation of minorities has occurred all along, because it is an intrinsic feature of the formation of urban labour markets in capitalist economies.

The procurement of workers from a source external to the society, and their exclusion from the host community after they are brought in, is a recurrent pattern of social organization in the history of western societies, in Europe and overseas. The dynamics at work can be summarized by way of a blunt phrase, 'Wanted but not Welcome'. The combination of a positive desire to recruit workers from particular groups and of a negative desire to keep them out makes for a classic 'dialectic', giving rise to social patterns that constitute 'solutions' to 'contradictions.' However, it should be expected that sooner or later, the contradictions will undermine the pattern, which is then likely to collapse and gives way to another.

The perennial use of 'stranger workers' arises not simply from the fact that they usually draw lower wages, but is grounded in the structure of the international economic system. In economies that experience significant fluctuations in demand for labour, there are some marked advantages in being able to maintain a 'reserve' to park workers when they are not needed. Because of differences of skills, there are advantages in distinguishing between 'permanent' and 'disposable' workers (Piore, 1979, and Gordon et al., 1982 analyse the economic dynamics in question). As when it comes to storing goods that are not immediately needed, it makes sense to store the reserve where this can be done at the lowest cost – in peripheral areas, or even in another country altogether. Since workers are also actors, there is a steady tendency to incorporate workers from older sources (in effect, 'natives') into the 'permanent' category who benefit from a broad array of rights, while replenishing the 'disposable' category with newcomers – who are likely to be culturally distinct. From the perspective of dominant groups, this has the added advantage of facilitating discipline: as suggested by the old Roman imperial dictum, 'divide in order to rule', marked cultural (including racial) divisions among the labour force – a pattern that has been termed 'split labour' – maximizes the bargaining power of employers by enhancing the difficulties of achieving solidarity (Bonacich, 1972: 547–9).

Selected according to rational economic criteria, notably willingness to work for very low wages and under harsh or dangerous conditions, 'disposable' workers are usually drawn from some less developed country or region, which belongs to the world of 'others' in opposition to which the hosts have elaborated their identity; and the work they do in the country of immigration as well as the living conditions to which they are subjected ensures that the separation between the segments widens. This process of 'differential incorporation' thus precipitates the formation of 'minorities' (Portes, 1981: 279–97).

Historically, this process was further induced by wilful state-enforced segregation, of which slavery and modern apartheid are the archetypes, as well as milder forms of control designed to prevent settlement, such as limiting the intake to single men or single women, rotating recruitment, restricting them to the jobs for which they were imported, and confining them to residence in special hostels. Other devices include the erection of obstacles to naturalization, either by way of the categoric exclusion of certain groups, as with people of colour in the United States from 1790 onward, or the imposition of long waiting periods and expensive procedures, as in Switzerland and Germany.

However, most of these practices conflict with contemporary norms regarding the treatment of human beings in democratic societies and hence are no longer acceptable. These constraints on their hosts enabled many of the 'disposable' workers recruited in the post-Second World War period to turn themselves along with their families into 'immigrants', and eventually into citizens – or at least, secured this status for their children. However, as amply demonstrated in the contributions to the present volume, in most cases this was not sufficient to overcome fully the dynamics of segmented incorporation.

Unfortunately, the advent of post-industrial society and of globalization exacerbate the inherent difficulties of the process of incorporation. The proportion of secondary-sector workers among the economically active population of the more developed countries peaked in the early postwar decades, when the latest 'disposable' workers were recruited, and is now well into an irreversible decline (Gordon, 1988: 24–65).[1] Moreover, even before the onset of the 'oil shock', industrialists 'reacted aggressively' to the 'increasing strangulation' effected by the welfare state (van der Wee, 1987). As is well known, multinationals began to look to the Third World, in particular to the newly industrialized countries, where enormous unemployment, both open and concealed, meant that wages could be kept low, and unions were weak or nonexistent. Operating with little or no interference from national governments in the Third World, and simultaneously escaping the control of Western governments, 'they were thus in a position to restore a liberal market system in the world economy'. This further accelerated the deindustrialization of the West, especially in the old industrial regions, in whose cities the growing ranks of unemployed natives found themselves sharing their misery with a growing body of unemployed immigrants.

One of the most ominous aspects of the present-day situation is the deterioration of the public sphere in the receiving societies, and particularly of institutions that hitherto played a major role in incorporating the lower classes, including successive waves of immigrants, into the body politic. Among the most important are the mass political parties that arose in the late nineteenth century on both sides of the Atlantic in response to the rapid expansion of electorates, as well as the labour unions. The decline of these organizations reflects major changes in the nature of work, notably the shrinking of the urban 'blue collar' sector, which commonly provided to immigrants reachable rungs on the ladder of mobility (see Zolberg, 1995, for elaboration of this point). As well, the universal military service institutions of the age of mass armies, which played a major role in incorporating male immigrants in the United States, the overseas Commonwealth, and France in the first half of the twentieth century, have generally been replaced by professional bodies. Given the waning of other institutions, much of the burden of incorporation rests by default on the urban educational sector, which consequently has emerged as a prime arena of contention.

Some of these changes are probably irreversible, and others may be highly desirable: hardly anyone would advocate the revival of major international conflicts so that young male natives and immigrants have an opportunity to learn to live together in the barracks, or of the iron discipline of Taylorized River Rouge and Boulogne-Billancourt automobile assembly plants just so that immigrants might be turned more easily into Frenchmen or Americans. But if not these, what can take their place?

Evidence from reliable research overwhelmingly indicates that current interactions between residents and newcomers are not undermining the integrity of host communities on either side of the Atlantic. However, on the down side, there are disturbing findings that low-skilled immigrants, including especially those of tenuous legal status, tend to be recruited into secondary labour markets, and concomitantly display isolated patterns of settlement, with little or no contact with the host society. Less of the immigrants' making than a result of structures and policies of the host society, in the absence of remedial action such undesirable patterns might be reinforced. It is therefore evident that the task of incorporation cannot be left to the free play of market forces, but requires a major commitment of public action. One thing is clear: the dismantling of the public sector, as advocated by new-breed conservatives is likely to be highly counterproductive. Democracies cannot survive as 'separate and unequal' societies.

As pioneering accounts, the observations and analyses of contemporary life in European cities assembled in this volume are reminiscent of the proliferation of efforts at understanding stimulated by the horrendous conditions prevailing in European cities in the middle third of the nineteenth century. One path led to the emergence of an entirely new literary genre, the social novel, which produced such enduring English classics as Dickens's *Oliver Twist* (1838), Benjamin Disraeli's *Sybil*, or the *Two Nations* (1845), or on the other side of the channel, Eugene Süe's unduly forgotten *Les Mystères de Paris* (1842–43). Another approach, purporting to decode the dynamics that produced these conditions in a more systematic manner, generated an entirely new intellectual pursuit, the social sciences. This transnational undertaking, involving Marx, Comte, Spencer, Le Play, Le Bon, and many others, produced seminal theories of social integration and social exclusion. Although they still speak to us today, we must also free ourselves of their limitations and reconstruct our theories in the light of a realistic understanding of our unique circumstances.

Note

1. However, Britain, historically the most industrialized country, reached its maximum proportion of 51.6 per cent as early as 1911; for second-run Belgium it was 48.6 per cent in 1947. In the United States the peak came on the eve of the Great Depression, and it is significant that the 'disposable' immigrant workers of the post-Second World War period were used mainly in agriculture.

1 Introduction: The Dynamics of Social Integration and Social Exclusion at the Neighbourhood Level

Sophie Body-Gendrot and Marco Martiniello

Without entering into the debates about the global city and the thesis of polarization (Mollenkopf and Castells, 1991; Sassen, 1991), no one will deny that the context of economic restructuring has an impact on the social integration of the most vulnerable groups, among them immigrant groups. The industrial European city was loaded with social problems but gradually, towards the end of the twentieth century, an almost full-salaried society was getting more benefits shared by more and more categories of the population, including both nationals and non-nationals (Castel, 1994). The new mutations impacting on cities concern:

1. technological developments transforming the job requirements and the modes of living of many populations;
2. the expansion of financial, capital and labour flux and their impact on national societies; and
3. the obsolescence of a welfare-state model according to which protections against risks and the continuity of social bonds came from the apparatus of the state (Habermas, 1990).

By and large, European states undergo similar trends of hollowing out. They fragment into structured, ramified and de-centred networks.

Immigrants have settled or moved to European cities submitted to such global/national changes. Variations occur according to national contexts, but convergences are also observed. Where there used to be a sense of social cohesion and progress, there are instead communication networking, selective markets and increased competition. Unlike the welfare state, the market produces neither global social cohesion nor a reduction of ine-qualities, but it widens socioeconomic and spatial inequalities in large cities as those located at the top of the social spectrum increase spectacularly their wealth. As the European state experiences difficulties cushioning dis-parities, new centralities and marginalities emerge via blurred definitions (McGregor, 1996; Mollenkopf, 1997a; Préteceille, 1998; Wilson, 1996).

Neighbourhoods are microcosms at the epicentre of larger problems; they exhibit forcefully the consequences of the choices political majorities do not make in our democracies. In other words, with the erosion of grand narratives, the former dramatic reading focusing on social classes and on their involvement in their future has given place to a topographic reading of contagion, flux, territorialization, disconnection and violence. In a binary logic, the emphasis is set as much on dangerous places, no-go areas, ghettos or barrios as on a so-called *underclass*. A recurrent dis-course of fear has taken place since the beginning of cities, but it gets its hyperbole with new immigrants, especially if they are undocumented and do not abide by the laws.

The public support given to deprived groups is a crucial question. In periods of accelerated mutations and fiscal austerity, what is at stake is not only how high the piles are but also who sits at the table (Gitlin, 1996). Poor immigrants and minorities know that they are unwelcome at the club called 'nation' and are not invited to participate in projects elaborated for their children's future. Yet the cleavage is not only between nationals and non-nationals but also between those who have rights and those who do not or are not even conscious that they have rights.

RACE AND ETHNICITY IN THE NEIGHBOURHOODS

At the same time, on such global phenomena abounding in Western post-industrial societies, European characteristics are noticeable. In such cross-national comparisons, the first striking difference from Anglo-American societies is in the importance given to identity politics and race, ethnicity and gender in the formation of neighbourhood identities. It is interesting that, on public disorder and ethnic and racial clashes in disadvantaged communities (Christopher (1991); Kerner (1968); and Scarman (1981) reports), numerous US and British reports emphasize the roles that discrim-inating factors and contexts of institutional racism weighing on minorities play in triggering events. Conversely, dominant French discourses (see Cardo (1992); Delarue (1991); Dray (1992); and Perez (1995) reports) hardly ever mention institutional racism or the problematic attitude of the police in conflict-ridden communities. Because of an ideology of assimilation, links between race, ethnicity and deprivation are rarely taken into account. In the USA, on the other hand, every urban issue evokes a discussion about race. The debt from slavery constantly recurs in sociopolitical debates. Just as race as a category cannot disappear from the census, race will remain a principle of mobilization (Winant, 1995). Immigrant success and mobility are therefore perceived with the black/ white background in mind (Steinberg, 1995). Take the strategy of Mayor Guliani in New York City: immigrants are the success story he likes to tell, as previous mayors of the Big Apple did, immigrants are his economic policy of development, immigrants make New York a global city.

In the UK, the colonial circumstances of exploitation are at the core of the race relations' literature. According to John Crowley, British sociology of race relations commits itself to the interests of minority groups. It asserts itself as a principle of analysis linked to a principle of political mobilization based on antiracism (Crowley, 1997). But in France, the obsession in the dominant discourse with 'a one and indivisible nation' imposed from the top by institutions has led to a general amnesia about the diversity of identity groups making the nation. Apart from a small group of social scientists focusing on inter-ethnic relations, most researchers (who tend to have a civil servant status) espouse institutional categories and do not allow themselves to follow the British path of research. Those who do have been given a hard time (Tribalat, 1995). A voluntary doubt seems to persist among researchers over whether concerned actors from poor neighbourhoods find more resources in and form their strategies from their ethnic/racial grievances or from their territorial identity. The question remains open, though a radicalization of identities is possibly based on territorialized ethnic logic, a territory that is both real and imagined, emotional and subjective.

INSTITUTIONAL INTERVENTIONS

Another European characteristic has to do with the role of the middle classes and with a less severe spatial segregation than in the United States. First, it is difficult to see at the core of European cities a mere interface of yuppies and Third World populations. In many European cities, the middle classes have not deserted the city centres to participate in suburbanization as massively as they have in the USA. Their strategic position is fundamental and infers on theoretical configurations. The middle classes interact with migrants and minorities both at work, for instance as civil servants, and in the neighbourhoods in which they live. They may therefore want the state to intervene to slow down the precariousness that is hitting those categories, but that could also sooner or later hit them or their children. It is a self-served solidarity (Body-Gendrot, 1996b).

Second, another major difference concerns state intervention and the public treatment of social protection. Non-intervention by the state and competition between groups is more a feature of a country like the USA, with its philosophy that oiling the wheels of the job machine and reducing the budget deficit will take care of social tensions. European analyses deconstruct such *laissez-faire* schemes and reintroduce national, regional and local variables. In France, where expectations of state intervention remain strong, at least for one vulnerable half of the population that did not support the referendum on the Maastricht treaty, restricted public resources imply that the days of the benevolent state are counted. It has an increasingly limited margin of action with which to respond to new social challenges: available funds are absorbed by the salaries of public employees (25 per cent of the active population), by pensions, by allocations for the unemployed, and other mandatory social transfers. The state is also caught in an internationally interdependent environment that has reordered its priorities: defence of the currency, sharp global economic competition, foreign relations and diplomatic ties. At budget time, these considerations take priority on the agenda over social redistribution and the reduction of inequalities.

The increasing complexity of society and the wide range of demands from users as well as citizens reveal the inability of central governments to impose rules from the top. According to that perspective, European countries, including France, tend to valorize a local treatment closer to the citizens. It is what some call a 'hyperlocalization of the social' and the relegation of the treatment of complex social problems to the local sphere. As the city becomes the mirror of globalization and experiences social and economic fractures, it also then becomes an arena of contention with major stakes. Everyone knows that the tide does not lift all the boats. The perplexing question relates to how movements of social action relate to elite behaviour, and how the actions of the elite mould the protest environment, in other words, how the structures play out from above, and not simply how they act from below (Schain, 1994: 67). Protest forms include immigrants and their children and the governance of complex societies (Le Galès and Bagnasco, 1997).

Mobilizations in immigrant and mixed neighbourhoods reveal that a state's functions are being questioned. Such mobilizations express the emergence of forms of transversal citizenship. They show how identities amalgamate and on which basis they support action. Democratic processes sometimes dissolve tensions, while spaces of memories sometimes exasperate them. The growth of inequalities, uneven upward mobility and the failure of redistributive policies also reinforce the depacification of our societies. When the rules of the democratic game seem biased in the housing, education, labour and civil rights' arenas, resorting to direct action makes sense. Controlling the margins of global centralities calls for tightening law and order at local, national and international levels.

THE STRUCTURE OF THE BOOK

The present volume is meant to be a European state-of-the-art examination of issues pertaining to immigrant minorities' dynamics of social integration and social exclusion at the neighbourhood level. To take the complexity of the subject into account, the volume is divided into four parts. In the first part, the question of the participation and exclusion of migrants in the field of economics is examined. In his analysis, Thomas Faist clarifies some basic concepts, such as transnational social space or social capital, which are seen as fulfilling crucial bridging functions, linking networks and collectives, in different nation-states. Focusing on the German end, he documents the emergence of ethnic Turkish businesses in Germany and the creation of transnational businesses spanning both countries with direct investment in Turkey from Turkish entrepreneurs living in Germany. However, such trends may become more limited in the future. For his part, Jan Rath deconstructs the patterns of economic incorporation as defined by Roger Waldinger for New York and Los Angeles. The situation is different in Amsterdam, where ethnic concentration and niche succession are not the only components necessary for economic incorporation. Market development has to be taken into account as well as the enforcement of rules and regulations in a specific country. The case of Marseilles illustrates such idiosyncrasies. There, Michel Péraldi explains that a real commercial system has progressively developed in the old central neighbourhoods of Marseilles, which are in deep crisis. This commercial dynamism has promoted unemployed youth living in huge public housing projects into informal commercial 'careers'. Péraldi analyses the conditions of access, the social and relational competencies displayed by these youth, as well as the reasons why they choose the underground economy. Christian Kesteloot adds the factor of housing in his analysis of the immigrants' economic incorporation in Brussels. Restriction to better segments of the housing market has given way to consolidated ethnic neighbourhoods distinguished from one another in terms of networks, location and infrastructures. These differences generate diverse economic potentials such as reciprocity, redistribution and market exchange.

The second part deals with social relations at the neighbourhood level and their impact on exclusion/inclusion. Bringing a dynamic perspective to the analysis of community integration, Sophie Body-Gendrot looks at diminished protection against risks and the erosion of welfare states in an era of globalization and increased competition. She shows that, as actors, immigrant and minority groups may pursue diverse strategies (calls for social justice, self-help or instrumental violence). Race and ethnicity may intervene in the mobilizations. A cross-national comparison examines the diversity of institutional responses. Jocelyne Cesari shows that three dimensions help define Islamic identities in the European urban context – the status of Islam in the home country, the status of ethnic groups in the host countries, and the context of globalization. Organizations and mobilizations are often based on ethnic or cultural ties and transnational networks rather than on a universal Islamic identity. In each country, the nation's political and cultural characteristics – the statuses of religion in France, of ethnicity in the UK, and of nationality in Germany – shape the issues. Patrick Simon examines an original model of local integration and social control in an historical working-class Parisian neighbourhood, Belleville. Jews and Arabs from the Maghreb, Asians, black Africans, Turks, old French workers and new residents from the middle and upper-middle classes all share a strong local identity. The Belleville model refers to a mosaic as both a topographic metaphor and a sociological concept.

Generally, the inclusion/exclusion debate focuses either on the social and economic aspects or on the law and order dimension. The political aspects of exclusion, and how they are articulated with social and economic exclusion, are often neglected. The incorporation of migrants and their offspring in a changing labour market has received wide attention, as has the issue of ethnic crime and social dislocation in urban settings. The various forms of political exclusion and/or of non-participation of migrant origin population in the local public sphere and in the political and policy-making processes of cities and underprivileged neighbourhoods are more rarely studied. However, they may be expected to have crucial implications for the development of an active local citizenship and for social integration and solidarity. This issue is examined in the third part of the book. In Chapter 9, Marco Martiniello deals with a specific aspect of the political participation and representation debate that is highly relevant at the neighbourhood level throughout Europe. This is the possible link between immigrant and ethnic-minority populations' residential concentration and their political mobilization, participation and representation. Hassan Bousetta (Chapter 10) analyses the collective dynamics, sociopolitical participation and ethnic mobilization of immigrant minorities. His chapter is based on comparative case studies of Moroccan communities in three medium-sized cities, namely Liège, Utrecht and Lille. John Solomos and Les Back, whose chapter is based on research conducted in Birmingham (UK), are concerned with three intertwined processes. These are the historical context that has shaped the political understandings of race within British political culture and institutions; the mechanisms ethnic minorities use to mobilize themselves politically; and the responses of political parties and institutions to racial and ethnic questions. In the final chapter of the third part, Sigrid Baringhorst looks at various public campaigns that have been launched to struggle against racism and to promote multicultural understanding in some German cities.

Finally, in the fourth part of the volume, we see how conceptions of law and order and security, as well as the institutional praxis they engender, affect migrants' exclusion/inclusion opportunities. Jef Huysmans examines the implications of the growing discourse on security in the migration area (Chapter 13). Simon Holdaway deals with the very delicate question of migration and crime in European cities. He draws attention to the need for small-scale studies, including research at the neighbourhood level. In Chapter 15, Fabio Quassoli looks at the construction of migrants as criminals in the Italian context. More precisely, drawing on ethnographic research in the courts of Milan, he shows how the judicial system can turn migrants into criminals in a northern Italian city. Finally, Jean-Pierre Bonafé-Schmitt deals with a specific attempt to find a solution to urban conflict in France, namely the process of mediation.

A theoretical or general chapter introduces each part of the volume. This is followed by three case studies that reflect what we know in Europe about the issues under investigation and rely on empirical data drawn from local studies. Among the cities covered are Amsterdam, Brussels, Marseilles, Milan, Paris, Birmingham, Utrecht and Lille. While these case studies show how diversified Europe can be, they also reveal some basic similarities with respect to the social exclusion and inclusion of migrants at the local level.

Part I

Participation/Exclusion of Migrants in the Field of Economics

2 Economic Activities of Migrants in Transnational Social Spaces

Thomas Faist

FROM INTERNATIONAL MIGRATION TO TRANSNATIONAL SOCIAL SPACES?[1]

For viewers of the Turkish government channel TRT Avraysa on German cable television, it is obvious that some Turkish immigrants' children in Germany have embarked on successful music careers in both Turkey and Germany. For example, during the summer of 1995, the German-based Turkish rap group 'Cartel' (now disbanded) replaced Michael Jackson as number one in the Turkish charts. Also, the nightly news on German TV usually features reports on the widely known Kurdish political-military organization – the *Partiya Karkarên Kurdistan* (PKK, Kurdistan Workers' Party). The PKK not only operates in Turkey but also tries to influence German politicians to exert pressure on its Turkish counterpart. Moreover, TV programmes for Turkey are often produced in Germany and vice versa. For example, the state television TRT produces about a quarter of its shows for viewers of TRT Avrasya in Germany. Another example of transnational linkages developing in the course of international migration is the growing presence of Islamist groups. Being denied a formal status in Turkey in the 1970s and 1980s, these organizations grew and flourished in Germany. Also, it has been obvious that Turkish migrants' remittances, though declining, have been complemented by a flow of goods and information in the other direction. In addition, capital flows are gradually replacing remittances. For example, some Turkish migrants' children have been investing in textile production in Turkey and marketing the products in Germany. Similar observations can be made for many of the origins and destinations of labour migrant and refugee flows in the contemporary world (see, for example, Pessar, 1997).

All these examples point to a circular flow of persons, goods, information and symbols that have been triggered by international labour migration and refugee flows. These circuits include the circulation of ideas, symbols and material culture, not only the movement of people. The question is how such transnational phenomena in economics, politics, culture and religion can be described, categorized and explained. As the above anecdotal examples suggest, these phenomena may not be limited to the first generation of migrants. Rather, even second and third generations have developed forms of transnational linkages of their own.

The analysis focuses on the *interstices* between nation-state and the global elements of economic activity. Transnational social spaces develop in two stages. In a first phase they are a by-product of international migration and are basically limited to first-generation migrants. Researchers have long recognized that migration is not simply a transfer from one place to another with few social and material links. Rather, migration usually generates continual exchanges between geographically distant communities and migrants do not automatically sever their ties to the sending countries (Werbner, 1990: 3). As a matter of fact, migrant networks characterize migration flows. In turn, international migrations are often also characterized by ongoing processes of return migration, where recurrent migrants regularly go home for varying periods each year, or migrants return for good to their communities of origin. After all, it has long been a truism that every migration stream breeds a counter stream.

In a second phase, transnational social spaces go beyond the migratory chains of the first generation of migrants and develop a life of their own. In the *economic realm*, there has been a partial movement from the remittances of the first-generation migrants working in Germany to ethnic businesses in Germany and further to direct investment in Turkey of second-generation Turkish entrepreneurs living in Germany (for example, production in Turkey, administration and distribution in Germany). When Turkish ethnic businesses such as restaurants and travel agencies started to emerge in Germany during the 1970s, this sector rapidly expanded in the 1980s. Yet in some fields Turkish entrepreneurs started to compete with German firms. This was one of the factors leading to investments of German-based Turkish entrepreneurs in Turkey. Transnational networks of entrepreneurs have begun to encompass both Turkey and Germany.

The development of transnational social spaces offers a unique opportunity to look into the formation of groups that span at least two nation-states. Some classics have argued that *propinquity* – among other factors, such as a shared common interest and a common language – is conducive to the formation of groups. For example, English trade unions first organized along patterns such as location (for example, city). Later, the trade as an organizing principle replaced this focus. However, international migrants living in transnational social spaces form networks, groups and 'communities without propinquity' (Webber, 1963). One of the questions is by what principles is propinquity supplemented? Physical location and geographical distance are by no means the only grid on which phenomena such as collective action, common culture and economic cooperation can be mapped.

First, this analysis tries to clarify basic concepts such as transnational social space and the main resources involved, such as social capital that are based on social and symbolic ties. Second, a few forays into the empirical realm serve to illustrate processes of development in these spaces, focusing on the German and neglecting the Turkish end: the emergence of ethnic Turkish businesses in Germany and transnational businesses spanning both countries. The discussion concludes with some trends that may limit the future growth of transnational social spaces.

TOWARDS A DEFINITION AND TYPOLOGY OF TRANSNATIONAL SOCIAL SPACES

The examples mentioned above attest to the ability of movers creatively to pattern their personal and collective experience. We need to develop concepts that can be applied not only to the sending or receiving regions, but also to emerging transnational linkages, such as those between Algeria and France, India and the United Kingdom, Turkey and Germany, and Mexico, the Caribbean and the USA. *Transnational social spaces* are combinations of social and symbolic ties, positions in networks and organizations and networks of organizations that can be found in at least two geographically and internationally distinct places. These spaces denote dynamic social processes, not static notions of ties and positions (see also Basch et al., 1994: 8). Cultural, political and economic processes in transnational social spaces involve the accumulation, use and effects of various sorts of capital, their volume and convertibility: economic capital (for example, financial capital), human capital (for example, skills and knowhow) and social capital (resources inherent in social and symbolic ties). The reality of transnational social spaces indicates, first, that migration and remigration may not be definite, irrevocable and irreversible decisions; transnational lives in themselves may become a strategy of survival and betterment. Second, even migrants and refugees who have settled for a considerable time outside the original sending country may entertain strong transnational links. The transnational social spaces inhabited by (former) migrants and refugees and immobile residents in both countries thus supplement the international space of sovereign nation-states. Transnational social spaces are constituted by the various forms of resources or capital of spatially mobile and immobile persons, on the one hand, and the regulations imposed by nation-states and various other opportunities and constraints, on the other – for example, state-controlled immigration and refugee policies and ethnic communities. Transnational social spaces are characterized by *triadic relationships* between groups and institutions in the host state, the sending state (sometimes viewed as an external homeland by diasporic communities) and the minority group – migrants and/or refugee groups or ethnic minorities.

Space here not only refers to physical features, but also to larger opportunity structures, the social life and the subjective images, values and meanings that the specific and limited place represents to migrants. Space is thus different from *place* in that it encompasses or spans various territorial locations. On a micro level, this has to be seen in conjunction with the use of time to form particular time–space strategies of potential migrants. In interacting with significant others, the potential migrants themselves constitute the context of decision-making, for example in kinship groups. Larger structural factors such as economic and political opportunities constitute a more remote, albeit an enabling and constraining, context in which individuals, collectives and networks operate.

The social capital embedded in social and symbolic ties is one resource in transnational social spaces that needs explaining. *Social ties* are a continuing series of interpersonal transactions to which participants attach shared interests, obligations, expectations and norms. *Symbolic ties* are a continuing series of transactions, both face-to-face and indirect, to which participants attach shared meanings, memories, future expectations and symbols. Symbolic ties often go beyond face-to-face relations, involving members of the same religious belief, language, ethnicity or nationality.

Social capital is the resources inherent in patterned social and symbolic ties that allow individuals to cooperate in networks and organizations. It also serves to connect individuals to networks and organizations through affiliations. We can differentiate the following forms of social capital:

1. reciprocity as a pattern of social *exchange*: mutual obligations and expectations of the actors, associated with specific social ties and based on exchanges and services rendered in the past (Coleman, 1990: 306–9). These obligations and expectations can be an outcome of instrumental activity, for example, the tit-for-tat principle.
2. reciprocity as a social *norm*: what one party receives from the other requires some return (Gouldner, 1960).

3. *solidarity* with others in a group that shares similar positions (Portes, 1995: 16). It is an expressive form of social interaction. The most important form of solidarity is 'collective representations' (Durkheim, 1965). These are shared ideas, beliefs, evaluations and symbols. Collective representations can be expressed in some sort of collective identity ('we-feeling' or 'we-consciousness') and refers to a social unit of action. It its ideal-typical form, these are cultural communities, such as families, ethnic groups, national groups, religious parishes, congregations, communities and nations. Solidarity can also be institutionalized: citizenship, for example, is an institutionalized form of solidarity (and thus social capital) that is in short supply among Turkish immigrants in Germany.

Social capital has two important characteristics. First, it is very hard to transfer from one country to another; it is primarily a *local asset*. Thus, in addition to political regulations of international migration, it is one of the main causes for the relatively low, albeit increasing, rates of international mobility. However, if transnational networks and chain migration emerge in the course of migration – often caused by labour recruitment and refugee flows and mediated by pioneer migrants and organizations (like recruitment bureaux and illegal intermediaries) – the transferability of social capital and other forms of capital increases. Second, social capital is a crucial mechanism for applying other forms of capital; it is a *transmission belt* that bridges collectives and networks in distinct and separate nation-states. Since social capital is necessary to mobilize other forms of capital, especially among those short of financial (economic) capital. And, often, immigrants need social ties to established immigrants or brokers to find work; in other words, they need to employ their human capital such as vocational skills and educational degrees in the receiving country. Social capital is also a sort of castor oil to establish a flourishing cultural life in the receiving country. Thus, social capital is crucial in the formation of a circular flow of goods and persons between countries and fulfils a bridging function. It is only when persons in distinct places are connected via social and symbolic ties, enabling the transfer of various forms of capital that transnational social spaces emerge.

Of course, social capital is contingent upon time and space. One macro structural trend may have accelerated the emergence of transnational social spaces. While the technological breakthrough in *long-distance communication and travel* occurred in the nineteenth century, new and improved methods of communication and travel, combined with increased levels of labour migrants and refugee flows after the Second World War set the necessary but not sufficient stage for the development of trans-national ties. The communication and transport revolution that started in the nineteenth century with transoceanic steamship passages and telegraph communication has considerably decreased the costs of bridging long geographical distances. This trend sharply accelerated after the Second World War. Trans-European commuting is now possible to a higher extent than during the 1960s and 1970s.

One may speculate that the full break-through of factors enabling long-distance communication and travel was significantly delayed by the two world wars and the period in between that was characterized by isolationism, immigration restriction to a level not known today and in the nineteenth century, and economic depression. In sum, a variety of structural and technological developments have liberated communities from the confines of territorially-defined neighbourhoods.

We can differentiate transnational social spaces along two dimensions – the degree of integration into structures of both the original sending and receiving states, and the length of time involved or durability of trans-national linkages. The first criterion involves the *spatial extension* and measures the degree of transnationalization. It does this by looking at the extent to which ties cross nation-state boundaries and the networks and groups involved have grown roots in at least two countries; the second refers to the duration, to the *temporal stability* of transnational linkages. There are at least four ideal-typical forms of transnational social spaces that can be ordered along the spatial and temporal dimensions (see Figure 2.1) – (1) assimilation; (2) transnational exchange and reciprocity; (3) transnational circuits; and (4) transnational communities. The underlying proposition is that as we move from type (1) to type (4), the amount of social capital in transnational social spaces increases.

Dispersion in the wake of violent conflicts and repression, or expansion of labour and trade are necessary prerequisites for all four forms of trans-national social spaces. First, *assimilation* (weak simultaneous embedding in sending and receiving countries and short-lived transnational social and symbolic ties) implies that immigrants in a receiving country eventually integrate and assimilate culturally (acculturation) into the host society within one to three generations. In most cases, the immigrants and refugees gradually break off most ties to the original sending country. Nevertheless, symbolic ties may still exist, even a form of 'symbolic ethnicity' (Gans, 1979) could emerge, that refer to ethnic collective identity without having a strong organizational basis among those who consider themselves belonging to an ethnic group. The case of 'white ethnics' in the United States, the descendants of European immigrants who arrived before the First World War, is a case in point.

integration into nation-state networks and organizations	mainly receiving country	spanning the original sending and receiving countries
duration		
short-lived	*assimilation*:	*transnational exchange and reciprocity*:
	gradual erosion or (forced) cut-off of social and symbolic ties to sending country; acculturation to life in the receiving country	ties to sending country upheld in the 'first' migrant generation; often: return migration
	1	2
long-lived	*transnational circuits*:	*transnational communities*:
	circular flow of persons, goods, information, ideas, etc.; social ties are used in one or several areas (for example, business, politics, religion)	dense networks of 'communities without propinquity' in both sending and receiving countries with a high degree of solidarity (for example, diasporas, borderlands)
	3	4

Figure 2.1 A Typology of Transnational Social Spaces

Transnational exchange and reciprocity (strong simultaneous embedding but rather short-lived social and symbolic ties) are typical for many first-generation labour migrants and refugees. Transnational *exchange* becomes very visible in the manifold 'export–import' businesses established by immigrants in the receiving countries so as to satisfy typical needs of immigrant communities for mother-tongue videos, food, clothing and other supplies. The establishment of enclave businesses and niche economies, homeland-oriented voluntary associations (for example, soccer clubs of Mexican immigrants in Chicago or tea houses of Turkish immigrants in Bremen), the transplant of homeland political organizations, and the emergence of religious congregations are regular features of these processes. *Reciprocity* can be seen, for example, in remitters sending back money to members of their kinship groups in the country of origin. This is especially evident in cases when (temporary) territorial exit is part of a strategy of economic survival or betterment among migrants and those who stay behind (for example, risk insurance). In those cases, the migrants remit money to those who run household affairs in the sending place. Often, seasonal, recurrent and eventual return migrations are part of these strategies. Yet, even a return to the sending country may not be permanent, as many older migrants temporarily migrate again in the opposite direction to secure medical care in the countries in which they once worked and some of their children or other kin still live.

Transnational circuits (weakly embedded and long-lived) are characterized by a constant circulation of goods, people and information crossing the borders of sending and receiving states (Rouse, 1991). In the context of international migration, for example, kinship ties stunningly cross-national boundaries. For example, by the end of the 1980s, about half of all adult Mexicans were related to someone living in the United States. Transnational circuits seem to be most developed in such cases of circular international migration. They also typically develop in a context in which we find (often rather successful) socioeconomic adaptation to the conditions in the receiving country, or successful reintegration in the sending country. Sometimes, we see the so-called 'second-and-plus-generations' involved in business activities in the former sending country of their parents or grandparents. The overseas Chinese family businesses in Southeast Asia and Indians in central or East Africa are cases in point. What is crucial is that these entrepreneurs and their dependants are firmly rooted in either the former sending or the former receiving country and use it as a sort of base from which to carry out entrepreneurial activities in the other country. Economic, political or cultural entrepreneurs use 'insider advantages' such as knowledge of the language, knowing friends and acquaintances in the other country to establish a foothold. For example, a second-generation Turkish textile manufacturer in Germany may use his or her contacts to establish production facilities in Turkey, taking advantage of cheaper priced Turkish labour. The above-mentioned Turkish rap band 'Cartel', based in Germany, stormed the Turkish hit charts and thus successfully widened its international market.

Transnational communities (strong embedding and long-lived in at least two countries) characterize situations in which international movers and stayers are connected by dense and strong social and symbolic ties over time and across space to patterns of networks and circuits in two countries. In addition to exchange and reciprocity, social capital as solidarity is necessary for the functioning of transnational communities. Such 'communities without propinquity' (Webber, 1963) in which community and spatial proximity are not coupled do not necessarily require individual persons living in two worlds simultaneously or between cultures in a total 'global village' of deterritorialized space. Living in two places simultaneously is true of only very few migrants, such as hyper-mobile Chinese businessmen on the west coast of the USA in the late twentieth century. This is an outgrowth of the growing interdependence of the US economy with the Chinese Pacific economies of Taiwan, Hong Kong, Singapore and China. For example, these astronauts establish a business in (say) Singapore, yet locate their families in Los Angeles or Toronto to maximize educational opportunities for their children, or as a safe haven in the event of political instability (Cohen, 1997: 93).

For the majority of international movers, the existence of transnational communities primarily means that social and symbolic ties crisscross nation-state boundaries for a considerable amount of time between persons and groups who are firmly grounded. After all, social capital flowing through and sometimes inherent in social ties is above all a local asset, although it may become mobile and is transplanted from one context to another via migrant and migration networks, which constitute accumulated, namely crystallized, social capital. Social capital constitutes a conduit or transmission belt to transnationalization because it is both firmly grounded in at least two local contexts and still has the capacity to link across borders. It helps transfer economic, cultural and human capital.

Diasporas, especially those made up of (first-generation) refugees represent a very distinct form of transnational community. There is a vision and remembrance of a lost or imagined homeland still to be established, often accompanied by the receiving society's refusal to recognize fully the immigrants' cultural distinctiveness. Diasporas often include a full cross-section of community members who are dispersed to many diverse regions of the world, and who yet retain a vision or myth of their uniqueness and an interest in their homeland (for a fuller list of characteristics, see Safran, 1991). Diasporas typically span collectives and networks in more than two nation-states. Diasporas have to be differentiated from *borderlands*. The latter imply a situation of bi-locality where an emerging syncretic culture is temporarily separated by nation-state border controls, but linked by legal and illegal migration. Good examples of borderlands are the riverain areas of the Rio Grande linking Mexico and the United States, and the Oder-Neisse linking Poland and Germany.

While transnational communities are typically embedded in an ongoing structure of social ties between sending and receiving countries, diasporas do not necessarily need contemporary and concrete social ties. It is possible that the memory of a homeland manifests itself primarily in symbolic ties. This has been the case for the Jewish diaspora for centuries after the destruction of the Second Temple, and for Sikhs after Indian troops had stormed the Golden Temple in 1984. The difference between diasporas and other transnational communities becomes clear when we compare the Jewish diaspora before the establishment of the state of Israel with global communities such as Chinese entrepreneurs and traders in many countries of Southeast Asia, Africa and the two Americas. The vision of the Chinese was (at first) much less oriented towards the ancestral homeland, and lacked components of exile.

We have now come full circle to the opposite end of the spectrum from where we began: diasporas vanish when we see gradual cultural assimilation or acculturation (assimilation, type 1), or a rupture of material, social and symbolic ties with the country of common origin. In the nineteenth and twentieth centuries labour diasporas have usually been of a transitory type, especially in the white settler colonies. The generations following the first advanced to middle-class status or returned home. Whether this pattern repeats itself in international migrations that have started in the 1960s is too early to say. This scenario requires that successive groups in a sort of queue fill 'immigrant jobs' or slots for immigrant entrepreneurs. What is certain, however, is that to flourish and survive diasporas need to distance themselves both from the culture of origin and of settlement if they are to choose appropriate political and economic strategies of moving 'in between' (Saint-Blancat, 1995: 10).

AN EXAMPLE: ECONOMIC TRANSNATIONALIZATION

In the Turkish–German case, we find a gradual transition from intra-household and intra-familial transnational exchange and reciprocity (type 2 in Figure 2.1) to partial transnational circuits that include families, but also larger groups such as ethnic communities (type 3). Three periods of self-feeding processes of economic transnationalization can be distinguished: first, remittances of labour migrants from Germany to Turkey; second, the inception and growth of ethnic businesses in Germany; and third, transnational production, distribution and sales.

The first period, from the early 1960s until the 1970s and 1980s, was characterized mainly by labour migrant remitters who transferred money to Turkey and returning migrants who invested in housing and consumer products. In the 1980s and 1990s, the share of remittances from Germany to Turkey as a percentage of foreign trade have decreased, probably because of family reunification; remittances from the Gulf states have partly compensated for this decline. Nonetheless, if migrants' participation in the tourist and housing industries and their investments in other sectors are taken together with family remittances, international migrants have become the single most important source of hard currency in Turkey.

The second period has been characterized by higher scales of economic activities in Germany, such as investments in housing and the growing importance of a thriving so-called ethnic economy in Germany (ethnic niche). The number of self-employed Turkish people in Germany tripled between 1983 and 1992 from about 10,000 to 35,000. In Germany, about 8 per cent of all immigrants are self-employed, with Turkish immigrants coming closer to the higher rates among Greeks and Italians. This overall rate of immigrant self-employment corresponds to the rate of self-employment among German citizens (*Bericht der Beauftragten*, 1994: II, 2, 10). Typical activities of Turkish migrants include crafts and running grocery shops, travel agencies and restaurants.

About 65 per cent of all these companies are family-owned, run mainly by the owner and employing family members (Zentrum für Türkeistudien, 1989: 177–8). Thus, new labour for businesses, serving the ethnic niche and a small but growing German clientele, has often come from the respective kinship group in Turkey (Goldberg, 1992). Therefore, many Turkish companies in Germany use a sort of ethnic social capital that emphasizes kinship groups as a recruiting pool. Kinship migration and marriage migration have enabled Turkish entrepreneurs in Germany to tap this pool of labour since the recruitment stopped in 1973. A well-known black side – excessive exploitation of new labour from Turkey – often accompanies kinship-based exchange, reciprocity and solidarity.

More recently, a transition has occurred from the second to a third period, from the ethnic niche to transnational coordination of business activities. Some Turkish entrepreneurs have entered fields in which they compete with German businesses, for example, software development and textile production (ATIAD, 1996). Because production costs, especially in the latter sector, are much lower in Turkey than in Germany, textile companies move production to Turkey while retaining their sales and distribution centres in Germany. A small group of German-based Turkish immigrant entrepreneurs can exploit various forms of social capital such as 'insider advantages'. They use their language skills (a form of human capital) and social ties with friends and acquaintances in Turkey to gain a foothold in a transnational market. In these cases, social capital is of the utmost importance because it helps lower transaction costs – the costs of enforcing contracts. Informal arrangements cover various areas such as credit, labour recruitment and dealing with the German and Turkish authorities (own interviews). In some cases, social capital even helps circumvent costly formal contracts, for example, in dealing with the Turkish authorities to establish production facilities and pay taxes.

One could argue that this latest stage of development is restricted to privileged entrepreneurs with relatively high amounts of financial capital; such as the textile entrepreneurs just mentioned. It certainly is important to emphasize that the majority of migrants have remained proletarians or – a small but growing minority – modest self-employed (for example shopkeepers), or being increasingly excluded from the labour market on the German side (Faist, 1995: Chapter 7). Yet, both small export–import businesses and middle sized textile firms benefit from the same set of innovations in communications and transport that underlie the larger-scale industrial relocations of textile production. Put more broadly, these grassroots economic initiatives do not arise in opposition to more general trends of transnational relocation of production and trade, but are partly driven by them. Petty transnational migrant entrepreneurs and middle-sized companies occupy specific niches in the international division of commerce and production. In doing so, some migrant labourers who become self-employed partly substitute social capital for financial capital.

A case study helps to illustrate the development of a transnational space. It involves smaller economic actors riding the crest of transnationaliz-ation.[2] In the case of international migrants from a small Anatolian village, Alihan in the 1970s, there was frequent contact between and among those men from Alihan who lived and worked abroad. Those in foreign countries such as Sweden (and Germany) also kept links with family members still living in Turkey. These ties extended to Turkish migrants from other regions and Turkish male clubs and associations. These wide networks of communication were used to transfer messages and information about situations in Europe and happenings in the home village. Yeniköy migrants from a village in the same region, by contrast, kept their social interactions and ties more exclusively in their own group. They had few ties with men from other regions or villages, even in men's clubs; their leisure activities were shared with men from the same kinship group.

Social capital enabled the Alihan men to use considerable ingenuity in the economic realm and they became much more heavily involved in the import–export business than their Yeniköy counterparts. For them, international migration formed part of a household survival and improvement strategy. In addition to building houses, virtually all those who returned to

Turkey became self-employed and settled outside Alihan, mostly in Konya, the provincial capital. Some of the returnees invested in joint projects not only with other Alihan returnees but also with people from other parts of Turkey. Alihan men often embarked on joint-ownership ventures with Turks outside their immediate circle, whereas the Yeniköy men never invested with anyone outside their group. Yeniköy migrants mostly returned to their own village and would save and invest within its local economic structure. One reason for their higher rate of return to the sending village was that they usually faced better economic opportunities than their Alihan counterparts.

The key to understanding these differences is found in the migrant's ability to mobilize the various sorts of social capital, such as reciprocity and solidarity, embedded in social and symbolic ties. Potential migrants from Alihan could call on strong social ties that encompassed more than one kinship group, whereas those interested in migrating from Yeniköy could not do this unless they belonged to the same kinship group as one of the first migrants who had left for Europe. Alihan was a village with strong social cohesion and relatively few economic differences. The population also shared strong feelings of solidarity derived from a common history dating back to the sixteenth century. The 'collective representation' of the village as a cohesive unit was pervasive. All villagers considered themselves descendants of the original settlers and most families had marital links with other families in the village. Marriages were mostly arranged within the village with few newcomers entering the resident kinship groups. Help was present in times of need. Reciprocity in the form of mutual obligations even extended beyond the kinship group; there was a non-kin reciprocity, embedded in a village-wide solidarity of a sense of common origin, shared history and multiple bonds of kinship (certainly not representative of all Anatolian villages). In other words, the various benefits of social capital derived from reciprocity and village solidarity, particularly information, partially substituted for financial capital. Alihan migrants could rely on a high degree of social capital. Migrants from Yeniköy, by contrast, only supported members of their own kinship group. Other potential migrants could not rely on the valuable social capital flowing from that kinship group. In the mid–1960s the village had been in existence for about 100 years and was grouped into various communities (Turks from Anatolia, Turkish refugees from Bulgaria, and Kurds) that had little contact with each other. It is thus not surprising that the one kinship group located in the poor Turkish community did not share its social capital concerning migration with other villagers.

In sum, when migrants from both villages found themselves abroad, the

Alihan community, with its higher amounts of social capital, more successfully exploited the new opportunities transnational social spaces offered than migrants from Yeniköy, who only kept close ties with their own kinship group. We can observe that transnational ties in the Yeniköy case existed for roughly one generation (type 2: transnational exchange and reciprocity in a single kinship group). Transnational economic activity effectively stopped when the migrants returned from Europe to Turkey, whereas it continued for longer in the Alihan case (type 3: transnational circuits, embedded in a socially and culturally cohesive community).

OUTLOOK: TRANSNATIONAL SOCIAL SPACES 'BETWEEN' AND 'IN' NATION-STATES

International migration is not restricted to migration as a set of self-feeding processes, typically producing migration flows that may last several decades with a clearly defined beginning and end (Faist, 1997). International migration is also accompanied by a transnationalization of migrants' activities, encompassing all spheres of life. There are distinct challenges to nation-state policies in receiving and sending contexts once transnational social spaces have unfolded. Although the relationship is still asymmetric in terms of power between sending and receiving country, the interdependence is stronger through migrants living in both contexts, either practically (for example, through commuting back and forth or exchanging goods and information) or symbolically (for example, through cultural practices spanning both countries). In this context, questions emerge such as: What happens to kinship systems and their traditional living together in one place when economic reproduction, risk diversification and betterment encompass various countries? What happens to notions of nationalism and nation-state unity when citizens move abroad and seek to establish a new homeland, carved out of the old one? What happens to notions of cultural uniqueness when persons acquire cultural repertoires that are transnational? Can the ancestral or desired future homeland also be a transnational space, such as the Islamic *umma*?

In particular, the existence of transnational social spaces calls into question the dominant focus on immigrant integration/disintegration and assimilation/non-assimilation at the nation-state level in receiving countries. As the initial empirical evidence presented here suggests, integration at the nation-state level (for example, national citizenship and participation in formal labour markets and social insurance) is a crucial element of the migrant experience. Yet, this dimension needs to be complemented by a stronger focus on transnational and sub-national levels of analysis so as to capture the dynamics of exclusive or complementary sending and receiving country orientations of transmigrants, or even the formation of social spaces in between, such as diasporas.

Migrations and refugee movements and the settlements of migrants and refugees are still at too early a stage to evaluate whether transnational ties and linkages have crystallized in transnational communities such as diasporas. To speak of a diaspora, a group should be dispersed to more than one country. Although this applies to Turkish labour migrants, for they settle not only in Germany but also in Belgium, the Netherlands, France and Switzerland, Germany is too dominating to speak of more than predominantly bi-national linkages and ties. This is somewhat different for the Kurds. They seem to have dispersed more evenly in European countries such as Germany, the Netherlands and Sweden.

Transnationalization may be attenuated when seen in the longer historical perspective. What seems like a comparative advantage at one point may be a springboard to something entirely different for some, while it becomes a kind of trap for others, preventing them from making more successful moves within the nation-state that has become their new home. There are several such comparative advantages. For example, some Turkish entrepreneurs in Germany have access to cheap labour in their garment factories in Turkey. Some Kurdish exiles have a secure political basis from which to struggle for more autonomy or even independence in the southeastern provinces of Turkey. Also, there are Turkish Muslims of various religious groups who use Germany as a base to fight against secularism and laicization in Turkey. It is only when these immigrants and their descendants find a basis for their economic, political and cultural activities other than those of the sending country or homeland that elements of transnationalization can remain beneficial to them in the long run. In short, we should not allow temporary transnationalization and 'multiculturalism' to cause us to lose sight of the ever-present trajectories of assimilation in the receiving countries.

Notes

1. For a detailed treatment of this topic, see Faist (1998).
2. The following account is based on a secondary analysis of Engelbrektsson's (1978: Chapter 2) superb ethnographic study of migration from two very different Turkish villages to Sweden (and Germany).

3 A Game of Ethnic Musical Chairs? Immigrant Businesses and Niches in the Amsterdam Economy

Jan Rath

For years, Amsterdam has been a place of settlement for large groups of immigrants. In the sixteenth century, residents from the south Netherlands arrived.[1] They could no longer bear to live under the yoke of the Spanish fury and fled to the Calvinist North (Lucassen and Penninx, 1994: 30ff.). In the seventeenth century, a new flood of Protestant refugees arrived – the Huguenots. Both groups, immigrants from the south Netherlands and the Huguenots, were well endowed with capital, trading contacts and skills, which enabled them to secure a prominent place in the Amsterdam economy. This was especially so for the first group of refugees who specialized in trade and industry, and were given certain privileges such as (free) civil rights and generous fiscal benefits by the city administration. Partly due to their energetic entrepreneurship, the city of Amsterdam – and with it the republic – became a focus of what was then the world economy. In this regard, it is significant that roughly one-third of the money invested in the Dutch East India Company came from immigrants from the south Netherlands.

There were, of course, other groups of immigrants. From the end of the sixteenth century onwards, large groups of Sephardic Jews from the Iberian Peninsula arrived in the *Mokum* and, in later periods – up until this century – also Ashkenazi Jews from central and eastern Europe. These immigrants became involved in trade and industry – partly because the non-Jewish majority excluded them from various occupations (Berg, Wijsenbeek and Fischer, 1994).[2] Jewish economic activity was concentrated in certain branches of industry, such as banking, the sugar trade and butchering. At the end of the nineteenth and beginning of the twentieth centuries – when the industrial economy developed further and the foundations of the welfare state were being laid – they were well represented in Amsterdam in the free professions. These included the entertainment industry, banking, insurance and the retail trade, as well as the production of ready-to-wear clothing, tobacco processing and cutting and polishing diamonds (Leydesdorff, 1987; Lucassen and Penninx, 1994). They also monopolized the market for kosher products and local traders in the Jewish quarters were partly protected from the 'open' market. Finally, a considerable proportion of Jews earned an income through irregular home working – this was widespread in the garment industry – and with small-scale street trading. Jewish street traders were over-represented in the vegetable and fruit trade, in the fish and flower trade and to a lesser degree as ice sellers. In the interwar period, one out of every three Amsterdam street traders was of Jewish origin; at one point their share in the rag-and-bone trade was 90 per cent.

In the second half of the nineteenth century, Roman Catholic immigrants of Westphalian origin settled in the city. Anton Sinkel was one of the first people to experiment with the concept of a 'modern' shop. Descendants of the German peddlers Clemens and August Brenninkmeijer followed in his footsteps. Though the first C & A department store was situated in the northern town of Sneek, it was in Amsterdam that the chain became really successful. There, at the turn of the century, a number of sales outlets were set up, as well as the first factory for garment manufacture. The retailers Willem Vroom and Anton Dreesmann also established their first manufacturing business in Amsterdam. They, and many other immigrants with a Roman Catholic, German background were able to penetrate the Dutch (especially Amsterdam) garment manufacturing industry using their trading skills and their knowledge of textiles (Miellet, 1987).

So much is clear: these immigrants, or at least a number of them, originating from different corners of the world, arrived in different historical eras each with their own ethnic and religious backgrounds, and concentrated themselves as entrepreneurs in certain branches of trade and industry. Other examples of such concentrations are those of Belgian straw hat makers; German bakers; German beer brewers; Oldenburg plasterers, whitewashers and masons; French umbrella peddlers; Italian street traders selling plaster of Paris statues, or terrazzo workers, chimney sweepers and ice-cream makers (Bovenkerk and Ruland, 1992; Schrover, 1996). Although all these examples suggest that economic concentrations only occurred with tradesmen and craftsmen, the case of German servants illustrates that this could also apply to hired labourers (Henkes, 1995).

That immigrants should funnel into certain occupations or branches of industry is intriguing. Such niches are not confined to history books. To this day, such concentrations can be observed in various forms. Walking through the city, one is likely to pass an Italian ice-cream seller or a Turkish or Moroccan Islamic butcher, or bump into the clothes rack of a Turkish sweatshop. With a bit of imagination we could even claim that they are the successors of the Jewish ice-cream sellers, kosher butchers and confectioners who determined the townscape before the war.

Does the process of economic incorporation really take place through concentrations in certain occupations or lines of business? Does a pattern of succession really occur? If so, what are its structural determinants? The answers to these questions could help us obtain more insight into the dynamic process of economic incorporation in which the immigrants of today participate. Immigrant self-employment in Amsterdam has been researched here and there, but the question of the succession of ethnic niches has not been systematically dealt with until now (see Rath and Kloosterman, 1998). This chapter is therefore to be seen, first and foremost, as an intellectual exercise. I use the theoretical insights of the American sociologist Roger Waldinger as a source of inspiration, and shall conclude by providing some commentary on his work.

A GAME OF ETHNIC MUSICAL CHAIRS

Waldinger (1996) expressively describes the process of succession of ethnic niches as 'a game of ethnic musical chairs'. In his cleverly written book on New York – as well as in his contribution to the prize-winning book on Los Angeles (Waldinger and Bozorgmehr, 1996) – he deals with the question of why various categories of the population take up certain positions in the urban economy. In particular, he asks which structural determinants trigger this process and keep it in motion. In contemporary literature, emphasis is placed on the economic and demographic trans-formations that metropolises such as New York, London and Los Angeles are going through and which, in turn, cause a mismatch of labour (see Kasarda, Friedrichs and Ehlers, 1992). Other scholars emphasize the process of globalization and point to the concentration of high-grade service activities in so-called global cities, which directly or indirectly create a demand for small-scale and partly low-quality activities (Sassen, 1988 and 1991). Waldinger is not enamoured with these approaches. In his opinion, they lack adequate empirical foundations (certainly in the case of New York and Los Angeles), are economically deterministic and ahistorical and do not take enough account of the real *dramatis personae*, the immigrants themselves.

Waldinger claims that in every market economy jobs are distributed according to the principles of desirability and availability, yet each market economy is affected by the social structure of the country within which it is embedded. In a society as 'race conscious' as the United States, people in the 'free' market economy are ranked in terms of ethnic or racial characteristics. In this way a *queue* is formed, a pecking order, with the members of the dominant cultural group at the head and the problematized groups somewhere towards the end. Immigrants coming into such a structure, whose economic orientation is still influenced by their land of origin, will, more often than not, be satisfied with this marginal position. However, changes in the economy affect the queue. Due to the vertical or horizontal mobility of those who are better situated, vacancies are created in the lower levels of the queue. Those in a lower position or by newcomers fill these in turn. These processes take years, sometimes developing quickly, sometimes slowly. This knowledge forces us to drop our all too popular preoccupation with short-term developments and enables us to go beyond worrying about the issues of the day.

How are niches formed? Waldinger (1996: 95; see also Waldinger and Bozorgmehr, 1996: 476–7) operationalizes a niche. On the basis of the work of Model (1993), he does this partly as 'an industry employing at least one thousand people, in which a group's representation is a least 150 per cent of its share of total employment'.[3] This definition is not limited to trade and industry, but includes the public sector. The government influences niche formation, not only as an agent that can strengthen or weaken it, but by influencing its location – for example by employing members of a certain ethnic group in the public sector. Niches develop in the interaction between a group and its surrounding society, in which the degree to which the players are embedded in social networks is of crucial importance. Lieberson (1980: 379) points out that:

> It is clear that most racial and ethnic groups tend to develop concentrations in certain jobs, which either reflect some distinctive cultural characteristics, special skills initially held by some members, or the opportunity structures at the time of their arrival. ... These concentrations are partially based on networks or ethnic contacts and experiences that in turn direct other compatriots in these directions.

Waldinger uses this line of thought and suggests that immigrants are funnelled towards specialized economic activities via their networks, the most important instruments being enforceable trust and bounded solidarity to one's own group (cf. Portes and Sensenbrenner, 1993 with Roberts, 1994). As soon as the first pioneers have established themselves, others follow and thus, in time, ethnic concentrations – or niches – are formed. As usual, the most attractive functions are reserved for *insiders,* while the *outsiders* at the end of the queue (for example, members of other immigrant groups) are excluded (Waldinger, 1995). This continues as long as there is space in the market (Light, 1998) or until vacancies occur elsewhere, enabling a group as a whole to shift to another line of business. The latter may be caused by the niche itself: once a concentration of entrepreneurs from a certain immigrant group grows, the demand for accountants, lawyers, carriers and so on from the same group also increases.

To summarize, the most important ingredients in Waldinger's recipe are:

- the permanent striving of all participants in economic life for social mobility;
- a continuous stream of new immigrants;
- a race-conscious society;
- restricted embedding in social networks;
- the formation of a labour queue with in-groups at the top and out-groups at the bottom;
- the formation of ethnic concentrations (niches) in certain occupations or branches of industry;
- an institutional framework formed by ethnic or racially based interest group activity; and
- a high level of continuity in market conditions and ethnic loyalty.

Together, these form the mixture from which the pattern of succession of ethnic niches develops.

To what extent does this viewpoint – with its empirical foundations on the other side of the Atlantic Ocean – give us something on which to build? True, Waldinger did not develop it with the intention of understanding and explaining the situation in Amsterdam. Yet, it does serve to assess the validity of his *theoretical* argument. There are, however, a few complications. First, use of Waldinger's definition of niches can lead to peculiar situations. Are we to consider the tens of thousands of guestworkers in the ageing industries of the 1960s as forming a niche, even if, as job hunters, they had no influence on the branch of industry in which they eventually landed? And what are we to think about slavery? A strict application of

Waldinger's definition could possibly be taken to justify statements suggesting those African slaves on the US cotton or Surinamese sugar plantations formed a niche. Such statements seem to me to be rather strange.

Second, Waldinger refers to occupations and branches of trade and industry in rather general terms. Because of this, he is in danger of missing important differentiations. A particular group may, for example, have formed a niche in the health care sector. In terms of their economic incorporation, there is a vast difference between being spread over the sector as a whole or concentrated in the positions of heart surgeon, nurse or domestic help. These are, after all, different labour markets.

Third, only when the number of people in a particular occupation or branch of industry exceeds 1000 does Waldinger consider it to fall within the definition of a niche, for only then does the concentration have any impact on the group as a whole. In the case of Amsterdam, this would mean that the 14 Greek cafés and restaurants, for example, would have absolutely no impact on the local Greek 'community', which then consisted of roughly 250 people (Vermeulen et al., 1985: 57, 114). This is hardly credible. I can think of no compelling theoretical reason to employ the huge scale used in the United States on cases such as Amsterdam.

Fourth, Waldinger assumes long historical periods of continuous immigration and strong social continuity. To some extent, these are necessary conditions for the game of ethnic musical chairs. However, in the Netherlands these conditions are only partially fulfilled. There is absolutely no question of continuous immigration (the Second World War was an important breaking point), which clearly affects the continuity of entrepreneurship. During the occupation, the Nazis destroyed the Jewish niches, making any eventual niche maintenance impossible.[4] For this reason, in the rest of this chapter, when using examples from the past, I will focus mostly on the postwar period. Whether this period is long enough to allow niches to mature remains to be seen.

Taking these restrictions into account, I return from what was New Amsterdam, to the would-be global city in the lowlands.

NICHES IN AMSTERDAM

Amsterdam, like New York, has always had a strong influx of immigrants. At present, almost at the end of the second millennium, the Dutch capital has, absolutely and relatively, the greatest number of immigrants. Some 42 per cent of the total population of the city (irrespective of

Table 3.1   Immigrant/ethnic groups in Amsterdam, 1 January 1996

Origin	Number
Surinam	69 600
Dutch Antilles	10 500
Turkey	31 000
Morocco	48 000
South European countries	16 300
Non-industrialized countries	59 700
Industrialized countries	69 500
The Netherlands	413 600
Total	718 100

Source: Hoolt and Scholten, 1996: 15.

nationality and including those born in the Netherlands) are immigrants. Most of the labour force among these groups is incorporated in the urban economy through employment as waged labourers. In this connection, it is interesting to note that the Chinese, who are well known for their entrepreneurship, came to Amsterdam in 1911 as hired seamen (van Heek, 1936). They were recruited to replace striking boilermen and coal trimmers. As blacklegs, they stood way back in the labour queue – to use Waldinger's terminology.[5] A similar position was later held by the guestworkers from Italy, Spain, Turkey and Morocco. During the 1950s and 1960s, economic expansion enabled native Dutch labourers with low levels of education, who were working in malfunctioning industries, to find employment in higher ranks of their own branch of industry or in branches with better prospects. The vacant places were filled by migrant workers who, being economically oriented towards their land of origin, saw little chance of obtaining – by Dutch standards – more attractive jobs (Marshall-Goldschvartz, 1973; Penninx and van Velzen, 1977). The government was most supportive of such recruiting practices. In Amsterdam, the guestworkers were hired in the factories of, for example, Ford or one of the offshore firms.

Between 1956 and 1963, industries also recruited in Surinam (Dutch Guiana) and the Dutch Antilles. Experiences with these labourers were, however, 'not so positive' and new recruits were not sought (Penninx, 1979: 50; see also van Amersfoort, 1973: 163–4, 182–6). The slow work

Table 3.2 Percentages of unemployed people in Amsterdam, 1995

Origin	% unemployed
Surinam	25
Dutch Antilles	23
Turkey	22
Morocco	27
South European countries	18
Non-industrialized countries	36
Industrialized countries	14
The Netherlands	8
Total	14

Source: Hoolt and Scholten, 1996: 68.

tempo, the high level of absenteeism and the lack of work experience made the Ford factory wary of hiring more Surinamese – which seems to prove the existence of a queue (Bayer, 1965: 64). On the other hand, Surinamese workers at an offshore firm accused their employers of not keeping to their agreements and complained about their salaries and housing (Schuster, 1998). Many of the present immigrants, however, arrived later, during periods of economic recession. The two immigration peaks from Surinam, for example, occurred at the same time as the two oil crises in the 1970s, thus hampering their economic incorporation.

During the 1970s and early 1980s, the position of immigrants in the Amsterdam labour market declined considerably – as in the rest of the country. Since then, immigrants have been more likely to experience unemployment than native Dutch people have and for longer periods; if they do have work, it is often in the less attractive areas of the labour market. The labour force classification of 1995 showed that, on average, 14 per cent of the urban population was *without* a paid job. The differences between the different population categories are marked.

Amsterdam residents *with* jobs work mainly in the service sector, particularly in health care, social work, banks, insurance companies and other commercial service sectors. The Surinamese and West Indians fit in with the general profile. Turks and Moroccans are almost non-existent in the commercial service sector; they work in industry in general and in trade and catering in particular. This pattern is explained not only by their lack of qualifications, but also by discrimination and the fact that their economically relevant networks rarely extend outside these sectors (see Veenman, 1994: 98). That the economy in Amsterdam is increasingly heavily dependent on the service sector (Amsterdam Municipal Council, 1996) does not make it easier for the Turks and Moroccans to quit their positions at the end of the queue.

In the Dutch welfare state, the government and, in its wake, numerous organizations and institutions in the private sector have made efforts to turn the tide. With inventive forms of flexible work – part-time work, temporary work and temporary contracts – and moderate wage increases, after 1985 employment levels increased considerably (Penninx et al., 1995; SCP, 1996). Dutch women have profited most from these measures and in Amsterdam this has been especially true of trade, and of the hotel and catering industry (Kloosterman, 1994, 1996a and 1996b). On top of all this, the government has developed a series of employment plans, training schemes, subsidized wage schemes, contracts, positive action measures and so on. Immigrants from non-industrial countries, especially from Surinam, are over-represented in the public sector's various job-creation programmes.[6] They constitute an average 43 per cent of the participants, while being 'only' 26 per cent of the labour force.[7] Furthermore, immigrants often find employment in areas of the public sector that are explicitly orientated to ethnic minorities as a target group. Examples of these would be so-called migrant workers in the welfare sector, teachers of mother tongue education or civil servants concerned with the implementation of ethnic minority policy (Bovenkerk, den Brok and Ruland, 1991; Koot and Uniken Venema, 1985).

This gravitating of immigrants towards the public sector is interesting. Waldinger had already emphasized the importance of this sector in New York and Los Angeles for African Americans. Previously, the civil rights movement had fought for the privileged admittance of African Americans to (among others) civil servant positions. This was a situation which, due to their political empowering, they could exploit to the full. Once inside the civil service, they could use their own networks to assist other African Americans to find better jobs. In this way they nestled themselves in the public sector niche.[8] It is difficult to say whether we are already witnessing similar developments in Amsterdam. In the Netherlands, this sector includes a mix of the most diverse services and establishments from both the civil service (in the strict sense of the word) and the subsidized sector such as education, welfare work and health care. The use of the concept 'niche' in this vast and colourful field of institutions seems at present inappropriate. The supplementary employment programmes only offer short-term jobs, which furthermore (at least officially) are not intended for one specific ethnic group. Having said this, experience in Amsterdam shows that people from Surinam or the West Indies work as government officials or in education almost as much as Dutch natives (Berdowski, 1994: 40). What has not yet materialized, still can. The fact that the Surinamese have not as yet been able to get to grips with the political system in order to influence the division of labour – assuming that they would wish to do this – hampers the possible formation of their own niche within certain public functions or sectors.[9]

An increasing number of immigrants no longer wait for a job as an employee, but, as the Jews or Roman Catholic Westphalians before them, set up their own businesses. Some of them emigrate with the intention of becoming an entrepreneur in the host country (Blom and Romeijn, 1981; Bovenkerk and Ruland, 1992; Choenni, 1997). In this way, they contribute greatly to the growth of self-employed entrepreneurs – a general trend over the last few years (cf. OECD, 1995 and Rath, 1998a).

On 1 January 1996, Amsterdam counted roughly 72 000 businesses (Amsterdam in Cijfers, 1996: 207–11). Exactly how many of these belong to immigrants is difficult to say. In 1986, it was assumed that about 1000 immigrant entrepreneurs were in business out of a total of 30 000 entrepreneurs, namely about 5 per cent (Kupers, 1995). In 1993, Choenni (1997: 58–9) researched the company trade register at the Chamber of Commerce and counted 4301 immigrant-run businesses. According to the register, 5097 entrepreneurs were involved in these establishments and they accounted for 6.7 per cent of the total population. However, registration at the Chamber of Commerce is imperfect: not all registered businesses actually start up, while not all those that close down are registered as such. A recently held (mini) count of the labour force showed the number of self-employed entrepreneurs in the city to be smaller (Hoolt and Scholten, 1996: 76–7). Of the 3328 entrepreneurs Choenni counted from Surinam and the Dutch Antilles, Aruba and the Mediterranean countries, the count does goes no further than 2600: roughly 4 per cent of the total. Its economic relevance stretches further than the interests of the entrepreneur do. The Economic Research Bureau (1994) claims – without proof – that each ethnic entrepreneur has three employees. Were this assumption to be correct, immigrant businesses in Amsterdam could be contributing an additional 8000 to 10 000 jobs to employment.

The Turks are the largest category of immigrant entrepreneurs, followed directly by Surinamese and less closely by Moroccans, Egyptians and Pakistanis. Together, they account for almost two-thirds of the registered immigrant entrepreneurs (see Table 3.3). If we study the number of entrepreneurs in the respective labour forces, we see that Italians and Turks, and especially Egyptians, Pakistanis and Indians are active: their entrepreneurship far exceeds the national average of 8.7 per cent (OECD, 1995: 314–15).

Table 3.3 The share of immigrant entrepreneurs in the 1993 Amsterdam labour force

	Turkey	Morocco	Surinam	China	Egypt	India	Pakistan
Entrepreneurs	1015	429	915	382	407	312	370
Share in labour force (%)	12.8	4.7	3.5	–	>33	>33	>33

Source: Choenni, 1997: 60.

Table 3.4 shows the sectors in which immigrants most often settle, and it is here that we should find the contours of their niches. Indeed, there appears to be some kind of ethnic specialization forming. As shown in the table, of all the researched categories, Surinamese and Turkish entrepreneurs are the most widely spread over the different sectors. Turks are the only category active in the manufacturing industry, particularly the garment industry – as far as this still exists today (Raes, 1996; Rath, 1998b). Besides the latter, Turks are active in the catering industry, in particular in their own coffee houses and in Italian restaurants (Larsen, 1995; Rekers, 1993), and in (Islamic) butchers and bakeries (Kloosterman, van der Leun and Rath, 1997b: 74–85). Recently, there has been a movement towards trading activities (Kloosterman, van der Leun and Rath, 1997a) although this is without clear traces of concentration.

The Surinamese, the other immigrant group spread widely over the different sectors, have also penetrated the service sector in such branches as insurance and property. They are most active in the distribution of advertising material (folders), in accountancy, in boosting trade and in assisting during events in the fields of sport and theatre, without, however, any traces of niche formation. In the rest of the service sector we come across Surinamese who have set themselves up in business as driving instructors, cleaners, or handymen or women.

Other remarkable concentrations of immigrant entrepreneurs are of course the Italians in their ice-cream parlours, the Chinese in their stores and restaurants,[10] the Greeks in their restaurants, Indians and Pakistanis in the (wholesale) trade in textiles and clothing, and Egyptians in snack bars (*shoarma*), currency exchange banks and teleshops.

Table 3.4 Immigrant enterprises in 1993 in Amsterdam by sector and country of origin

Sector	Tur	Mor	Sur	Chi	Egy	Ind	Pak	O im	T im
Manufacturing	224	6	17	2	6	7	3	18	283
Wholesale/distributive trades	141	37	162	44	41	91	111	370	997
Retail business	183	127	223	40	24	100	109	181	987
Restaurants	235	143	176	147	226	38	47	278	1290
Production services	7	3	32	8	5	1	1	37	94
Other services	84	46	79	6	16	1	24	107	363
Other	26	18	83	22	15	19	5	99	287
Total	900	380	772	269	333	257	300	1090	4301

Note: Tur = Turkey; Mor = Morocco; Sur = Surinam; Chi = China; Ind = India; Pak = Pakistan; O im = other immigrants; T im – total immigrants

Source: Choenni, 1997: 61.

This overview shows that quite a number of immigrants set up shop without niches being formed, and that some 'older' niches have almost or totally disappeared. In certain cases, the disappearance of the occupation or branch of industry, such as straw-hat makers, caused this. In others, it was due to the location of the activities being changed. The diamond industry in Amsterdam – an outstanding example of the Jewish niche – has almost disappeared; before the Second World War, businesses were already being moved to Antwerp or elsewhere. The baking trade, in the nineteenth century a niche for immigrants of German origin (Schrover, 1996: 103), still exists today, albeit with a strong industrial influence and no longer in the hands of one specific group. Although one in six bakers in Amsterdam are Turkish, they represent a minute segment of the market (Kloosterman, van der Leun and Rath, 1997b: 74–80). The market trade, previously the domain of Jewish entrepreneurs, has not (yet?) developed into a niche for immigrant groups. The strict system of assigning market stalls according to registration based on a subscription period, seems systematically to disadvantage immigrants (Kupers, 1995; see Kehla, Engbersen and Snel, 1997: 54–5). Finally, it is noticeable that there are

38   *Jan Rath*

hardly any immigrants active in the street trade, such as the Jewish paupers or the Chinese peanut sellers before the war (van Heek, 1936). A few exceptions are perhaps Vietnamese pancake roll sellers, Italian ice-cream sellers, musicians from Ecuador or (undocumented) Indian rose sellers (Staring, 1998), which is not to say that these *per se* form niches. The small number of hawkers could be explained by the – by now – fairly strict regulations on ambulant trading, by changed consumption patterns, or by the fact that it is no longer necessary to earn a pittance by trading door-to-door. The present welfare state guarantees social security: every (legal) resident has a right to an income, either from supplementary benefits or otherwise (which is not to say that people never have financial problems). This is very different in 'liberal welfare states' like the USA.[11]

ETHNIC SUCCESSION

In as much as immigrants now form niches, to what extent are they part of an historical chain, as Waldinger claims? In the interwar years, Italian ice-cream makers forced Jewish ice-cream sellers from the market; more recently, Egyptians have supplanted Israeli *shoarma* sellers and Turks have nestled in what was previously the Jewish niche in the garment industry. Ethnic succession also takes place in the more infamous sectors of the economy. Moroccan cannabis dealers, for example, have pushed Dutch drug barons out of the market (Bovenkerk and Fijnaut, 1996: 129).

However, these examples do not in the least prove that the settlement of immigrant entrepreneurs takes place according to the rules of Waldinger's game of ethnic musical chairs. At second glance, the case seems some-what more complicated.

Take, for example, the *Italian ice-cream makers* (Bovenkerk, Eijken and Bovenkerk-Teerink, 1984). These young migrants prepared excellent fruit ices, a product many customers appreciated. On the basis of this popular product and with the help of their own networks, they were able to form a niche. Although Italians are still well represented in the ice-cream trade, the continuity of their niche is in jeopardy. Second – and later – generations of *gelatieri* are disinclined to take over their parent's business and move out into other economic sectors. Nowadays, commu-nity forming hardly exists and the role of ethnic networks has corres-pondingly decreased (see Lindo, 1994). Moreover, the preparation and selling of quality ice-creams faces competition from other (internationally operating) factories such as Häagen Dasz, or concerns such as Unilever.

During the 1960s, Italian guestworkers did make a run at the ice-cream selling business (as street traders), so much so that the local authorities started to regulate the branch. They thus enforced a legal ceiling, limiting the growth in the number of entrepreneurs in the ice-cream trade. Most ice-cream sellers, however, have no wish to establish themselves as self-employed ice-cream makers – among other things because of the many rules and regulations with which they must comply – and consider the trade only as an extra source of income.

Take, as another example, the *Turkish garment manufacturers* (Raes, 1996; Rath, 1998b). When the garment industry was struggling to get to its feet during the years of recovery after the war, various Jewish entrepreneurs participated, but they did so without reinstalling their niche. Jewish entrepreneurs could no longer rely on the help of Jewish women for the workshop and instead recruited labour on the Dutch open market and later also in the Mediterranean countries. The sector began to decline during the 1960s, due to international competition, and one business after another closed, or moved its clothing assembly to lower-wage countries. A few Turkish workers, who had learned the trade from Jewish entrepreneurs, eventually set up their own establishments. These entrepreneurs only really got started once market developments were favourable. Partly as a result of changing consumer demands, customers – especially those in the so-called short-cycle ladies fashion – needed shorter and faster supply lines. Local workshops could meet this demand. Both immigrants with experience in the (craft) clothing industry in Turkey and unemployed guestworkers got lucky, and, partly through their networks, a cluster of Turkish trade and industry evolved. The mushrooming of the Turkish garment industry at the end of the 1980s and the beginning of the 1990s is also linked with the extremely accommodating attitude of the authorities towards their informal practices. Since 1994, however, the public prosecutor has intensified controls on fraud and illegalities in the garment industry. Partly forced by the operations of the garment industry's intervention team and partly due to the opening of new markets in east Europe and Turkey, garment sweatshops were forced to close one after another. As far as the Turkish niche has disappeared, no new successors have appeared to take their place as yet.

Or, take the *Egyptian shoarma sellers* (Choenni, 1997: 71–9). Israelis introduced *shoarma* (kebab) to Amsterdam during the 1970s. During the busy holiday periods they hired Coptic student workers from Egypt who knew the product. When the snack became popular, these first temporary workers changed tack and became self-employed entrepreneurs. One thing leads to another and, within a few years, the Egyptian immigrants had completely overshadowed the Israeli *shoarma* sellers. In 1993, in a 'community' of roughly 3200 Egyptians, some 145 snack bars and lunchrooms were counted. The rise of these *shoarma* bars has been so quick that the question arises of whether this falls under the heading 'ethnic musical chairs'. After all, the Israelis had hardly had a chance to form their own niche.

CONCLUSION

The time has now come to make up the balance. Immigrants who have come to Amsterdam over the years have all followed their own route of economic incorporation. In earlier historical periods, immigrants mostly sought refuge in trade or in certain traditional craft industries. This was because their skills and trading contacts were aimed at these sectors, but also because they had been denied access to other more regular economic areas. In more recent periods, the majority of immigrants have taken their refuge first and foremost as employees. Lately, however, self-employed entrepreneurship is on the rise, a development in which immigrants participate disproportionally. Here, Amsterdam shows an increasing similarity with the world's most classic immigrant city, New York. Within groups of immigrants, though, we sometimes see a large degree of heterogeneity.

The sociologist, Waldinger, has discovered in New York – and also in Los Angeles – a remarkable pattern of economic incorporation: immigrants settle in niches and become – via these niches – engaged in what resembles a game of ethnic musical chairs. Further examination, however, shows that this pattern of incorporation is not automatically applicable to Amsterdam. There *are* forms of ethnic concentration, but these do not seem to be the only – or necessary – route to economic incorporation. Moreover, there is not always a continuing historical chain: sometimes niche succession takes place falteringly, other times, not at all.

Although the present state of research in Amsterdam demands modesty, the above economic sociological exercise still leads to questions regarding Waldinger's theoretical assumptions. Waldinger does point to important factors and processes, such as the role of social networks, but fails to take the following points adequately into consideration.

First, Waldinger stipulates the need for a hierarchy of preferred population categories. This must, moreover, be practical, for example through the formation of a labour queue. Generally, such processes also take place in the Netherlands. There are, however, important differences, for we are now talking about different 'imagined communities' (see Rath, 1991). In the United States, ethnic and racial characteristics form important *markers* (it is no coincidence that Waldinger calls the society 'race conscious'), while in the Netherlands, the main *markers* were primarily religious in the past and are sociocultural in the present. In the present Dutch system, the significance of sociocultural characteristics inspires all kinds of attempts at the 'controlled integration' of minority groups; attempts that assume that sociocultural characteristics are changeable are often of an extremely paternalistic nature. This specific signification and its sociopolitical dynamics produce changing orders of ranking and queues. This means that attention should be paid to their dynamics, that is the possibility that the society's appreciation of these characteristics can rise or fall. Although only 30 years ago, Spanish and Italian immigrants in the Netherlands figured as problem categories at the back of the queue, although not as far back as 'long-haired louts' (see Bagley, 1973), they are now considered 'relatively non-problematical' (Lindo, 1994: 117).

Second, but related to the first point, Waldinger supposes the long-term existence of more or less cohesive ethnic groups, with a large measure of solidarity and trust. However, in reality, social relationships are not often that harmonious. Especially when entrepreneurs are operating from one niche, namely in the same market, there is a strong chance that they become each other's competitors. This can undermine the niche. Furthermore, we must bear in mind that some immigrant groups assimilate, so their niches are not permanent *per se*. Italian immigrants are less and less using their own ethnic networks for their economic activities.

Third, Waldinger focuses on the sociological and not the economic field when explaining the economic incorporation process. Although he certainly does take market developments into consideration – he sees these as one of the factors that lead to changes in the labour queue – he regards networks as being of central importance for the incorporation process. However, if we are to explain the rise and fall of the Turkish garment industry in Amsterdam, for example, we cannot ignore such factors as the changes in consumer demand or the international division of labour. Without such changes, the small Turkish businesses would never have had so much opportunity to develop. In this connection, we must also point out the role of technological change. The fall of the Jewish niche in the sugar trade and industry, halfway through the nineteenth century, can be explained, for the most part, by the technological innovations that made it possible to make sugar from sugar beet instead of from imported sugar cane. Although the Jews had not lost their control over the processing of sugar beet, the Roman Catholics from the southern province of Brabant were able to take over the market simply because they were able to offer a considerably cheaper product (Schrover, 1994: 164).

Fourth, Waldinger limits the role of the institutional framework to political arrangements steered by ethnic or racially based interest groups with the aim of influencing the allocation of jobs in the public sector. The political system in New York is certainly not a blueprint for 'the' institutional framework. The government and its nimbus of quangos, 'quasi non-governmental organizations', determine the latter. In the Dutch corporate welfare state, this framework has expanded enormously, certainly in comparison with the rather meagre US welfare state. This has far-reaching consequences for spending power. Even the long-term unemployed have a fairly high minimum wage in the Netherlands, which influences the need to start up and make a success of one's own business (Kloosterman, 1998). The mixture of rules and regulations steering economic traffic – and the way the authorities enforce these – have more direct influence. The Jewish street trade before the Second World War, the preparation and selling of ice-cream by Italians, as well as Turkish garment manufacture, would have developed to a greater extent if regulations had been less strict and investigators less active. On the other hand, we see that the institutional framework can contribute to the endurance of certain niches. The establishment of Islamic butchers (of Turkish or Moroccan origin) is subjected to a special legal regime. Moreover, the ritual slaughter necessary for obtaining halal meat falls under a different regulation. Interestingly, this regulation is based on rules and regulations that were once made for Jewish butchers (Rath et al., 1996: 74).

All in all, the game of ethnic musical chairs, described by Waldinger, cannot be accepted without reservation as *the* model for understanding and explaining the incorporation of immigrants in Amsterdam. Although he points to a number of important processes – which deserves our appreciation – others remain underexposed. His viewpoint would certainly be strengthened if he were to give more credit to the role of the market, to technological innovations and to the institutional framework

Notes

1. The author thanks Frank Buijs, Mies van Niekerk, Rinus Penninx and Marlou Schrover for their commentary on an earlier version of this paper and Sanna Ravestein-Willis for her editorial support.

2. In the beginning they were excluded from most of the guilds. However, those of the surgeons, estate agents and booksellers allowed them to become members – under strict conditions – even before the Batavian Republic (Kockelkorn, 1994; Lucassen and Penninx, 1994). Furthermore, the exclusion from the (other) guilds in the republic was far less extensive than in some other neighbouring countries (see Lucassen, 1997).

3. I would like to point out that I am concerned here with *niches*, not with the seemingly related concept of the *ethnic enclave* (see Wilson and Portes, 1980). The concentration of ethnic groups in a certain trade or line of business is determined by dividing the share of a certain group in employment in a certain industry by its share in the total employment.

4. This, of course, also applies to other countries on the European continent. Morokvasic, Phizacklea and Rudolf (1986) contribute the absence of immigrant-run sewing workshops in Germany partly to the persecution of the Jews.

5. Admittedly, those with restaurants nowadays have little in common with the labourers of the past. The Chinese form in many ways a rather heterogeneous group, see Benton and Vermeulen, 1987.

6. This applies to immigrants and their children from the ex-colonies, Mediterranean countries and all other non-industrial countries. In the jargon of the Amsterdam civil servant, these are collectively named 'minorities'.

7. At the end of December 1996 these programmes totalled 6492 participants, of which 2799 were from the above mentioned target groups. See the Amsterdam Work Monitor (1996: 10). The share of ethnic minorities in the Melkert 1 Supervision Programme is a good 60 per cent. According to Hoolt and Scholten (1996: 73–5), Surinamese and Moroccans were the main participants in the joint working group. See also Smeets, 1993: 16–17.

8. This niche has proven vulnerable. Both in New York and Los Angeles, African Americans are losing political influence, while the continuation of programmes for affirmative action is under discussion. Concentration on networks in this sector has led to a lack of relevant networks in other ones. This is now leading to their downfall. See Waldinger (1996) and Grant, Oliver and James (1996: 399–400).

9. This does not, however, alter the fact that they may profit more than other immigrant categories from the space afforded to immigrants within the political system or that they may be better equipped to fight for this space. Compare Rath (1988: 631) or consider the adventures of the so-called Black Caucus (*Zwart Beraad*) in the district of the Bijlmer.

10. Indo-Chinese are generally strongly represented in the medical profession, whether this is the case in Amsterdam I cannot say (see The, 1989).

11. It is no coincidence that one often finds hawkers in the *global cities* such as New York or Los Angeles (see Austin, 1994).

4 Migrants' Careers and Commercial Expertise in Marseilles

Michel Péraldi

It is taken for granted in all Western societies that phenomena such as chronic unemployment among young people, a gradual slip into economic uncertainty for whole sectors of the labour market, and extreme poverty can no longer be understood merely as alarming signals of a conjunctural crisis. They are endemic manifestations of a new economic and social order emerging from the dislocation of former industrial worlds.

These manifestations can no longer be analysed in terms of issues such as the treatment of residual zones of extreme poverty. They should rather be linked to the far more enigmatic question raised by R. Castel (1995). This is the question of the 'apparently increasing and insistent presence of individuals placed in a situation of wavering within the social structure, and occupying its gaps, unable to find a designated niche'. This problem seems particularly serious when we consider the current period as the second of a cycle of general mutations. As a continuation of the previous decade's dislocation of the industrial economy, a phase of reassignment occurred in certain economic sectors at the end of the 1980s. There is no doubt that this trend falls far short of the return to full employment the public expected. In fact, all indications are that we have to deal with highly selective reassignments characterized by an inherent lack of security in newly created jobs, and an increase in informal economic activities within the context of a general reduction in the number of stable work contracts.

The social sciences must examine these forms of mobilization and describe the circumstances in which they emerge, as well as the new combinations they operate. More particularly, they must give an account of social spheres that no longer focus on a face-to-face confrontation between 'left out' and 'well off' populations. They need to show instead how complex the situation becomes when the gaps are used by a new category of 'free people'[1] who generally remain assigned to the margins of the symbolic and normative values of Fordist wage-earning society.

After a few years in Marseilles, it became noticeable that ethnic entre-preneurs, traders, door-to-door sales people, craft workers and occasional 'go-betweens' constituted as much a part of this modernity as the other more traditional craft workers do through their insertion in the worlds of urban trade and production. In this sense, their activities and initiatives represent neither individual solutions to the ongoing crisis nor simple remedies in a struggle for survival, but, both socially and economically, they are strategic forms of 'productive mobilization'.

MARSEILLES: UNPRODUCTIVE PLACE OR TRADING-CITY?

Like most European cities, Marseilles gradually lost the industries that had been creating its prosperity since the nineteenth century (metallurgy, ship maintenance and chemical engineering). The local economy was par-ticularly vulnerable to this erosion, which began early in the postwar period, for it was not replenished with new industries and services; instead, these have been established on the metropolitan outskirts of the city (in Aix-en-Provence, Aubagne and around the Etang de Berre). The presence of this economically prosperous circle around Marseilles emphasizes the urban decay into which the city has slid. Since the mid-1970s, Marseilles has been losing an average of 10,000 inhabitants a year (it now contains fewer than 800,000 people). These are mainly lost to its metropolitan outskirts where towns like Aix and Aubagne have registered some of the highest rates of increase in France in the past 15 years. More than 40,000 indus-trial jobs disappeared between 1975 and 1990, and most of the great factory complexes now lie empty. The social consequences of this situ-ation are proportional to the radical changes: approximately 20 per cent of the people in Marseilles are unemployed. In the city's northern districts, where most of the working class has been concentrated since the nine-teenth century, this rate can reach up to 30 or even 40 per cent of the active population. In some council housing estates located in the northern part of the city, whole generations are affected. Migrants' children, who have been opting out of the education system since the 1980s, have nothing to replace chronic unemployment other than the stopgap jobs offered by urban and social development policies – the public NGO and institutional programmes that provide social support in the poor districts. Nearly 15 per cent of the people in Marseilles live below the poverty line. Recent migrants, mainly from the Maghreb, bear a heavy cost, for they constitute a large part of the outcasts emerging from the above figures.

This crisis divides the local urban society into opposing factions that are socially and spatially segregated. Most of the civil servants employed by the state and city council are situated in the southern half of the city, the traditional trading district, where there is also private housing. The northern half of the city is where the working class and unemployed live in council housing (70 per cent of which is located in the four northern districts) amid broad expanses of former industrial sites lying fallow. Caught between these two halves and carved from its imaginary function as federal public space, the historical centre has become the symbol of this industrially unproductive town. Regarded as an area of decay, it constitutes both the target of a political crusade that plans its reassignment and an appropriate dwelling place for populations looked upon as dangerous outsiders (Medam, 1995).

This zone has become an important landing stage for Maghrebian and, more recently, black African communities coming in from both sides of the Mediterranean Sea. Bounded by a railway station to the north and a commercial harbour to the south, it is where ethnic street-corner shopkeepers have been establishing their business premises since the beginning of the century. Between 1980 and 1988, it was estimated that an average of 400 stores in this area produced a turnover of FF3000 million ($500 million). This was from the steady stream of more than 40 000 weekend customers from the Maghreb, over and above the local and regional consumers (Tarrius, 1995). This landing stage not only attracts food products that European stores do not provide, such as *halal* meat, spices and various other supplies, but it also allows people access to all sorts of manufactured goods that may still be difficult to find in their countries of origin. These include textiles, car spare parts, household electrical goods, and new and second-hand cars.

Algerian vendors who arrived in Marseilles between 1970 and 1975 opened up this commercial front, which has since been taken over by Tunisian, Senegalese and Moroccan traders. The framework of this landing stage also consists of its connections with broad commercial networks. There are the wholesalers of ready-made clothing, such as the Sephardic Jews from Morocco or Algeria, who settled in Marseilles after decolonization. The area also depends on suppliers and wholesalers in Belgium (carpets), Germany (cars), Italy (leather, shoes and Asian-made household electrical goods), and Turkey (jewellery and ready-made clothes). The whole system of circulation within this commercial framework is, in most cases, completely alien to normal standards of transport logistics, for the traders themselves organize it through networks of 'ants' and door-to-door sales persons. Apart from being a district of intense commercial and trading activity, Belsunce is also a nodal area in which the economic and social conditions necessary for the exchange of goods prohibited or subject to political embargoes are negotiated on a Mediterranean-wide scale. The unregulated gold on its way from Istanbul or Naples to the Maghreb and Africa, the German cars destined for Libya and the baskets of cost-price American shoes, imitation luxury items and various other odds and ends pass through Belsunce. These examples demonstrate that Belsunce is above all a trading place in which actors rely on oral agreements and in which mutual obligations maintain the circulation of supply and the cyclical increase in profits suspended by social and political boundaries.

Despite fluctuating relations between Europe and the Maghreb, currently exacerbated by the Algerian crisis, and notwithstanding the urban pressures of local institutions or the continuing promotion of diabolical public attitudes, the trading post is in constant evolution as it concentrates on an ever increasing range of enterprising initiatives. The different waves of migrants become integrated into the process of succession and cooperation that characterizes this central district, which has become a place of settlement as well as a centre for trade and business. Established patterns of cooperation between 'old hands' and 'newcomers' constantly regenerate the various sources and areas of supplies, commercial routes and even available labour power. Belsunce is a rare example of an intercultural framework of commercial functions in which, instead of ethnic relations, it is the migration streams themselves and their differences that constitute the economically available resources.

The most significant example of this evolution is the opening of new market places and the extension of the commercial landing stage to new spaces in the city. Some of these are located in the immediate neighbourhood of the historical seat of Belsunce. Others, such as the flea market (Péraldi, 1995), have appeared on disused factory sites in the industrial heartland of the northern districts. These new commercial spaces, which have been opened up by the prosperous vendors of an earlier wave, are characterized by a distinct shift in business strategy. While not necessarily disconnected from the Maghrebi stream of customers, these new markets are more systematically oriented towards local consumers, for they offer food, ready-made clothes and household goods at very low prices. Theirs is the strategy of the 'huge discount'. Such a redeployment of commercial activities produces greater accessibility for local populations, whether in the precarious spheres of society or in that fringe of the middle class that remains relatively uncontaminated by cultural divisions or by the symbolic importance of marking their social distance from the working class. Out of these latest and most original markets have emerged new types of entrepreneurs, sons of migrants more precisely, young unemployed boys or men excluded from the wage-earning labour market. They are attempting new social and professional careers grounded in their special competence as 'go-betweens' or mediators among the different cultural worlds that rub shoulders in the market place. This is how young people from the poor districts (who up until now had been excluded from commercial life by migrants recruited from within family trade networks in the host country) eventually entered this domain of activities.

THE COMPETENCIES OF AN '*AFFRANCHI*'[2]

The presence of structured commercial spaces available to a wide variety of customers in the heart of the city provides a strategic condition for the increase in careers outside the conventional wage-earning framework. The dynamism of this sector of informal employment seems to be viable so long as people can enter the commercial arena at any point along the deployed activity lines. To produce this flexibility, these markets rely on three ethical rules:

1. It is acknowledged as a collective norm that all the actors are potential entrepreneurs.
2. It is taken for granted that everyone is in the business for themselves and can open their own businesses whenever they want, regardless of what initial status allowed them to enter the arena, for example as sales persons, occasional go-betweens, or even as simple informants or suppliers of small services. It is common to see employees set up their own businesses with a former boss sometimes helping them by lending start-up capital, offering preferential access to suppliers, or providing stock in advance of payment.
3. Every commercial arena gradually develops a set of complex networks built up around gifts and counter-gifts, debts and interdependencies.

However, not everyone has access to these initial positions. Entry to and participation in the arena are strictly related to whether or not one belongs to certain social circles. As one sales person put it: 'You must be straight and well-known', or in other words, integrated through personal relations. These circles are generally ethnic or family linked, but they extend to relations formed in commercial spaces or residential neighbourhoods. These are sometimes formed during moments of leisure in 'moral zones', like cafés or restaurants, as well as in places of worship, especially mosques. Another of their features is the primacy of oral agreements over any other form of structured exchange. This applies as much to moral values (trust, respect of the given word) as to performance – being a 'smooth talker', good company, having the gift of the gab, or knowing how to be persuasive. This clever mix of cultural skills and performance organizes the regulated extension of the trader's milieu beyond the initial ethnic circles.

The following illustration of a typical route into this line of commerce shows how the ethical rules operate and stand the test. Slimane is the son of a labourer. He left school early with a poor scholastic record. His father, who had political links in Algeria, had been involved in the transit business there at a fairly senior level. The family now owns a bar in the flea market and a butcher's shop in a council housing estate in the fifteenth district. Slimane explained: 'When I was a kid, my dad used to send me to the council estate and to the flea market to sell stuff that his boss [his supplier, a Belsunce wholesaler] gave him. My dad was doing extra hours in return without being paid. The boss used to give us clothes, chocolate and chewing gum.' Having left school, Slimane entered a Sephardic wholesaler's firm as a storekeeper:

It was just as if I belonged to them. I was at their disposal. I wasn't making my 39 hours a week like everyone else, but 60 instead. Just because I was a registered worker, I owed them everything. He was often calling me in the middle of the night asking me to come and unload stuff from a van I had to drive elsewhere afterwards. It was too much!

Slimane left his boss under a friendly arrangement: the wholesaler would supply the stock on credit, which Slimane would then sell on his own account in market places or housing estates.

It was I who came out to him with this deal, and he said OK immediately. I think he owed me something in a way. It's as if I had been working for him too much and now, it is just like he's paying for all the nights he woke me up, and all the extra hours I made.

Slimane only sells high-quality clothing he gets from wholesalers, or he very carefully resells to reliable clients small quantities of items embezzled through the network of dockers and haulage contractors in the harbour. Let us see what he says about how he organizes his activities:

Q Why do you sell in the council housing estates?

A Many people who used to live here have moved and came to live in these housing estates. I know many people there; we grew up together. It's better for me, the estate is my world, and I feel at home even if I don't live there. I live near there.

Q How much do you earn?

A When I was a kid working for my dad, I used to bring him in 100 francs ($16) a day. At the flea market, I was making between 400 and 500 francs ($66–$83). Now I get an average of 700 to 900 francs ($116–150) every evening. I only go there from Monday to Friday. It's hard to find people on weekends.

Q How did you manage to get yourself a clientele?

A It was hard at the beginning. I used to knock at every door in every building. Doors slammed in my face very often. I got my clients little by little and now, they are still the same. I have 15 regular clients, 30 occasional ones and about another 50 buy stuff from me exceptionally.

Q Do you sell for cash or do you agree to give credit?

A It's rare people pay me cash. They pay me when they want, that's the deal between me and them. Some forget to pay me, I don't forget them. They hug the walls when they see me. Some of them still want to buy my stuff so I sell to them only if they pay cash. I never ask for the money they owe me. I make gifts but I don't forget. I've trusted people too much and it's made me suspicious. Now, I do like the police, there are checks at every border. A tradesman has to test people in front of him or else he gets eaten. People who don't keep their word, they're out. Automatic.

Q What is your definition of business?

A It's relations with others, that's all. And you need all your time to keep them going. In the things I do, money has never been my first principle. The biggest mistake is when you mix money and business. Many tradesmen have gone under because of that. You can be in the business without money. It's as if people, acquaintances, replace the money. You don't need to handle maximum money, you need to handle maximum people. That is business. Look, I have no money and I'm a businessman. It's all a question of relations. People can be red, green, yellow or white, that's not a problem. As long as they are in the business, they're interesting people to know. You just have to win their trust and it's OK, but that's the tough bit of it all.

Slimane is a door-to-door salesman in the traditional sense of the word. Of course, he does not cross mountains as rural traders do, but he crosses the social and economic barriers to the urban social space. It is difficult to evaluate the economic impact of door-to-door trade in council housing estates, not because this activity is clandestine or invisible, but because it is 'informal' and, as such, slips outside national accountancy or wage-earning norms. However, unlike certain criminal activities such as petty theft, delinquency or drug trafficking, it is neither legally restricted nor morally prohibited. The invisibility of door-to-door trade stems from the very nature of the exchanges it organizes and from the muddling of the social divisions and frontiers it operates, for its function is to promote the circulation of supplies across these boundaries. What remains out of sight is the economic arena's transverse action within which door-to-door trade is but one piece: seeing it as a whole would mean identifying the conspicuous consumption – especially of clothes – that governs the ordinary aspects of young people's social lives. It would also mean identifying the extravagant and equally conspicuous consumption patterns that animate community relations and the ordinary ways in which migrants cope with their link to those who stayed 'over there'. This would then reveal the ordinary role of luxury and ostentation in the urban middle class, as well as the social and symbolic closeness between these middle classes and the 'left out' populations. It would eventually reveal that the consumption of hashish has become commonplace, not only in council housing estates (as most witnesses have noted), but among young people in general. Indeed, the very marginality of the door-to-door trader who sells in social spheres in which he or she is a foreigner, is an essential condition for opening up new distribution networks. Yet, simultaneously, it helps hide the extension of the commercial arenas in which the transit of goods being passed on is articulated as well as the complex organizations and networks underlying them.

INFORMAL TRADE AND SOCIAL ADVANCEMENT

The individual paths and career narratives that have been analysed and reconstructed so far have led us to a double finding. Contrary to a widespread prejudice, choosing an informal commercial activity is neither an ultimate survival strategy in the face of no other opportunities to gain an income, nor a social position acquired through techniques or in continuity of a family tradition. Although the media and social services associate 'easy money' with informal activities, it is obvious that those who have nothing are able to survive because of their access to social benefits and, above all, to public allowances such as the subsistence grant. Those who start up a commercial career radically reject this type of income. They are more likely to boycott the institutional relations they regard as allegiance rituals, or simply refuse to accept the low wages provided by social benefits. Instead, as an alternative to giving up, their commitment to the world of trade constitutes an active form of resistance, a struggle in the name of honour and dignity, while any form of administrative supervision is perceived as a disgrace. Furthermore, many live out their commitment as an 'intense experience' (Simmel, 1971), or as a personal adventure that is likely to 'restore ordinary life's originality' on the same basis as sport and leisure (Wacquant, 1994).

Knowing how to 'cope', 'play the game', 'be in on the tricks', as activities in these spheres are variously named, also means saving face. This is not because they provide enough to live on at subsistence level, but because they ensure a kind of social status: they maintain a certain lifestyle, sartorial elegance and, more frequently, independence from the family.

Young people who launch into this type of activity have generally had a brief and troubled schooling. In these social spheres, we have yet to meet anyone who had trained as a trader or accountant before starting up in business. Most are the sons or daughters of labourers or former labourers. At first sight, nothing outside their individual choice seems to have led them to this type of 'career'. Many, however, refer to a phase of initiation, as shown in our previous example, under the authority of a father, brother or uncle who himself had been in the business. Yet, in the narratives, these family episodes constitute no more than initiation ordeals; they do not generate integration through apprenticeship or natural succession, but require in all cases individual proof of one's reliability. It is also common for parents to disapprove of their child's choice to take up business, for they would prefer to see them stay on at school. Indeed, young businesspersons often have brothers and sisters who go on to higher education or to jobs that require a firm stock of knowledge acquired at school, as in the social services, education or sociocultural activities.

Everything indicates, therefore, that taking up business constitutes neither a way of surviving nor of mastering and preserving acquired professional skills, as is often the case in moonlighting (Laé, 1989). The traders described here, whether occasional or aiming at stability, seek to guarantee for themselves a 'standing' and social status that their current position fails to provide. It can be asserted, albeit tentatively, that even though some traders initiate genuine businesses through informal activities and others do so to avoid ruination, the people worked on the council housing estates as an alternative to what a now broken but once upwardly mobile 'social elevator' can no longer provide. In this sense, these commercial activities can be seen as a way of perpetuating the dream generated by postwar economic growth, namely social advancement for all. What characterizes these young tradesmen is that they do it on their own behalf and with a conscious wish to show their resistance and personal challenge to established social rules, which have changed. There is no doubt that the institutional channels and systems of logic that once produced ascending careers are today, for those who remain their outcasts, also generating regressive and captive destinies.

Notes

1. In French, the term *affranchis* (here used as a notion) contains the idea both of somebody who has been freed from slavery and somebody who is a sort of outlaw.
2. See note 1.

5 Segregation and Economic Integration of Immigrants in Brussels

Christian Kesteloot and Henk Meert

During the 1960s and early 1970s, suburbanization was the most important process shaping Brussels' socio-spatial structure. Fordist accumulation was based on the distribution of productivity gains over profit and wage increases. As such, growing mass production found a market in growing mass consumption. Houses, cars and consumer durables fuelled this growth. These goods required space and became visible because people bought or built houses on the urban fringe, commuted daily by car and accumulated consumer durables at home. Thus, suburbanization in Belgium was the spatial expression of Fordist economic growth. The changing class structure also supported the suburbanization process. Rising levels of education and the development of tertiary activities pushed the Belgian population into upward social mobility. The population of Brussels became increasingly middle class and could draw on its growing incomes to become the owner-occupiers of individual buildings of dwellings outside the city, in a green environment where land prices were affordable.

Several conditions explain the strength of this process in Belgium (especially in Brussels as the main urban centre) compared with other European countries. The first is the national economy's prompt entrance into Fordist accumulation. As early as 1944, the government fostered a social contract between employers and trade unions, which established the national social security system and the principle of regular wage rises in response to productivity gains. The ideology of access to home ownership through self promotion and self building had been well established by the Christian democrat policies in operation since the end of the nineteenth century. It was regarded as a means of stressing Christian family values rather than the collective interests of the workers and to keep workers away from the cities and socialism (Goossens, 1988). After the Second World War, a new law providing grants to families buying and especially building their own homes was introduced. It yielded more than half a million grants for one-third of the postwar housing stock. Another law, promoted by the socialist party, tried to revive a construction programme for rented council housing, but ended up with a grant scheme for building on housing estates. Cheap mortgages for large households as well as building in the countryside remained subsidized (Goossens, 1983). Building activity following these state interventions resulted in a large spatial expansion of the city, but through the diffusion of car ownership it became a sprawl rather than a development of urban satellites. Finally, the absence of any physical planning to contain the urban sprawl made cheap construction land available on the peripheries of cities and along main roads in the countryside. This huge construction activity – predominantly through self-building and self-promotion – was sustained by rising real wages, job security and income security funded by the social contract and expansion of the credit system. The promotion of suburbanization as a key element in a Keynesian economic policy also discharged the state from the responsibility of financing a complete social housing policy and massive urban renewal.

The arrival of the guestworkers, mainly between the mid-1960s and 1974 when migration stopped, was directly related to the Belgians' upward social mobility and spatial shift towards the urban fringe. They filled the socioeconomic and spatial positions in the urban system that the middle and upper classes had vacated. Though now employed in public transport, catering and low-skilled services, they at first worked in the declining urban industries and, significantly, in the construction industry, which was heavily involved in the Fordist transformation of urban space. The city has been reshaped to provide more office space, a transport and communications infrastructure, and parking spaces for the suburban middle classes making the daily commute to work. The guestworkers are concentrated in a belt of vacant nineteenth-century houses. Much of the Fordist restructuring of the city, for which the guestworkers were used as a cheap labour force, has had a considerable impact on the function of housing and quality of life in the inner city. While the guestworkers helped build the Fordist inner city, they have also suffered from its restructuring, for they are trapped in its cheapest dwellings (Deslé, 1990).

Thus, suburbanization generated a new social division of urban space, for the migratory process was socially selective. The rich were the first to leave the city. Later, with the general rise in real incomes, they were followed by a less affluent strata of the middle class. As a result, the inner city lost its high-income groups and entered into decline. Only those who could not follow the movement remained trapped in the inner city. These included the elderly poor, unskilled workers, artisans, small shopkeepers, first-time buyers trying to enter the housing market, and guestworkers. Suburbanization during the 1960s and 1970s turned the city into a large urban region, characterized by clear socioeconomic, demographic and ethnic spatial differentiation. The periphery houses an affluent, relatively young population of Belgian families and rich foreigners who participate in the city's international functions. Decayed inner city areas house large immigrant families and both young and old single person households. In every way, these people are less affluent than their suburban counterparts. Without any demographic pressure on the housing market, itself a result of the economic and social processes behind suburbanization, there are no lower-class peripheral estates; the council housing stock remains small and accommodates mainly lower-middle-class households.

The effects of suburbanization are dramatic. While in 1963, Brussels Capital Region had an average income per person 60 per cent above the national average, it dropped to 28 per cent in 1975. At the same time, the figures in both surrounding districts rose from 5 and 12 per cent to 15 and 19 per cent respectively (Table 5.1).[1] Thanks to the immigration of guest-workers, the population is stable.

Table 5.1   Population and average taxable income per person compared with the national average 1963–95

	1963		1975		1985		1995	
	pop	income	pop	income	pop	income	pop	income
Brussels Capital Region	100	160	101	128	94	106	92	93
Halle-Vilvoorde district	100	105	116	115	121	117	127	120
Nivelles district	100	112	120	119	141	116	159	116
Kingdom	–	100	–	100	–	100	–	100

Note: Population in percentage of 1963 population; average income in percentage of average income per person of the Kingdom.

Source: NIS.

THE ECONOMIC CRISIS AND THE LOCKING OF IMMIGRANTS IN THE INNER CITY

With suburbanization based on economic growth, increasing incomes and income security, it is no surprise that the process slowed down during the second half of the 1970s and early 1980s. At first sight, this could be seen as a positive development for the inner city areas, for crises limit inner-city decay. However, it also curbs opportunities for upward mobility in the labour and housing markets among the lower income groups, which results in increased competition in these markets. This strengthened a second contrast within cities, which is visible through the spatial structure of the housing market (see Map 5.1).

As a result of suburbanization, the residual private rental sector came to dominate inner city housing (about 30 per cent of the total housing stock). Landlords ceased to invest in these old houses, for they had already recovered their original investments several times over through rent (Kesteloot et al., 1997). Living conditions deteriorated quickly because of a lack of either private or public interest. The earliest residential belt to surround the city centre and the nineteenth-century working-class areas contrast sharply with the more recent outer belts. The latter offer better quality and more expensive rental and owner-occupied dwellings (39 per cent of the Brussels housing stock is owner-occupied and about 20 per cent belongs to the more expensive rental sector). Although the share of council housing is relatively small (8 per cent of the total stock), most council housing estates are, interestingly, located in the outer belts. This is because, ever since council housing was introduced after the First World War, it has been built on cheap land at the edge of (or even outside) the city. A few estates were built in the inner city, especially after 1953 when a programme against hovels was launched. Most people entering the housing market for the first time can only afford cheap rented accommodation. They are likely to locate in the nineteenth-century belt and join those members of the original population who were too old or too poor to become suburbanized. The dominant group in the inner city is, however, of migrant origin. Thus, apart from a few areas, one can say that in the Brussels Capital Region, the inner city, the residual housing sector and the areas of immigrant concentration coincide.[2]

However, the operation of the housing market is not the only reason for the endurance of ethnic neighbourhoods. While such concentrations are a precondition for creating an ethnic infrastructure, it was the crisis that drove some immigrants into ethnic entrepreneurship, thus generating an ever-richer infrastructure. This move into ethnic entrepreneurship can be seen as a strategy to escape unemployment at the individual level, but it also makes living in ethnic areas cheaper at a local community level. Because over-investment and tough competition reduce prices, products and services are well tuned to the local population's needs, offering

Map 5.1   The housing market structure of the Brussels Capital Region, 1991

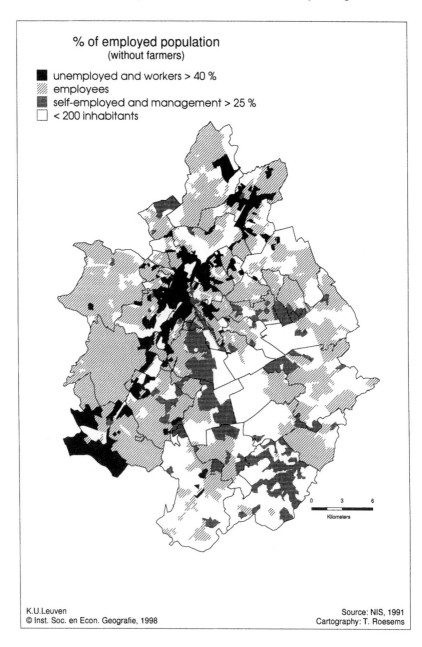

% of employed population
(without farmers)

■ unemployed and workers > 40 %
▨ employees
▦ self-employed and management > 25 %
☐ < 200 inhabitants

0   3   6
Kilometers

K.U.Leuven
© Inst. Soc. en Econ. Geografie, 1998

Source: NIS, 1991
Cartography: T. Roesems

widespread opportunities to buy on credit. All this relies on strong social networks within the ethnic community (Meert et al., 1997). Thus, the consolidation of ethnic neighbourhoods can also be seen as a spatial strategy for coping with the effects of the crisis, which brought higher levels of unemployment and income insecurity to immigrants than to Belgians (Kesteloot, 1995). In the same way, the nineteenth-century inner city neighbourhoods appear as rich environments for the development of survival strategies, including several forms of informal economy (Kesteloot and Meert, 1993).

POST-FORDISM AND DEEPENING POLARIZATION

Since the mid-1980s, there has been some renewed, but cyclical, economic growth. This growth, which does not match that of the golden 1960s, is closely associated with economic and spatial restructuring. Permanent jobs with good prospects for low-skilled workers have virtually disappeared. Industrial employment in the larger cities has been declining since the 1960s, and those jobs that have survived both deindustrialization and the economic crisis are being adapted to new production processes, which demand flexibility. Flexibility is linked not only to the organization of working hours, but also to changing production processes, consumption patterns and investment policies, to the multiplication and exchange of internal and external company relations and, finally, to the use of space. Thus, economic and spatial restructuring go hand in hand. Although they have not generated dramatic changes in Brussels' socio-spatial patterns, they have increased the city's dual character in several respects.

A flexible economy is accompanied by increased mobility of capital. The more mobile the capital, the more the cities and regions struggle with each other to attract investments, or simply keep them where they are. Regional competition for international investment, and consequently for jobs, intensifies as capital becomes increasingly footloose. Many recent urban developments can be linked to this competition. Cities are equipped with new research and industrial facilities, information, communications and decision-making infrastructures, and cultural and social assets. They develop a new image to reflect their position as attractive centres for inward investment in the global economy. In Brussels, nearly all these investments are located in the inner city, whether they be TGV-stations, luxury hotels, offices, shopping centres or up-market residential renovation projects (see Map 5.2).

Map 5.2   Urban restructuring in the Brussels Capital Region, 1985–95

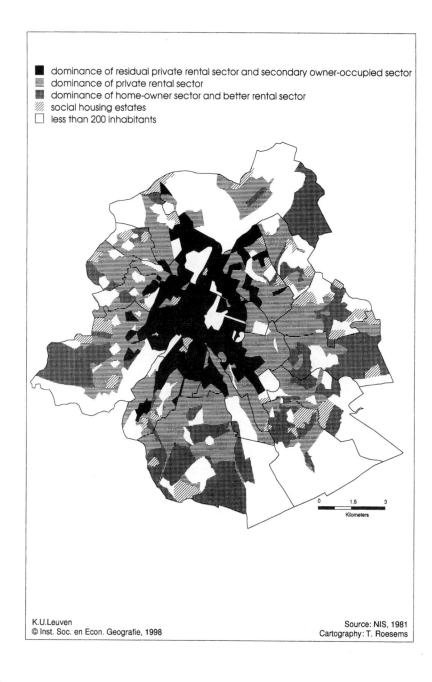

dominance of residual private rental sector and secondary owner-occupied sector
dominance of private rental sector
dominance of home-owner sector and better rental sector
social housing estates
less than 200 inhabitants

0   1.5   3
Kilometers

K.U.Leuven
© Inst. Soc. en Econ. Geografie, 1998

Source: NIS, 1981
Cartography: T. Roesems

The Brussels' municipalities and Brussels Capital Region are more interested in new developments than they were in the 1960s. As their population decreases and as part of the remaining population becomes more impoverished, they try to increase population and/or income in an attempt to generate enough finances from local taxes to maintain the required standards. Hence, urban policy seems to boil down to a careful scanning of the city's social map to select areas or apartment blocks that lend themselves to one or other of the three strategies dictated by the local and regional authorities' increasingly difficult financial situation. These are to increase population, to increase income, or to replace the poor population with richer people. The Regional Development Plan, launched in 1994, aims to bring 35 000 new inhabitants, mainly affluent single persons, to the capital region (Vandermotten, 1994). The plan, which is considered realistic, is based on changes in the labour market; demographic changes, particularly the so-called second demographic transition generating important shifts in household composition, namely the dramatic increase in one-person households (see Lesthaeghe, 1995); and the cultural and symbolic use of urban space (Harvey, 1987).[3] Also, large projects like the TGV-station (and possibly a second one in the north of the city), the European district, developments in the 'Quartier Nord' and adjacent Leopold II lane, and the more recent Music City project, clearly fit in this municipal logic of social recomposition (Kesteloot, 1995). Even in cases of socially inspired urban renewal, when all the actors concerned made the maximum effort to keep inhabitants in their area, it is noticeable that there are fewer poor families. There is also evidence of a careful move having been made to encourage a financially and politically more interesting mix (see, for example, Vanden Eede and Martens, 1994).

This post-Fordist urban restructuring has two effects on immigrant concentration areas – social displacement of the poorest and a rise in home ownership among immigrants. Urban restructuring puts the residential function to more profitable uses and introduces land speculation. As a result, prices on the housing market, particularly in the residual rental sector, doubled between 1988 and 1992 (ASLK, 1997). These pressures are strongest in the eastern part of the inner city and many immigrants (especially Moroccans) were displaced to the western part of the inner city (de Corte and de Lannoy, 1994; see also Map 5.3). Overcrowding, insufficient social infrastructure and the diffusion of housing price increases often make their new living conditions worse than before. Others (especially Turks) achieved both housing and location security through the purchase of a cheap low-quality house in a neighbourhood

Map 5.3   The consolidation of ethnic neighbourhoods: population change of Turks and Moroccans, Brussels Capital Region, 1981–91

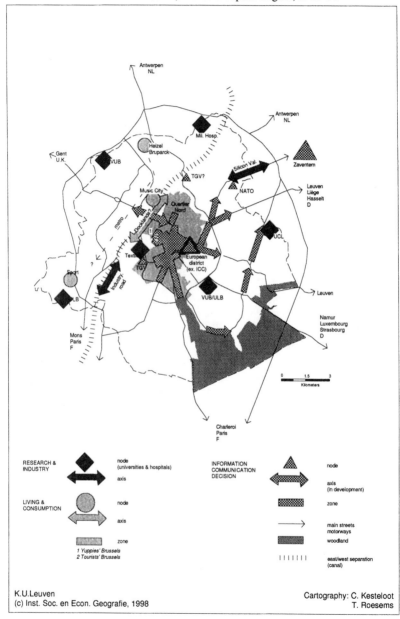

under pressure, especially in the northeastern part of the inner city, thus creating a secondary owner occupied sector. Because they no longer rent, they are protected against further increases in housing costs and at the same time they secure their location in a neighbourhood with access to an ethnic infrastructure, to social networks and to other assets for developing survival strategies. Thus, the number of owner occupiers among the Turkish households increased from 13 to 37 per cent between 1981 and 1991; the figures for the Moroccans were 10 and 30 per cent respectively (Kesteloot et al., 1997). These processes explain the further consolidation of ethnic neighbourhoods in the inner city, but they also worsen living conditions through rising housing costs in the face of stagnating incomes, the impossibility of being able to improve housing conditions, and over-crowding relative to housing as well as the neighbourhood infrastructure.

Economic Integration in Segregated Areas

The economic crisis of the 1970s transformed the immigrants from a cheap urban labour force into an unemployed labour force reserve and prevented the filtering of the immigrants into better segments of the housing market. The post-Fordist restructuring of the city consolidated these ethnic neighbourhoods even further, especially in the western part of the inner-city belt. Today, they form the city's most deprived areas (Kesteloot et al., 1998) and, clearly, deprivation is strongly linked to the immigrants and their offspring being trapped in these neighbourhoods. But, precisely because the inner city neighbourhoods are heterogeneous and mixed, rather than monotonous and monofunctional like the council housing estates on the periphery, they offer a range of opportunities for the economic integration of their inhabitants. To examine them closely, we first introduce the modes of economic integration, as conceptualized by Polanyi. We then use them as analytical tools to unravel local prospects (see also Kesteloot, 1998).

MARKET EXCHANGE, REDISTRIBUTION AND RECIPROCITY

Economic integration can be equated with access to the socioeconomic resources necessary for a decent living and the reproduction of the house-hold. This is because most of these resources are not produced directly by the households but by producers engaged in the economic system. Thus, access to these resources is not direct, but depends on how the household is integrated into the economic system. This problem of access to resources has been theorized by Polanyi and is encapsulated in his concept of modes of socioeconomic integration (Polanyi, 1944). Based on his economic and anthropological work, the concept distinguishes three fundamental ways to obtain resources produced in common: reciprocity, redistribution and market exchange (see also Harvey, 1973; and Mingione, 1991).[4]

In the Western world, market exchange dominates access to resources. In other words, individuals and households must develop a social utility, that is they must produce goods or services others need. This gives them an income that allows them to buy the goods and services they need and cannot produce for themselves. Most households put their labour on the market. Their wage is the price they get when they succeed in selling it. Others are self-employed and sell goods or services. The law of supply and demand indicates whether or not they made a good decision in bringing their labour or product onto the market. Bad decisions are sanctioned by loss of income, which reduces access to the resources produced by others. As a result, the market generates stratification – unequal access to resources based on strong or weak positions on the market.

These inequalities are inherent in market exchange and can be socially destructive because households without utility (those whose labour is not needed) have no access to resources. This is the structural reason why these inequalities are partially compensated for by state redistribution. From a household's point of view, redistribution means that everybody contributes to a common stock of resources, which are then redistributed according to a set of rules. The slow but steady development of welfare from the end of the nineteenth century resulted in a massive redistribution system controlled by the state and supplied mainly by taxes and social security contributions. From this viewpoint, political rights correspond to the power to participate directly or indirectly in decisions about the redistribution flow; and citizenship is the condition for participating in the system.[5] However, because of the actual rules of redistribution, especially in the social security system, taking part in redistribution is still largely determined by taking part in the labour market.

Finally, reciprocity helps people acquire resources through mutual exchange. It implies a social network with symmetrical links between members. Resources given to one of these members are returned by others, generally in the form of different goods or services, and very often not at the same moment. These features of the exchange process involve mutual trust between the members of an exchange network and the lasting ties of each member to that network. This type of relation to a network is termed affiliation. Hence, the most obvious networks are the extended family, ethnic communities and sometimes neighbourhood networks. Each mode of economic integration requires a different set of socio-spatial conditions. Therefore, economic integration, which necessarily involves one or more of the modes discussed above, will be promoted or hindered by the features of each neighbourhood in question. Three main dimensions of this geography of economic integration can be distinguished (Figure 5.1). The first one concerns the intrinsic spatial logic of each mode of integration. The second concerns the presence or absence of the material and social infrastructure that supports the integration activities. And the third relates to the historical layers of the socio-spatial structure of the city in which symbols, habits and relations from the past are embedded and possibly reactivated (Meert, 1998).

In general, one can say that the spatial range of the goods and services offered determines the spatial dimension of market relations. This can be seen in both production and consumption. Access to employment from each neighbourhood, be it in the neighbourhood itself or in other areas (in the case of labour being sold), and access to enough customers (in the case of self-employment) are crucial on the production side. The availability in one's place of residence of all the necessary goods and services sold on the market is crucial on the consumption side. This geography of economic integration through the market is well documented by the classical location theories where centrality and access (distance and transport costs) are the key concepts.

Redistribution is usually spatially organized within a delimited territory in which resources are both collected and distributed. In an urban environment, however, the political partition of the city and the interrelations between national, regional and local authorities (to which one can add the small but growing intervention of the EU) will differentiate cities and even, as in Brussels, neighbourhoods and municipalities within the same city. Thus, the strength of the redistribution system and immigrants' access to resources through this system will differ from country to country, city to city and municipality to municipality. Moreover, local authorities are particularly responsible for collective resources, the social and cultural infrastructures at the neighbourhood level. The same location theories can be used to describe access to these resources and unveil inequalities in their location, which derive from local authority decisions.

Reciprocity implies networks, as well as the material exchange of goods and services within these networks. Spatial proximity is an asset because it facilitates the dialectical relationship between exchange and maintaining the network, thus generating the necessary trust. However, strong family, kin-

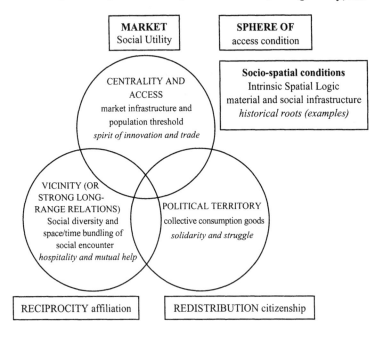

Source: Adapted from Kestelbot (ISEG KU Leuven, 1998).

Figure 5.1   Spheres of economic integration and their socio-spatial conditions

ship or community ties can compensate for loose spatial relations between members of a reciprocity network.

Each mode of economic integration also involves a set of social and material infrastructures. Thus, market exchange supposes a concentration of population, offering the necessary thresholds for production and distribution. Redistribution entails the actual presence of means of collective consumption and of agents for this redistribution. Reciprocity needs an appropriate arrangement of public and private space, offering places that foster social networks through bundling social relations in space and time. Of course, reciprocal exchange will gain in efficiency if the resources the members of the network hold are sufficiently differentiated. Thus, reciprocity has more potential in a socially heterogeneous area than in an area where all the people have similar demands and resources.

Finally, space carries a history, which potentially reinforces certain mechanisms of economic integration over others. These could include a long tradition of hospitality and mutual help, a history of worker participation in the struggle to build a strong welfare state, or traditions of trade and innovation.

Neighbourhood Potentials for Economic Integration

At first sight, the inner city reveals only the weaknesses and barriers to economic integration, especially for immigrants. Empirical research on deprived neighbourhoods in Flanders and Brussels shows that these weaknesses are manifest in four domains (Kesteloot et al., 1996):

- social isolation (expressed by the high rate of single people and the absence of telephones),
- poor access to goods and services redistributed by the state (especially for immigrants in the absence of political rights),
- difficult access to the labour market (expressed by a high rate of unemployment, high ratio of manual to non-manual workers, indicating poor educational levels, job insecurity in the context of deindustrialization) and, finally,
- poor housing conditions (which can hit both tenants and owner occupiers in the neighbourhoods concerned).

The last three show strong interrelations with income.[6] These four domains can be reduced to three spheres of economic integration. Social isolation is related to reciprocity, access to the labour market to market exchange and the two others to redistribution. The durable character of housing and its necessary claim on land explain market failure and therefore state intervention in the provision of decent housing to the whole population. Geographically, the four domains strongly confirm the segregation of immigrants (especially Turks and Moroccans) in the city's most deprived areas (Map 5.4).[7] Concentration and segregation of the poor reinforce their deprivation (Friedrichs, 1997a). At the same time, an analysis of these areas in terms of socio-spatial conditions for economic integration reveals interesting possibilities.

Contrary to many deprived areas in other European cities, which are situated in peripheral housing estates, the immigrant areas of Brussels at least have the advantage of a central location. This provides access to a

Map 5.4 Indicators of deprivation, Brussels Capital Region, 1991

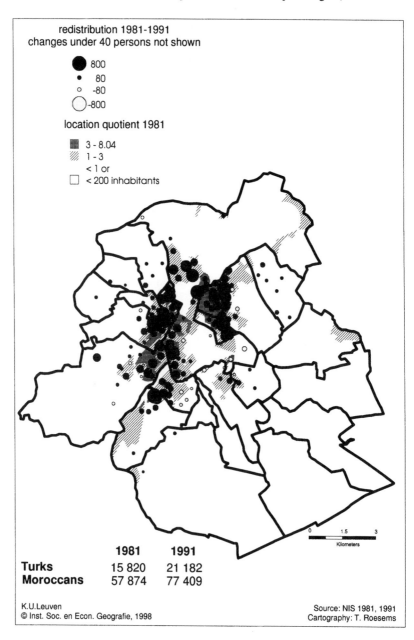

redistribution 1981-1991
changes under 40 persons not shown

- ● 800
- • 80
- ○ -80
- ◯ -800

location quotient 1981

- ▦ 3 - 8.04
- ▨ 1 - 3
- □ < 1 or
  < 200 inhabitants

	1981	1991
Turks	15 820	21 182
Moroccans	57 874	77 409

K.U.Leuven
© Inst. Soc. en Econ. Geografie, 1998

Source: NIS 1981, 1991
Cartography: T. Roesems

large clientele, and the high population densities of the nineteenth-century neighbourhoods, where specific ethnic demands are concentrated, open up opportunities for ethnic entrepreneurship. By contrast, deindustrialization, labour market polarization, and a growing employment mismatch between the urban centre and the periphery, hamper access to the labour market. Thus, paradoxically, these neighbourhoods relate with market exchange. On the one hand, their growing marginalization results from economic restructuring. On the other hand, the inhabitants systematically use (a part of) the market and its mechanisms when they orient themselves to ethnic entrepreneurship or to specific market niches (mostly the cheapest) as strategies through which to gain access to basic resources.

Many collective goods provided by the state in the immigrant areas of the city were inherited from the nineteenth century at a time when education and leisure were limited and state intervention in social matters was considered a weird idea. Schools, sports and cultural facilities are thus poorer than those of the affluent periphery are. Moreover, since immigrants are not recognized as full citizens, they do not have the right to participate in decisions about how and what is redistributed. They are thus easily neglected by local politicians whenever decisions about the allocation of resources are to be made (for example council housing). However, their spatial concentration adds a collective dimension to their incomplete citizenship. Since they are not represented on the municipal councils, a political class that has no relationship with them neglects the infrastructures and services of their neighbourhoods (ranging from schools, sports and cultural facilities to street cleaning and security). Of course, Belgian people living in the same areas experience the same infrastructural deprivations. The lack of state intervention is also caused by shortages of money at the regional and municipal levels as a result of suburbanization and the local authorities' system of financing, which is heavily dependent on the size of the population and its income. However, depending on what coalition is in office and sometimes even on which political figures, differences between municipalities can be substantial (see Dassetto, 1991). Nevertheless, to bring about a more positive redistribution, it would be necessary to generate new flows between the Brussels Capital Region and its periphery. At present, people living in the suburbs make use of the city every day, but pay taxes only in their own rich suburban communes.

The weakness of redistributive flows is partly tempered by the Brussels Capital Region's efforts to fight against the city's dual socio-spatial structure, though these efforts are always triggered by youth riots in the deprived areas. Therefore, they address security more than integration problems. For the same reasons, but also because of the historical inertia since the nineteenth-century charity movement operated in working-class areas, the neighbourhood contains many subsidized private initiatives – welfare activities in the fields of health, housing, youngsters, the elderly, training and employment. They offer survival strategies to poor households, which are aimed at maximizing the aid these institutions receive. However, one should not overestimate the power and impact of these initiatives. An absence of structural support from the authorities, the specific and complex character of the problems and even party-political considerations all are responsible for their poor results. Apart from the authorities, churches and their charity initiatives also play a role as redistributors, as do mosques in some ethnic areas. In the Turkish area, some Turkish shops contribute to an alternative redistributive system controlled by the central mosque, which collects some of their profits for redistribution to those in need of assistance.

As mentioned earlier, reciprocity is more efficient in the case of social mixing. Through their strategy of owner occupation in their area of concentration, northeast of the city centre, Turks tend to stick together, which indicates that their socioeconomic differentiation is growing, allowing for solidarity between rich and poor. Moroccans are more likely to leave their area of concentration if they have the financial means to do so and their areas of concentration are also socioeconomically selective. Moreover, most Turks arrived through chain migration in the late 1960s, when clandestine migration was tolerated. This type of migration allowed for the reproduction of the original village structures. Each Turkish pub is a meeting place for village-centred networks. Finally, due to this area's nineteenth-century genesis, with the king regularly travelling to work between the city centre and his castle in Laken, it was always more socially mixed than the city's other working-class areas.[8] All these elements open up opportunities for reciprocity, which is often a springboard for integration strategies in the two other spheres (Mistiaen et al., 1995). By contrast, deprived neighbourhoods dominated by single persons, one-parent families or atomized ethnic groups are lower performers in the sphere of reciprocity because of the weakness of their social networks (as in the medium deprived areas shown in Map 5.4).

It would be possible to undertake a more detailed geographical analysis of the zone of immigrant concentration. It would be helpful to look at employment opportunities, retail centres and actual ethnic enterprises (for market exchange), at council housing, quality of schools, public transport, communications and welfare agencies (for redistribution) and at social networks and meeting places (for reciprocity). This would yield important information on local economic and social development strategies. It would be necessary to classify every possible asset or infrastructure in one of the integration spheres, which would unveil the strong interaction between them. Economic integration through market exchange is particularly dependent on assets in other spheres. This can be illustrated, with many examples, as the need for adequate training to get a job, cheap public transport to get to work, and the know-how gathered from one's network to start an enterprise. But these are all instances of one theoretical fact, namely that market exchange does not pull people together in a comprehensive and unified economic system, but brings every economic actor into competition with all others and denies access to resources to those who are inefficient. Therefore, market exchange as the dominant mode of economic integration cannot exist without combining with the other two, which are actually keeping society together (Mingione, 1991).

This analysis of integration strategies in terms of the three spheres of economic integration also shows the limits of territorial based actions. All efforts to insert educationally and professionally marginalized persons into employment, especially those without any positive experience of work, will yield no more than a few thousands jobs, whereas about 60 000 people are unemployed in Brussels. Political participation as a key element in redistribution also transcends the local level. Only the fostering of reciprocity has a clear local basis. Structural solutions beyond these limits lie particularly in the field of redistribution. First, access to labour, or at least access to an income allowing a decent standard of living, must be secured for every household. This would entail a radical reduction in working hours or the creation of a universal allowance – solutions that are not generated by market exchange, but can only be forced by redistribution. Redistribution has a centralized, often hierarchical structure to enable the steering of the redistribution system. Market exchange and reciprocity are, on the contrary, 'blind' routes to economic integration, for they have no inherent assessment of their effects and no decisions can be taken to influence these effects in one way or another. Because of its steering capacity, redistribution is the only mode of economic integration through which access to basic resources for everybody can be guaranteed, without exception. It is a matter of political decision. The granting of full citizenship, with all the political rights this implies, is thus essential for improving the economic integration of future generations of immigrants.

Notes

1. Of the 45 peripheral communes of the urban region (outside the Brussels Capital Region), 42 are in the districts of Halle-Vilvoorde and Nivelles, in the Flemish and Walloon regions respectively. The northern half of the Brussels urban region corresponds nearly perfectly with the Halle-Vilvoorde district. The northern and western parts of the Nivelles district, which are the most densely populated, correspond with the southern part of the Brussels urban region. Figures for both districts give a good approximation of the urban region's suburban belt. More accurate figures on the Brussels urban region are difficult to compute because of municipal amalgamation in 1976.

2. The most relevant exceptions here are those areas in the inner city where the residual rental sector has been partly replaced by immigrant owner occupation and a few small high rise council housing estates on the periphery in which mainly foreigners live.

3. Gentrification is surprisingly modest given the impressive restructuring of the city. There has been a gentle increase in immigration into Brussels Capital Region from the urban periphery since the 1990s (but suburbanization has also resumed). Small-scale gentrification is reported in the central city, but no dramatic socio-spatial change is detected at the neighbourhood level in the concentration of immigrant workers. The modest dimensions of the urban region and relatively good access to the centre are probably the main reasons for this. In other words, Brussels is a small global city and the trade-off between central and peripheral locations is less relevant than in large cities.

4. We exclude autarky, because it does not entail economic integration.

5. Marshall's (1950) conception of citizenship includes both social and political citizenship and necessarily implies civil citizenship.

6. These four dimensions were obtained from a principal component analysis of 23 indicators, which themselves were selected in a set of 65 variables. The seven indicators mentioned in the text and shown on Map 5.4 are those used to delimit Brussels' deprived neighbourhoods. The lower value is the threshold used for each indicator; when a neighbourhood exceeds the threshold value for at least four indicators, it is considered deprived; the degree of deprivation results from a cluster analysis on the seven indicators. Four of them are the best representations of each dimension. The three others are endowed with great heuristic relevance, but relate to more than one dimension.

7. Turks and Moroccans are the largest non-EU communities (20 000 and 80 000 respectively in a total population of 950 000). By the year 2000, EU nationals will be enfranchized, according to the Maastricht Treaty. Thus, both groups represent the city's politically excluded. Due to a strong concentration of immigrants with large families in the poor western crescent of the inner city, the share of single person household is highest in the other parts of the inner city.

8. This is visible on Map 5.4 for all indicators except unemployment, and the presence of Turks and Moroccans and of single person households.

Part II

Social Life at the Neighbourhood Level

6 Urban Violence and Community Mobilizations

Sophie Body-Gendrot

In the city the society's large problems are revealed when economic development impacts unevenly on urban territories and their populations. Certain elected and administrative officials find that the presence of numerous migrants and minority members in a city makes problems more difficult to control and the task of social integration elusive. Conversely, others argue that the vitality and initiatives taken by such groups in the social and urban arena are trump cards for city development. The urban question leads to a redefinition of the former question on social integration. It sets both the problems of urbanization, of dehumanized universes produced by hasty and cheap architectural design, of residents with no experience of upward social mobility, of their symbolic and material phasing out of the mainstream and of social panics (Body-Gendrot, 1995). At the beginning of this century, there were obviously marginalized and peripheral working class and immigrant neighbourhoods, there were hoboes and bums and workers seen as different and unmeltable. There is little difference between the current discourse on marginalization (exclusion) and the label given to the dangerous classes of the past. But the residents of shantytowns and urban zones who were frequently migrants to cities had kept former links with the hinterland. Many of them experienced the same fate and commonalities. Currently, the new form is a vacuum bristling here and there with high rise blocks where heterogeneous populations are forced to live together.

Such form generates sparks of violence. Is the spatial urbanized form at the core of tensions and violence in populations? Is the representation of distressed neighbourhoods by the media and dominant discourse a self-fulfilling prophecy, stigmatizing residents who no longer dare give their address when they look for a job, ask for bank credit or seek new relationships? Because they resent an imposed discourse of stigmatization on the place where they live, do some of the residents, especially immigrants and the young, act accordingly while others turn the stigma around? We would then speak of space effects. Or, do the social deprivation and lack

75

of reference points on the part of some of the residents have a bearing on the whole community in which they live, thus modifying the community's identity? My approach focuses on the articulation of the spatial and social processes and on the context in which urban violence and community mobilizations – the object of this chapter – take place.

The term *violence* has many applications deriving from disciplines that constrain its use in different ways. I refer here to the sociological and political interpretations of violence involving migrants, ethnic and racial groups in decaying neighbourhoods.

By *community*, I refer here to neighbourhoods or urban territories and focus on disadvantaged low-income urban neighbourhoods. I use the definition of a neighbourhood as an ecological sub-unit of a larger community conditioned by cultural and political forces, a locality with sentiments, traditions and a history of its own. Then, I emphasize that it is also a mosaic of overlapping boundaries, an imbricated structure reflecting the society at large and processing the global and the local.

THE CONTENDERS ARE ACTORS AND VICTIMS

In a disproportionate way, urban violence hits youths from minority groups (as in the USA, Canada and the UK) and from immigrant groups (as in France and other European countries) in neighbourhoods in crisis. Several questions need to be asked.

Are we allowed to think that the more a minority group is stigmatized, the more it is submitted to the violence of majority groups, whether it instigates violence or not? Differentials in violence across groups reveal that the more severely a minority has been stigmatized by a dominant society, the greater its levels of interpersonal violence are likely to be. For instance, in Canada, which has the second highest violent crime rate in the Western world, black people face a risk of being murdered that is roughly three times that of other Canadians. Their male counterparts in the USA are approximately eight times as likely to be murdered as white males. Native Indians (first nations), who are the most stigmatized people in Canada, experience homicide victimization rates seven to ten times those of other Canadians. Native Americans, by contrast, are less than half as likely as blacks to be victims of homicide (Gurr, 1995: xi). A sociology of complex social relations is greatly needed. The effects of macro and micro changes are always mediated and subject to local contingencies.

For instance, does ethnic diversity in the same types of neighbourhoods breed patterns of violence? It is a common wisdom that ethnically diverse societies tend to have higher levels of social and interpersonal violence than more homogeneous ones: the USA and Japan are often contrasted in that way (Gurr, 1995: x). In France, where 30 to 40 different nationalities frequently live together in 800 neighbourhoods categorized by the police as experiencing 'problems', the police (*renseignements généraux*) reported more than 3000 disorders in 1992 and almost 7000 in 1997 with 800 injured persons. Not only do planned attacks against policemen, bus drivers and firemen, as well as arson and stone attacks, reveal a general and collective distrust of society, but clashes between territorial gangs are increasingly involving weapons and are becoming more vicious. They caused 17 injuries in 1992 and, in 1995, 46 injuries and six deaths. In September 1996, the police reported 12 deaths of youths through being stabbed or hit by their peers. Youths of minority origin (especially French West Indians and Algerian French) were over-represented in the homicides (Bui Trong, 1996).

Once we agree that European neighbourhoods are diverse, made up of poor and non-poor, nationals and non-nationals, minorities and mainstream, we want to know what community strategies poorly positioned minority groups use in our competitive post-industrial democracies and which resort to violence and which do not. Among several strategies, I have chosen to focus on three because they allow comparative points of view from American, British and French contexts. In the USA, however, no urban issue can avoid a discussion of race. The fate of African Americans who experienced slavery was unique and a principle of mobilization (Winant, 1995). Immigrants' mobility is therefore perceived with the black/white background in mind. The European story with the focus on nationals and immigrants, with variations related to citizenship, as in the British case, is therefore quite different and should be kept in mind as a limit of the comparison. The second part of the chapter focuses on differentiated institutional reactions.

STRATEGIES OF VICTIMIZATION AND CALLS FOR SOCIAL JUSTICE

The first form of mobilization is a search for specific protections based on the status of minorities. In the USA, *affirmative action* programmes have attempted to redress the harm the status of slavery has caused in terms of discrimination and segregation. Even though at least one-third of African

Americans were able to join the middle classes via the trampoline of affirmative action programmes, this strategy has only been partially successful: ghettoized blacks, especially single-parent families, have been bypassed by more recently arrived groups and given welfare as a handout. Yet, many positive changes occurred to remedy racial discrimination following the civil rights movement. The challenges of black activists in the 1960s forced the political and judicial systems to react and important anti-discrimination legislation was passed. Voting districts were redistricted to allow a better political representation of minorities; discrimination was banned in public housing with the Fair Housing Law passed in 1968; hate speeches were forbidden by law and minorities were allowed to have access to legal aid to protect their interests.

Most of the legislation was passed before the post-1965 immigrants from the Third World flooded into the USA. As a consequence, new immigrants were spared nativist resistance due to major civil rights statutes and to judicial decisions giving close scrutiny to aliens as 'a protected class' (*Graham v. Richardson*). As minorities, Latinos, Asians and native Americans were able to take advantage of the civil rights' revolution and become participants in the political process. The judicialization of immigrant and religious minorities' rights over the centuries has been a unique American feature. Soon feminists, gays, environmentalists and other groups joined identity politics and took advantage of such rights provided by the constitution and the law. To a moral ideal based on equal opportunity and non-discrimination, was substituted numerical equality of result or proportional representation for racial, gender and ethnic groups.

The unity of the contest movement eroded rapidly because not only rights but also power, control, resources and concrete goods were at stake. Divisions over matters of identity were the inheritance of centuries-long conflicts in the US social structure. Though groups were fragmented by definitions of differences and by their class positions, gender and age identities, their opponents were similarly divided. Today, difference seems more salient than commonality and less energy is being devoted to common bonds than to the boundaries of distinction (Young, 1990; Body-Gendrot, 1998). Every group is eager to portray its own victimization based on the most widely shared identity, that of victim. The political authorities' complacency in allowing all kinds of clienteles to benefit from non-discrimination measures has caused an unbalance in the merit system and a backlash from more privileged individuals excluded from this form of protection. Recently, as a frontline political laboratory, California (and Texas) decided by means of popular initiatives and referendums, that is approved by majority votes, to stop protecting minorities and illegal immigrants (Proposition 187 and 209) and to let the 'automatic society' and *laissez-faire* processes take place (Lowi, 1977). Divisions in minority leaderships have prevented the formation of a rainbow coalition to fight such measures. Legal action will show if some aspects of those propositions will be judged unconstitutional.

Is there a similar legal strategy in Europe? In the UK, one could refer to the symbolic importance of the Equal Rights Commission in gaining minority groups access to the courts and to the political empowerment it has created for them. The budget allocated to the Equal Rights Commission is small compared with its US counterpart and even with the French Social Fund catering to populations of migrant origin. Yet, since 1976, when the law was passed, the existence of specific socioeconomic handicaps experienced by racial minorities has led to affirmative action programmes and contract compliance, regarded as temporary, as in the USA, and meant to reduce racial tensions. But such programmes have remained controversial. Under the race relations legislation, it is possible to provide targeted training and recruitment so that excluded populations have the opportunity to increase their representation in a particular workforce (Moore, 1997; Modood, 1997). These programmes are defended with a 'business case', namely that employers can neither afford to have talented potential employees overlooked nor have a workforce that is not equipped to engage with minority populations as customers or clients. But, UK programmes deal essentially with UK citizens and permanent residents. The latter are singled out for special treatment because they are the victims of special circumstances that may be in the employers' interest to overcome. In the UK, identity politics and the question of difference have recently remobilized energies. Some militant nationalist groups want to support antiracist legal actions, whereas others refuse to reify race (Gilroy, 1990; Crowley, 1992; Body-Gendrot, 1997)

In France, where the judicial arena is under pressures from the political decision-makers, the situation is more ambiguous. The French authorities do not recognize minorities or communities as potential partners, and intermediary bodies are weak. The case of the French from the West Indies illustrates how, after understanding the weakness of the state apparatus over various issues, they have diversified their struggles and successfully gone to court on very pragmatic points related to their status. The question of the Islamic scarf also reveals that the central state can no longer impose diktats from the top on sensitive matters. The courts have sent back the decision to local school authorities.

It appears that groups that have already accumulated gains in the host society or nation are not eager to jeopardize them. In France, after the civic marches at the beginning of the 1980s on the theme of 'respect my difference', youths of immigrant origin from the neighbourhoods of Lyons, Marseilles and Paris understood that they were heading into a blind alley. At that point the extreme right started to fuel hatred by evoking themes of 'false nationals' and 'dubious French'. Many of the marchers subsequently adopted the motto of 'respect my *in*difference'. While discrimination remains strong in the labour and housing arenas, it seems that the settled migrant groups and their children evaluated the risks. In the French context, they would have more to lose by asserting their ethnic and cultural differences in the public sphere to have wrongs redressed than by keeping a low profile. Because of their particular attitude towards ethnicity and race, the French élite does not want to identify the waste there is in not hiring well-qualified immigrant youths with French citizenship. A recent official report pointed out that in Roubaix, for instance, hundreds of such youths are discriminated against on the labour market and that employers clearly specify their racial preference (BBR – *bleu blanc rouge*) without embarrassment.[1]

GRASS-ROOTS STRATEGIES AND SELF-HELP

From an analytical European point of view, US violence in ghettoized areas is less rooted in behavioural pathologies than in structural deficiencies. It appears to be generated by extreme socioeconomic inequalities, by racial segregation and by a lack of economic redistribution approved by the mainstream and enforced by lawmakers. This ethnically and racially diverse society occupying a very large territory with a federal structure seems less obsessed with social cohesion than most European societies. Political choices support the society's winners, while individualism and localism yield a fragmented view of people's problems. American ethics dictate that all Americans have a duty to protect themselves and their kin and to refuse handouts. Newcomers and minorities have to fight for themselves and begin by joining ranks in their own community to enter the societal contest with resources.

For some observers, however, community politics marks 'the twilight of common dreams'. Top public and private actors who give their support to community organizations to do the work they, are convinced of the benefits of having multiple actors tackle multidimensional problems in their neighbourhoods. Continuous micro initiatives in all kinds of ethnic and racial communities, which are aimed at various social segments in terms of age, gender and occupation, reveal the setting in motion of social capital in fragmented urban spaces (Sampson et al., 1997). It is unusual for a cause not to find a support group. Even poor, gay, African American inmates with Aids may find support groups for their own specific problem. This approach makes sense in a society based, at best, on communities, at worst, on enclaves, gated communities, ghettos and barrios. Following a binary logic, the dominant discourse constantly focuses on a Horatio Alger model and on success stories. Its intent is to blame those who cannot cope with their problems and reward those who commit them-selves to solutions. For many Americans, what is important is what takes place at the community level. The American notion of citizenship is anchored in the local community and in the empowerment that results from collective action.

Fiscal austerity and political conservatism explain why groups that rely on their own resources have to compete in the public arena to obtain better goods and services. Education, public jobs and housing are spheres in which inequalities of resources are frequently masked by a rhetoric of mobilization based on ethnic or racial identity. References to ethnicity in mobilizations seem to deny any 'reciprocity of perspectives' (Borgogno, 1990) that might allow the identification of commonalities and the emer-gence of processes of conflict resolution. In a city like New York or Chicago, the capture of some public services by various ethnic groups of European origin makes the notion of public service dubious and reveals situations of ethnic inequality according to which some groups are deceived by unfair rules (Waldinger, 1996). But, to combat this Darwinian situation with a strategy of ethnic/racial community mobilization implies risks. Focusing on a group's self worth can create forms of ethnocentrism and lead to a patrolling of frontiers within the city verging on tribalism. If this trend develops, groups then speak only for themselves and forget about the general interest (Minow, 1997). Black Muslims, for instance, help the most deprived in the African American community to get free lunches, to obtain emotional and educational support in prison, or to have their housing projects policed. Orthodox Jews behave similarly in their own neighbourhoods, as do Haitians and Cubans. From a European outsider's point of view, identity politics is not a healthy sign of demo-cratic processes; it strains community bonds while at the same time constraining individual identities by artificially reducing them to a single category of race, gender or disability. In a neighbourhood, conflicting demands may harm the interests of other groups living in the same area, such as one ethnic group controlling state schools. The politicization of demands may escalate, prevent compromise and pit one group against another.[2] It can be in the interest of no political system to let such tensions erupt. Social cohesion is a goal as well as a must in local governance.

Is there a similar grass-roots strategy in Europe? Research in the UK has shown that community mobilizations based on ethnic identities often manifest the same logic as the American minorities display. In Spitalfields, Catherine Neveu analysed the actions of Bangladeshis drawing on their resources to cope with poverty and security problems. In that example, their actions revealed the existence of strong tensions with the dominant society (especially with the police, schools and discriminating bureaucracies) as well as with other competing groups (Neveu, 1993).

In France, members of the so-called 'second generation' often undertake community work in their own neighbourhoods. It is the territory in which these young people live that gives coherence to their actions. Whereas their fathers mobilized to gain recognition for Islam, communication remains difficult for their children, especially since rampant drug trafficking, caches of illegal weapons and Algerian terrorist threats have led to increased demands from the general public for searches, arrests and raids in immigrant neighbourhoods. An effort was made after 1993 to create thousands of 'city jobs', a form of preferential treatment giving poor youths an opportunity to show their *savoir-faire* as security guards on the buses or as porters in public buildings (Obadia, 1997). After 1996, the social-democrat government put some effort into creating 150 000 new jobs for these young people in the public sector. So far, no one can tell whether this preferential treatment will reach its target group or whether, as in the case of the poor African Americans, dropouts from the inner cities (7 per cent of an age group) will be bypassed by more privileged youths seizing the jobs. Will mayors, state representatives (*préfets*) and other authorities be willing to allocate the jobs to those who rarely vote for them? Short-term views may lead them to play safe cards.

Discouraged youths may then choose other options. If they become convinced that there is no possible future for them in society as it is, a withdrawal into fundamentalism may appear as an assertion of autonomy. No one will decide for them without them (Cesari, 1997a). A religious assertion is a way of anchoring oneself in a controlled space of belonging and, in a micro society, resisting change. Other youths will search for expressions of deterritorialized citizenship to avoid subordination by the local arena, while the small number who fail at everything (school, work and relationships) may deviate and resort to 'institutional vandalism' every week or so.

STRATEGIES BASED ON VIOLENT MOBILIZATIONS

Strategies based on violent actions of contest are infrequent, despite the visibility they receive in the media. They can be interpreted a posteriori as a prelude to negotiation within a 'riot culture' (Hobsbawn, 1966). At the *macro level*, destruction, disorder and riots occur in contexts of urban deprivation. Jobs and their integrating function have vanished, drug markets offer resources to young entrepreneurs. The logic of the housing market has isolated numerous families with numerous handicaps from various trajectories. Despite architectural renewals, the middle classes, upper working classes and most public and private services have deserted such areas. Violence is not, however, the act of the most marginalized individuals in the bleakest neighbourhoods. It relates to real or imaginary boundaries at the margins of which groups mark their differences. It involves an identity emanating from space. In negatively connoted places with strong social homogeneity, ethnic, racial or cultural differentiations are over-valorized. The game of setting distinctions and frontiers goes from the housing project to stairs A, B, C and from the buildings to the surrounding ground. It attempts to establish hierarchies of social relations, the function of which is to compensate for the representation the populations have of their own marginalization (de Rudder, 1991).

Tension is extreme between partial, blurred identities, articulated in various ways and expressed in daily life on the one hand and global, abstract and universal identities on the other. When someone says, 'I am not French, I am from Marseilles,' there is no objective basis for that assertion, which is constructed here and now for a specific interlocutor.

Several factors may trigger violent mobilizations. First, they are likely to occur as an *acting out* in a context of frustration due to a perception that the residents' situation is unfair *compared* with that of the rest of society, or to the provocations of a hostile proximate group. Frustration may come from schools, which are perceived as not fulfilling their function of social promotion; parents realize that schools are at best a triage centre; children resent some teachers, whom they perceive as hostile, and schools become a locus of violence, inside the precincts or in the adjacent areas. Numerous studies show that family dislocations impinge on neighbourhoods. If the neighbourhood is itself surrounded by an ocean of poverty, it becomes even more difficult for residents to cope with their own deprivation (Jargowsky, 1996). They are aware of how 'the other half' lives, but, as described in *All Our Kin*, they need a double culture to survive in a brutal and violent environment (Stack, 1977). A stratum of young males, who leave school early, never leave their neighbourhood and have few contacts with the outside world besides television, may express their disempowerment through violent actions. They are not tempted to venture outside their housing estate and when they do, because of their mental enclosure, they say that they feel estranged and insecure (Sachs, 1997).

The second motivation to violence, the capacity to intimidate the rest of society and target precious public goods, is also instrumental. By rioting, youths create unity out of a fragmented universe and cultures in disarray. Just as young, poor African Americans find themselves in isolated, depopulated housing estates from which other categories have fled, so poor European youths – of immigrant origin or not – feel excluded from the larger contesting movement based on exploitation and want to express their rage.

These youths interact daily with disenchanted, hostile residents and exhausted, frequently offensive frontline civil servants (teachers, postmen, policemen, janitors and administrators). All of them accumulate grievances towards one another and a sense of being globally useless. The context for social conflict is therefore explosive.

At the *micro level*, petty delinquency destroys social efficacy in the neighbourhood. Broken windows are not repaired, graffiti are not cleaned up, and the police are not to be seen. This is usually the situation in the French inner cities, but in a context that is different from that experienced in North-American cities in terms of crime rates and in the nature and quantity of the violence (Fagan and Wilkinson, forthcoming). Transgressions by local institutions, corruption and perceptions of police abuse or denials of justice are frequent triggers to mobilization, especially when amplified by unfounded rumours. Through the media cover they receive, such mobilizations give rioters a sense of being one, of writing history. Diverging interests and identities amalgamate around a sub-neighbourhood and violence may last long after the triggering cause has operated. Young males are the actors of an urban moment with a banner and a cause in a youth culture valorizing fighters and rites (Canada, 1995). But this moment does not last. This is where the dehumanized urban context plays its own part. Instead of acting together to calm down young rioters, adults remain at their windows or locked up behind their doors.

In sum, if the strategy of violence is less often used, it is because it is costly, ephemeral and difficult to handle. Demonstrations appear as they go. They can be interpreted as alternative modes of action and a search for social bonding when the system of representation is in crisis. These 'weapons of the weak' reintroduce direct democracy in a system weakened by the widening gap between national elites and citizens.

At this point, a caveat must be introduced. It is not legitimate to put together strategies that look alike but may be different according to national contexts. More needs to be written to deconstruct the types of strategies presented above according to national and urban contexts and economic circumstances. Few major differences need be mentioned.

INSTITUTIONS IN THE VORTEX

On the first strategy requiring social justice and preferential treatment for minorities, in the current conservative context of the USA, the institution of justice seems to be becoming more and more isolated. It is not unusual to see local politicians campaigning against judges accused of being too lenient. The politicization of crime correlated with the *underclass*, a code word for poor, black and in the streets, is a lucrative business for politicians, the administration, the media and special interests. In a context of compassion fatigue, it allows populists to dismantle the affirmative action and welfare that benefits 'unworthy' minorities and migrants in poor neighbourhoods. Judges who pursue their own logic based on constitutional rights are likely to be increasingly accused by demagogues of being too 'soft' in their protection of minorities. Conservative public opinion in favour of the death penalty, of the 'lock them up and throw away the key' school of thought, will withdraw its support from them.

A certain number of French and British judges want to remain the keepers of 'democratic promises' in a context of general disenchantment with the political elites. In France, there have been several instances of them having supported social movements in favour of deprived minorities, such as the Right to Housing, a movement occupying vacant public buildings for the benefit of African and North African families. A poll taken at the beginning of 1994 showed that 64 per cent of French people thought that homelessness was one of the most critical problems in Paris and 81 per cent of the French approved requisitions (up from 70 per cent in a previous poll). The Constitutional Council's decision to consider the right to housing 'an objective with constitutional values' is important.

Other signs of resistance have come from French judges in the juvenile courts, who have protested against reforms requiring tougher sentencing, the criminalization of parents and speedy procedures for youths at risk. The characteristically French fights of multi-positioned intellectuals eager to defend 'fair' causes, sign petitions and support, for instance, immigrants with an ill-defined status, accelerate changes in mentalities and force central elites to act.

Finally, human rights legislation based on conventions the states have signed may give more protection to minorities and immigrant groups. Resorting to justice is more fruitful at a supranational level via the European Court of Justice, for instance, which recognizes the concept of minority and may eventually force national countries to redress phenotypical discrimination beyond the protection given by national citizenship. It seems that the European juridical space has not been fully exploited by the dominated groups precisely because the strategy is not a winner-take-all game and implies losses as well.

On the second strategy, built on self-help and community mobilizations that might threaten commonalities, the claims of groups with the power to sanction will be heard or not according to electoral politics and alliances. Non decision-making is also a resource of urban governance (Bachrach and Baratz, 1980). But, whereas decision-makers can accommodate cultural pluralism, majorities always perceive structural pluralism and separatism as threats. Following R. Hall, one could say that if 'others are a problem for separatists, separatism may be a problem for others' (Hall, 1978).

In the USA, the Clinton administration's federal policy to enforce empowerment zones is one of the very few initiatives to address the abandonment of ghettoized areas. It requires the residents of poor communities to get together, as would village residents, to imagine solutions to their multidimensional problems and to get to work with a minimum of support from the federal government and from other actors (Body-Gendrot, 1996). The symbolic involvement of federal and local policy-makers may help contain the violence: the leadership in the poor communities is mobilized within partnerships to produce social harmony, to cooperate with the police and to appease tensions (Goetz, 1996).

Not surprisingly, in France, the same policy (*zones franches*) is based on a top-down approach. City mayors tend to cooperate with the central state over the welfare of citizens as defined by elites. Because of their ceremonial top-down tradition, they are less eager than their counterparts in the USA and UK to support self-help and autonomous grass-roots actions.

As for the last strategy based on violence, in most Western societies, the repressive apparatus has become more sophisticated. Convictions for young offenders are longer and heavier, especially if they are poor and non-white, and it is unlikely that majorities will demonstrate in the streets to support the residents of poor neighbourhoods taking action. A routine mode of institutional action is to discredit rioters and emergent leaders and to play on stereotypes. Protest movements, or 'voices' in some cases, are, however, likely to continue. At the margins of legal processes, they are an ultimate and desperate call for participation and negotiation triggered by the crisis of regulation of the state and by its weakening capacity to respond to new and complex demands.

Notes

1. The question of migrants with ill-defined statuses requiring papers from the administration in France became largely a police matter in 1996/7. For some, it is a struggle for civil rights based on a citizenship beyond nation-states. Others claim that nation-states have a right to impose their rules of admission and select who will be part of the nation. The heated debate was still open at the time of writing.
2. It was the case of Koreans or Latinos versus African Americans in US neighbourhoods; Comorians, North Africans and gypsies in neighbourhoods of Marseilles, or Pakistanis versus Afro-Caribbeans in London suburbs (see Smith and Faegin, 1995).

7 Islam in European Cities

Jocelyne Cesari

Nearly 15 million Muslims live in western Europe. Their presence mainly results from migration flows to Europe from the old colonial empires of Asia, Africa and the Caribbean at the beginning of the 1960s. The existence of Muslim minorities in democratic societies is an unexpected consequence of drastic changes in European immigration policy during the 1972–74 recession when governments stopped labour immigration but allowed family unification. In the 1970s, the religio-cultural dimension became important in relations between Muslim and European communities because the contact surface between immigrants and the host society expanded greatly. Islam played an important part in the settlement process. It was because of its visibility that questions were raised, doubts were cast and, on occasions, violent opposition arose, all of which were linked to the integration of these newcomers in different national communities. The confrontation no longer occurred in the temporary, discrete and sometimes shameful context of the 1950s, but within that of a stable religion with a growing will to be recognized. Muslims are becoming increasingly politically active and these actions are reinforced by the emergence of a 'second generation'. The main issues surrounding migration are now cultural and political and not only economic.

Conflicts between Muslims and host societies, as seen in the Ruhsdie affair in Britain and the 'headscarf affair' in France, have centred on Muslims questioning the secular principles of Western sociopolitical life. Questions of citizenship, citizens' duties, the social contract and the relationship between religion and the state were considered solved until the cultural and religious integration of Muslim communities become an issue.

Western clichés, derived from the colonial past and an 'essentialist' vision of Islam as unique and changeless, provide the main and inappropriate framework within which this new and innovative situation is understood. Samuel Huntington's *Clash of Civilizations*, despite its ideological content, offers a fashionable interpretation of this perspective. It refers to a primordial and static vision of Islamic civilization that requires Muslims to conform to Islamic law whenever and wherever they live *because* they are Muslims. Although Islam is now a part of Western society, it is

88

persistently viewed as strange and totally different from Christianity or Judaism. This reluctance is due partially to the connection between Islam, poverty and violence at the international level. Events like the Rushdie affair or the Gulf War reinforce this perception. But it has also to do with the controversial question of Islam and modernity and the key debate on the compatibility of Islamic values with the secular organizing principles of western European societies.

This question needs to be viewed from a dynamic perspective that takes the new context into account: being a minority in Europe itself implies deep changes in Muslim identities and practices, especially among new generations born in the West. The analysis should consider changes that concern not only the Muslim groups but the host societies as well. From this perspective, multiculturalism becomes a real issue because it implies competition between different sets of universal values.

In Europe, the debate does not concern Islamic governance as it does in Muslim societies, but the experience of pluralism and democracy.[1] The dominant tendency is to consider that the situation of Muslims in Europe is the same as it is in their country of origin.

To give way to this illusion would be to forget the transformations of mentalities and behaviour that occur on discovering a minority condition. One should not forget that the great majority of Muslims in Europe originate from countries where Islam is either the state religion or the main religion. For this reason, transplantation, meaning interacting with a mainly non-Muslim environment is going to represent a unique challenge. Muslims have to innovate because the Muslim law elaborated between the eighth and ninth centuries, at a time when Islam was dominant both culturally and economically, did not examine the minority condition created by voluntary migration.

An objective understanding of Islam in Europe is a key factor in the management of multiculturalism – how political bodies face the increasing demand for cultural diversity. To achieve this, it is necessary to examine the status of religions in civil societies in a context of globalization.

In Europe, the so-called antagonism between Islam and modernity is associated with the larger debate about the 'return of religions', although this approach seems to be inappropriate. The modern sociological imagination is reluctant to consider religious formations as components of civil societies. Because religious affiliations are assigned by ascription, they are regarded as inherited rather than chosen identities. But, is the acquisition of a religious identity at birth really the same as acquiring blue eyes or left-handedness? Religious identities are subject to individual, collective and institutional construction and reconstruction.

New kinds of relationships are developing between religion and politics, even in societies with separate political and religious spheres. In a period of considerable doubt about the basic values of Western society (individualism, science and progress), religions try to provide new frameworks for individual and collective identities. From this perspective, the state of Islam has to be analysed within the context of changing democracies. It is necessary to refine a new conceptual framework to take into account this new use of religion.[2] In fact, an increasing circulation and dissemination of beliefs now characterize religious and political spheres. However, religion remains a particular sort of belief because it needs the legitimization of tradition. It carries two risks – dogmatic rigidity on the one hand and the control of consciousness and behaviour on the other. The propensity to control may be exerted in two opposite directions – *ad extra* as a way of extending religious influence in the society, or *ad intra* as a way of separating from the society as a whole all those who share the same tradition or faith.

The combination of these internal and external dimensions may be extremely diverse, according to the cultural or social context in which they occur. Islamization in a Western context is a means of maintaining and reinforcing the sense of belonging to Islam in a non-Muslim context, while in Muslim countries it can refer to a process of politicization. The experience of belonging to a minority in a context of political and cultural pluralism is the major difference between Muslim and Western countries.

In the context of globalization, this new approach to religion has to be combined with the new definition of ethnic minorities as diasporas. Steady improvements in communications and transport, as well as a striking increase in recent international migration, have contributed to a new theoretical interest in this term, which extends the meaning of diaspora beyond its historical association with the Jewish condition. The concept of a diaspora has three main dimensions – awareness of an ethnic identity, the existence of communal organizations, and the persistence of relations (even imaginary ones) with the homeland (Sheffer, 1996: 39). In fact, diaspora refers to a specific relationship to time (memory) and space, so can be considered as an ethnic transnational network. Religion is an important aspect of these transnational networks and activities: in Europe it increases the need for circulation and mobility from South to North and from North to South. To consider diasporas as ethnic transnational networks makes it possible to avoid a 'primordial' conception of ethnicity and to combine 'macro' and 'micro' analyses (Cesari, 1996).

From this perspective, European Islam can only be transnational, shaped by solidarity networks and mobility in connection with different national and geographical spaces. It may thus be defined as an emerging diaspora. This term enables us to understand the tension between Islamic space and Europe, which characterizes the settlement process of this religion. These transnational networks are visible in the main European capital cities, which have become capitals of Islam – Paris, London, Berlin, Turin and Madrid. Mobility between Europe and the Islamic world is going on in these metropolises, beyond national bonds and state borders. Our observations of these places will enable us to grasp what transformations lead to different minority conditions for the various ethnic backgrounds and contexts in which settlement takes place.

Islam, like other religions, is a vehicle for both conflict and cooperation – conflict where the security of borders, especially in Europe, is one of the main political issues; cooperation where Islam is an element of integration into different European societies. The tension arises because mosques or associations can both have an integrative function and, in certain cases, receive fundamentalists. The various political references are little by little turned into religious references for settled Muslim populations, which problematizes the role of Islam with respect to conflict and cooperation. Under what conditions is Islam a cause of conflict but, above all, a means for regulation?

The definition of Islamic identities in the European urban context has three dimensions: the status of Islam in the home country, the status of ethnic groups in different host countries, and globalization.

ISLAM AND ETHNICITY

According to the first dimension, the determining factor is each home country's specific relationship to Islam, which is shaped by its history and culture. Islamic membership is embedded in national or ethnic bonds. Organizations and mobilizations are often based on ethnic and cultural ties rather than on universal Islamic ones. For example, the religious sanction against Muslim women marrying outside the group often leads fathers of immigrant families to seek husbands for their daughters in their original environment. Or, vice versa, young women from Muslim lands (North Africa, Middle-East, Asia) are sometimes imported to the host societies: they are considered to be better wives in that they conform to the traditional model.

Besides, the first migrants who tried to interpret their religious demands without recourse to any external influence soon found themselves incapable of facing up to the new requirements of the Koranic teachings. For this reason, places of worship in Europe have been invested with imams from the various countries of origin. This management of religious activities has allowed educated people without any social perspectives from within their society of origin, especially from North Africa, to settle in Europe and create networks that assure them relative political security. It has also provided them with the financial means to lead from the outside political opposition against the regimes of their country of origin. However, the implications of these networks for immigrant populations are limited, for political activity can be organized outside immigrant associations and places of worship, even if it sometimes uses transplanted Islamic organizations. In fact, immigrant circles in Europe can function as sounding boards for political issues from the countries of origin, for they are able to voice 'illegitimate' points of view. Examples of this can be seen in the 'Berber' culture in France and the Islamist movement in Germany.

Finally, the characteristics of the 'triangular' interaction between the group, the receiving country and the home country also have an influence. For example, the diasporic condition may come about through homeland governments trying to profit from the settlement of migrants in different European host countries, with a view to improving either bilateral or European relationships. North African governments tried to present migration to Europe as an advantage in the context of the Euro-Mediterranean policy initiated at the Barcelona Conference in November 1995. Likewise, Turkey takes political advantage of the settlement of migrants in Germany.

However, ethnic influences can decline. In fact, competition between Islamic and ethnic ties is noticeable, especially for new generations born in Europe. For example, though the major centres of Islamic law are outside Europe, they are also outside the Maghrebian countries; a young adept can receive an intensive religious training in Saudi Arabia or Egypt, but not necessarily in the homeland of his parents. Islamic ties refer to the concept of *Umma* (Community of Believers) and not to ethnic or national bonds. This transnational identity is discernible during events such as the Rushdie affair, the Gulf War and the war in Bosnia when European Muslims expressed their solidarity with their 'brothers' abroad. The difficulty of demarcating the religious group, irrespective of whether or not it includes ethnic bonds, is the main issue confronting the organization of Islam in a

Western context. This explains why there is so much competition between the various actors in different European countries to impose their leadership and their own conception of the community. Some try to maintain a relationship with the homeland and a sort of ethnic partition of the religious community, while others defend a global view of Islam beyond the ethnic features (Cesari, 1997). It is, however, an illusion to think that European Islam is going to cut itself off from this external influence.

There are thus different ways of being a Muslim in Europe and these are related to this transnational dimension. The competition that exists between ethnic and Islamic ties has played, and continues to play, a large part in shaping some of the most important cleavages among Muslims communities in Europe.

PLURALISM AND MULTICULTURALISM

The condition of Muslim minorities also depends on the specific political and cultural features of each receiving country. The political and cultural effects of migrant settlement create controversy around each nation's political 'pillars'. The Muslim condition is shaped by the various conceptions of society existing in Europe, by the different routes towards acquiring citizenship, by the content of citizenship, as well as by the status of religion in the civil society. Han Entzinger has identified three European models for dealing with non-European immigration. The first is the guestworker model adopted mainly by the Germanic countries (Germany, Austria and Switzerland) in which the presence of immigrants is considered temporary in perpetuity. These governments make no attempt to integrate the immigrants or their families into the new environment, despite their children being born and raised in these countries and them showing no desire to be repatriated. The second is the assimilation model, which is promoted in France. This model insists that if immigrants seek to become French citizens, they must eschew their foreign cultural, religious, political and ideological allegiances. In other words, they must accept the already existing consensus of reality and polity of the prevailing system and assimilate into it, shedding all alien characteristics. The French policy of Gallicization sees the end result of integration as the privatization of religious practice, with the Muslim individuals becoming socially and economically assimilated. The third model is the ethnic minority model prevalent in a variety of guises in the United Kingdom, Netherlands, Luxembourg and Scandinavia. It recognizes that immigrants have alternative cultural identities that can be preserved and accommodated within the larger context.

Germany's *Gastarbeiter* policy – which allows workers provisional entry as economic migrants but makes it very difficult for them to acquire German citizenship – leads to self-organization within a framework of structures depending mostly on the state of origin. France's principle of *jus soli* (the right to the nationality of the territory in which you are born) enables the children of migrants automatically to become nationals and therefore citizens. The political tradition in the Netherlands and Great Britain, however, is to respect other identities and to recognize communities as components of the civil society, which is not the case in France where the nation is based on the exclusive allegiance of individual citizens to the state.

Moreover, despite the common acceptance of the separation of church and state and of the freedom of cults, the extreme diversity of religious statuses within European states has had an influence. The emergence of Islam in European secular societies has introduced controversy over religious freedom, tolerance and the limits to public expressions of faith. Against French secularism in the face of a persistent 'headscarf affair', one can contrast Germany's recognition of religions by social legislation, while in England, where the Queen is head of the Anglican Church, Islam is brought right into the schools. From now on, each country has to face up to a new challenge, namely the institutionalization of Islam within the framework of existing legislation. Different initiatives have been launched to deal with questions related to issues such as the building of mosques, the status of imams and the slaughter of halal meat. These include the Charter for the Islamic Cult Islam in France, the Superior Council of Muslims in Belgium, and national coordination in Great Britain and the Netherlands.

Moreover, when pluralism is linked with democracy, it ceases to be about the integration of dominated groups or the representation of the citizens' diversity, but about striking a balance between multiculturalism and the communities. In each European country, the issue is shaped by the nation's own political and cultural preoccupations – the status of religion in France and Italy, the status of ethnicity in the United Kingdom, the Netherlands, Denmark and Spain, and the status of nationality in Germany. This is why it is necessary to compare the conditions of Muslims in different European countries.

MUSLIMS IN EUROPE: WHAT KIND OF DIASPORAS?

The localization of transnational networks in large metropolises makes it possible to discern the existence, if not all the features, of a diaspora. The awareness of common membership is one determining feature and this embraces the whole social sphere. It is central to any definition of a diaspora, for it refers not only to a shared awareness of ethnic origin but also, and more ambitiously, to a set of specific values and norms that have formed as a direct result of the dispersion within different nations. This explains why the definition of a diaspora is so controversial with each group of migrants, especially North African ones. In fact, each feature defined by Gabi Sheffer (1996) can be questioned, namely preservation/ reconstruction of an ethnic identity, solidarity of the community, defence of their interests or the interests of their homeland, and attachment to a country or place of origin.

In receiving countries in which they have been settled for more than 20 years, as in France, Germany or Belgium, it is preferable to consider these North African groups as constituting an incipient diaspora. In new receiving countries, such as Italy or Spain, they are a dormant diaspora. When this new culture is not yet discernible, although objective behaviour rooted in transnational networks can be observed, the group can be called an *incipient* diaspora. When this behaviour is relatively new in a context of very recent migration, the group may be defined as a *dormant* diaspora. From this perspective, a diaspora is not the automatic consequence of migration and exile but refers to a voluntary identification with a common group of origin, even if the tie with the home country no longer exists. It thus implies *the perception of extra-territoriality*, which is a specific form of spatial self-representation. In the constituting of diasporas, both multipolar and interpolar relationships are therefore determining. This applies to Chinese migration, for Chinese migrants have gradually come to see themselves as an extra-territorial group (Ma Mung, 1996). Such a perception serves to generate and improve the group's operation as a diaspora, which in turn leads to a kind of utopia that consists of imagining oneself living independently of any territory.

So, for incipient diasporas, the main question refers to the degree of consciousness and capacity for self-denomination. It is a matter of fact that whereas an observer can detect many indicators of a diaspora in a group's behaviour, the actors themselves may neither refer to this term in defining themselves collectively nor prove that such a multipolarized culture exists. This is particularly true of the majority of people who, for all kinds of reasons, feel themselves at home in both Maghrebian and European spaces. In each family, the minimalist relationship with the homeland is demonstrated by regular trips, despite political crises in countries such as Algeria. While attachment to the homeland exists through family ties, it takes on a number of different forms – sending official or non-official remittances, dealing in the homeland black market, consulting religious authorities, or taking advantage of the larger matrimonial market for their children living in France. Other forms are more explicit, for example more and more Algerian families are acquiring parabolas with which to receive Arab channels directly from Algeria. Since the 1996 presidential elections, Algerians abroad have had the right to vote and were allowed to elect their own representative for the 1997 parliamentary elections. For four years, there has been a Ministry for the Moroccan Community Abroad. These recent dispositions prove that states are about to recognize this condition, even though they intend to control it for their own profit.

Social stratification and different socialization practices create important contrasts within the taken-for-granted cohesiveness of groups. Though social mobility in this migration group is on the increase, low levels of education and of social class have hindered the appearance of a diasporic consciousness. Consequently, there have been too few active mediators between the group and the receiving country, as well as the homeland. The situation is now changing with the emergence of an elite in different sectors. The group of entrepreneurs may become such a group of mediators but certain social conditions are necessary, if not sufficient, namely high levels of education and political involvement. The failure of the association of Algerian businessmen, Club 92, proves how difficult it has been to achieve cohesiveness despite a common professional interest. Several Algerian entrepreneurs living in France created this association in 1992. They come from different social levels: some belong to the Algerian urban middle class, others are working class, and yet others are the French children of first-generation migrants. The conditions under which the migration occurred – when it happened, at what age and under what circumstances – introduce important differences in the relationship with the receiving country as well as with Algeria. Those who left Algeria as adults within the last ten years are better educated than the earlier migrants of the 1960s or 1970s. Better-educated migrants in the two national systems are more likely to become aware of the existence of a diaspora. Club 92 failed to operate as an intermediary between France and Algeria because it lacked a homogeneous approach. While the common ambition was to acquire the status of a transnational lobby, the members of the different societies were in unequal positions. Some wanted the action to be confined to economic activities; others saw economic action as only one way of creating a global structure or organization with which to preserve the community's status in both France and Algeria. Those born and educated in Algeria shared the first approach, while those educated in France agreed with the second.

Moreover, the delimitation of this transnational minority remains uncertain. What forms the basis of a community? Is it the relationship to the homeland, to Islam or to a common Arabic culture? Is it derived from common experiences like immigration and discrimination? The answer depends on the national and political context of the receiving country as well as the history of the migration. For example, the willingness to maintain specific features of French society derives from the colonial origins of the North African migration, which influences the group's collective definition. In other words, it is difficult (if not impossible) for North Africans to assimilate because the majority in the receiving country discriminates against them: for example, in France they are considered more visible and more 'problematic' than other equally 'exotic' migrants. The political specificity of the receiving country is also important. In countries that accord political and legal recognition to differences and ethnicity, it is easier to institutionalize and organize diasporas than it is in countries such as France, which has a tradition of assimilation.

Besides, Islamic membership modifies the delimitation of the diaspora. While transnational economic activity may continue to be connected with a homeland, in the framework of an Islamic diaspora, the relationship with the homeland is no longer central, especially for new generations born in Europe.

For the 'dormant' diasporas in new receiving countries like Italy or Spain, ethnic enclaves seem to be the predominant form. In the older receiving countries, by contrast, economic activities tend to overlap ethnic frontiers. Continuous mobility from North Africa helps reinforce diaspora consciousness. Systematic mobility of entrepreneurs between the two shores can be observed. However, diaspora implies duration as well as experiences in different receiving countries. In fact, for the Maghrebian people, it seems that the main missing feature is the existence of this memory and experiences of the minority condition. Most of them have to face new and original circumstances for which they are ill prepared, especially among the first generation of migrants who are accustomed to a perfect overlap of religious, cultural, political and national memberships. Diasporic conditions, on the other hand, are characterized by a growing differentiation between all those dimensions. This is why the persistence of ethnic and cultural differences in the host countries is a central factor.

Besides the general definition of diaporas, it seems that certain conditions are required to make diasporas possible:

- the existence of mediators linking different places and cultures and, despite social heterogeneity, creating a collective consciousness in the group. It implies a sort of institutionalization of the diaspora in different national and political contexts. To achieve this goal, socialization and education are determining factors;
- a 'triangular' interaction between the group, receiving country and home country. A diaspora may occur through homeland governments trying to use to their profit the settlement of migrants in different European host countries with a view to improving either bilateral or European relationships. The Moroccan and Algerian governments' influence over the Muslim community is an example of the former and the European policy of these countries is an example of the latter. An interesting feature of ongoing debates is the emphasis they place on the role of migrants in promoting the development of their own countries and the need to redefine existing initiatives within a new policy framework;[3]
- a specific memory of the diaspora in different places and the group's permanence. However, definitional boundaries are rather blurred between tourists (as individuals or in groups), international migrants, guestworkers, asylum seekers and refugees who reside in host countries for long periods on the one hand and permanent diasporas on the other. This ambiguity occurs because, for emotional, political and legal reasons, the time period that individuals can and wish to spend in host countries before they settle down is highly variable. This means that there is no satisfactory general definition of the point at which groups of migrants form a diaspora.

It is essential to recognize that, to qualify, potential members of a diaspora must agree to be thought of as such. In the European context, assimilation and diaspora formation occur simultaneously. The relevant question to ask is why do people consciously choose to become members of a diaspora?

Finally, one must consider how the European Union influences the form and content of Islamic expressions. The year 1986 saw the introduction of visas for countries south of the Mediterranean Sea and, with the approval of the Schengen agreements by Italy, Spain and Portugal between 1990 and 1991, reinforcement of the enclosure of Europe. Also, crises like the Rushdie affair and the Gulf War have sparked hostile reactions towards settled Muslims. All these events raise questions about their collective presence and radicalize Islamic identity in Europe, which could eventually match the fundamentalism on the other side of the Mediterranean Sea.

Notes

1. The primordial vision legitimates the artificial and wrong opposition of Islam and modernity. This opposition hinders the understanding of major changes in the Arab and Muslim world. There a reference to Islamic law, or even more so to the vocabulary of Islam, does not automatically refer to the persistence of 'archaic' attitudes, but expresses the capacity of this culture to deal with social and political modernization.

2. French sociologists of religion like Danièle Hervieu-Leger (1993) and Patrick Michel (1996) are making this theoretical change.

3. Unfortunately, a European initiative like the Med-Migrations programme is disappointing because it does not go beyond organizing seminars and data collection. Over this period, migrants have accumulated financial reserves in their country of residence amounting to FF35 billion. For the whole of Europe, these reserves are estimated to be between 10 and 12 billion ECU.

8 The Mosaic Pattern: Cohabitation between Ethnic Groups in Belleville, Paris

Patrick Simon

The image of Paris as a 'cosmopolitan' city is as old as Paris itself is. However, only in the 1920s and 1930s did Paris earn its reputation of being a writers' city, an 'international republic of artists', to quote Alejo Carpentier. It became a centre of attraction for the intelligentsia worldwide.[1] After a period of decline, Paris has once again become a centre of convergence for the world's elite, a 'global city' where international executives and financiers run the global economy and redistribute the world's resources. The City of Light owes its cosmopolitan nature not only to its cultural and artistic aura, or to its role in economic exchanges and technological innovation. It also, and maybe even especially, owes it to the fact that from the end of the nineteenth century onwards, immigrants from foreign countries and from the provinces began to flow in massively, fostering an unprecedented economic and demographic boom.

As in all the other international metropolises, immigrants arriving in Paris were sorted and oriented towards different parts of the segmented city. Throughout the twentieth century, Paris has consistently been a centre of attraction and integration. The 1901 census shows that, at the time, a little over 9 per cent of the population was of foreign origin and 56 per cent had been born in the provinces. In 1990, over 25 per cent of the population of Paris were of foreign origin. Since 1982, the proportion of immigrants, which had risen sharply between 1954 and 1975 (from 6 to 14 per cent), has not much changed. As the presence of immigrants in the city increased, two main transformations occurred. First, the origins of the migrants changed as new waves of immigration followed in the wake of those of the 1920s and 1930s. And second, the city's functional reorganization modified their distribution in space (Guillon, 1996). One can identify a succession process according to the classical model established by the urban ecologists of the Chicago school. The Italians, Belgians and Poles who came in the 1920s were followed in the 1950s and 1960s by Algerian, Portuguese and Spanish immigrants. Thus emerged the 'ethnic neighbourhoods', as they are now called, and as a result, the immigrants became highly visible in the city.

The aim of this chapter, however, is not to provide a detailed list of Paris's immigrant neighbourhoods, but to study their multiethnic aspects.[2] One of the most striking characteristics of Paris's 'ethnic neighbourhoods' is that they bring together people of many different origins. In addition to ethnic diversity, there is also a certain amount of social diversity. Indeed, the social and symbolic value of neighbourhoods with high immigrant concentration has changed since the 1970s. 'Gentrification' has led many middle- and upper-class households to move to immigrant and working-class neighbourhoods. For these reasons, the bipolar model, such as the 'whites versus blacks' model, does not really apply to the patterns of segregation and cohabitation observed in Paris. We must imagine a complex network of relations involving many different groups that are more or less organized around cultural associations, community services or economic 'niches', and often circumscribed within a specific area. The various 'integration models' – assimilation, multiculturalism, pluralism, melting-pot – whose context of reference is always the nation, can thus be re-examined and contrasted with actual local situations of ethnic cohabitation. Indeed, by analysing situations from a local point of view, one can avoid the political implications of an analysis of social interactions carried out at the national level. By looking at a neighbourhood, we need not be concerned by questions of nationality and citizenship, which are of crucial importance in France. Their importance there results from the historical significance of the nation as a political concept in the organization of French society.

In a local context, social and ethnic groups negotiate their position with their own rationale, which often differs from the national integration model. To quote de Certeau (1986), theirs is a 'pedagogy of diversity'. We study 'inter-ethnic' situations to 'analyse the conditions for the creation of new sociopolitical *contracts* and in particular shed light on the internal transformations which occur within a dominant group as a result of the presence of other groups' (de Certeau, 1986: 790–1). To illustrate this point, we have chosen to look at ethnic and class relationships in a formerly working-class neighbourhood of Paris, the Belleville quarter, which has become today an emblematic place for several ethnic groups.

Our approach is to study the system of regulation of ethnic differences by examining how urban, political, symbolic space is shared between different groups that play an active role on the local scene. We will show how this system, by ensuring a certain degree of social cohesion, promotes the integration of the inhabitants into the city, if not into the nation.

THE BELLEVILLE CONTEXT

The Belleville quarter, one of Paris's former working-class neighbourhoods, is located in the eastern part of the city. It was urbanized at the end of the nineteenth century and its architecture is typical of working-class areas, with artisan workshops and low-quality apartment buildings. By the early 1960s, the state of upkeep of these buildings was so poor that Belleville had become one of the most insalubrious neighbourhoods in Paris. The first massive demolitions, carried out in 1956, forced much of the native population out of the neighbourhood. As a consequence of urban renewal, the area ceased to act as a 'shelter' for needy people, as it had since the end of the nineteenth century. We have chosen the term 'shelter' in reference to Belleville's role in the wider context of the Paris area housing market. Indeed, since housing in this neighbourhood was cheap, poor households still wishing to remain in Paris could, as a last resort, find affordable housing in Belleville. The low level of rents was also due to the neighbourhood's poor reputation. Belleville, home of the lower classes, was considered a dangerous hideout for criminals and political troublemakers, anarchists or communists; for this reason, the area came to represent the epitome of all social ills.

Those who first came to live in Belleville were the households evicted from the centre of Paris during Haussmann's renovations in the 1860s. This population was socially homogeneous: for the most part skilled workers working in small artisan industries. In 1871, during the Paris Commune, this working-class identity was emphasized: the actions of revolutionaries from Belleville gave the neighbourhood the reputation of a hotbed of rebellion, a reputation it has practically never lost since (Merriman, 1994; Jacquemet, 1984). As a result, Belleville became a socially isolated area with a strong sense of its own identity. In the 1920s, Armenians, Greeks and Polish Jews began to move in. At this time, Belleville became the social and political centre of the Yiddish and Armenian communities. Stores, workshops, cafés, places of religious worship or assembly, political newspapers, Zionist, Bundist or communist discussion groups, common interest groups, Jewish or Armenian trade unions formed a dense and dynamic network of community organizations (Roland, 1962). During the 1950s, the neighbourhood's 'Yiddish period' slowly became history, while a new era of immigration dawned with the arrival of massive contingents from Algeria; also came the Tunisian Jews fleeing North Africa in the throes of decolonization. This new wave marked the beginning of Belleville's 'North African' period. At the same time, the neighbourhood's social composition was changing as French workers, who previously lived in insalubrious housing, moved to the new public housing buildings at the city's outskirts, or to the suburbs. Immigrants from the transit housing projects or other forms of temporary housing then replaced them and, as a result, the insalubrious housing stock remained permanently occupied. Contrary to what is commonly thought, the departure of French residents was not caused by the arrival of immigrants; instead, the latter's arrival was made possible by the departure of French residents and the resulting vacancies. Between 1954 and 1982, in a context where the overall density of the neighbourhood dropped considerably, the population of French citizens fell to one-half of what it had been (from 45,263 to 24,654), whereas the number of foreigners doubled (from 4696 to 9470). The diversity of origins is quite impressive. In 1990, the major groups were Algerians (15 per cent of immigrants), Tunisians (15 per cent), sub-Saharan Africans (9 per cent), Moroccans (8 per cent) and former Yugoslavs (7 per cent). Asians, Turks and Sri Lankans complete the picture of Belleville as a global village (Simon, 1993).

Added to the diversity of ethnic origins, there has been a recent increase in the variety of socio-professional statuses. Whereas in 1954 the neighbourhood was essentially working class, the professional profile of the working population is now changing. The gentrification process began in 1980, after the partial renovation of several old buildings and the launching of urban renewal programmes. Middle- and upper-class households moved into new apartment buildings and into existing buildings that were still in good condition; the numerous new public housing programmes in renovated areas also attracted new residents. The working-class population fell from 59 per cent in 1954 to 31 per cent in 1990, whereas the proportion of liberal and upper-level professionals increased from 4 per cent to 13 per cent.

Over a period of 30 years, from 1955 to approximately 1985, the neighbourhood underwent several population changes. The pace of these transformations was relatively swift, a fact that partially explains why the recently arrived populations were able to take over the area's public space with such ease. Indeed, according to the paradigm of Elias and Scotson (1965), 'established' residents strongly resist the efforts of new residents, or 'outsiders', to penetrate the various spheres of local power. In most cases, the transfer of power from one group to the other occurs over a long period of time. However, in the case of Belleville, the massive departure of part of the population led to the disappearance of traditional forms of neighbourhood organization; the loss of original structures made it easier for the newcomers to take over. This situation occurs quite frequently in run-down neighbourhoods, before they are renovated (Coing, 1966).

Due to the departure of a portion of the 'established' population and the ageing of another portion, many small businesses and artisan workshops closed and a large share of the quarter's economic infrastructure was left vacant. Since, due to the neighbourhood's bad reputation, real estate prices were extremely low, commercial leases became available to people who in normal circumstances would not have been able to afford them. At the same time, immigrants began to purchase property in 'rundown' apartment buildings. The fact that the 'native population' of Belleville lost interest in the neighbourhood's public social life is apparent today in the surprising visibility of several ethnic groups. North African Muslims and Jews, Asians and to a lesser extent Africans can be observed mainly in the local businesses and in the public space. Linked to 'territorialization strategies', each group has created highly structured enclaves to serve its own needs; they represent the organizational basis of ethnic cohabitation.

A FRAGMENTED AREA

Though Belleville as a whole ranks quite low in the hierarchy of Parisian neighbourhoods, it is far from being socially and ethnically homogeneous. At the local level, one can observe the same inequalities in the distribution of social or ethnic groups as in the city overall and as in its different parts. Thus, the middle and upper classes live in the high-quality apartment buildings of Belleville heights, whereas the working classes and lower-level staff live in the nether part of the neighbourhood, in rundown buildings awaiting demolition. Between 1954 and 1982, the area's social geography changed as the demolition programmes progressed. As a result of the demolitions, the affordable housing space available to immigrants became scarcer, while the latter's numbers increased. This led to the 'crowding' of many people into a small area, almost reminiscent of a

ghetto, unmarked by material boundaries but in fact strictly circumscribed, owing to the pressure of the housing market.

Immigrants ended up all living in the same buildings because they used
family and community networks whose market was limited. Usually,
upon their arrival, Algerian immigrants temporarily settled in cheap hotels
whose managers came from the same district as they did (Sayad, 1977).
Later on, when their families joined them, they moved to neighbouring
flats. A few years later, African immigrants followed the same itinerary,
though the starting points were hostels for migrant workers instead of
cheap hotels. Community networks also played an important role in helping immigrants from former Yugoslavia or Portugal settle into vacant
apartments with their families. The Tunisian Jews were helped not only by
family and friends but also by community associations. The Unified
Jewish Social Fund[3] helped 'refugees' who had had to flee Tunisia during
the political crises the country was going through after independence. A
strategy consisting of channelling the poorest fringe of immigrants
towards Belleville apparently led to the emergence of a 'Tunisian Jewish
ghetto' (Simon and Tapia, 1998). Finally, the Asians moved into the
renovated stock. The latter's strategy involved property investments
thanks to collective funding. Furthermore, special aid programmes also
entitled Asian refugees to public housing space.

Despite these 'channelized migration flows', as B. Thompson (1983)
calls them, buildings are never wholly occupied by a single ethnic group.
The distribution of apartments among immigrant groups reflects their
diversity, except in the case of hostels and cheap hotels. Thus, at this
level, the only really active type of segregation is social segregation.
Housing status is determined by income: there are no upper-level professionals living in rundown buildings. Conversely, very few members of
the working class can afford to live in renovated buildings with amenities,
even if these buildings belong to the public housing stock. From one
building to the next, the difference in rent can range from one to ten!
Insalubrious buildings thus house immigrants of all origins, and their only
'native' neighbours are working class. The mixing of different immigrant
groups is thus reinforced by social segregation.

Although the different ethnic groups tend to mix inside the residential
area, the more dynamic groups have divided up public space through a
strategy of occupation and control. This strategy is based on the presence
of numerous businesses managed by members of the community and
aimed mainly at meeting the community's needs. The shops are used as
identity markers (Raulin, 1986): the shop windows convey specific

signals (through signs, displays, and linguistic and colour codes) and sell specific products. When several shops belonging to the same ethnic group are located side by side, they constitute a continuous 'area' through the repetition of these 'community markers'. 'Centres of activity' thus develop around the business areas with community services, leisure clubs, cafés, cultural centres, doctors and places of religious worship. In Belleville, not only are there many shops and businesses, but these are playing an important role in establishing a community's territory. For example, out of 86 shops in the lower Belleville area, 46 can be considered 'ethnic' in the sense that they carry mainly imported products that are sold in a specific decor or display according to specific, culturally determined selling practices. (For a description of ethnic shops, see de Rudder, 1987.) Of these15 belong to the 'exotic' type, meaning that though their clientele is not restricted to a single ethnic group, they still refer to a specific culture, visible in the shop windows and on the signs. The three largest communities of the neighbourhood – Sephardic Jews (mainly from Tunisia), Southeast Asians and North African Muslims – manage two-thirds of the local stores.

The Sephardic Jewish neighbourhood is located in a small area between the Ramponneau and Dénoyez streets and along the Boulevard de Belleville. Originally, it was much larger, but renovations and the departure of part of the Tunisian Jewish community have reduced the 'little Goulette' of Paris to its tiny dimensions. Jewish commercial activity in this neighbourhood is linked mainly to the food industry, with kosher butchers, oriental bakeries and grocery shops. There are 'bazaars' that sell kitchen utensils and various plastic items, a religious bookshop and several services. Most members of this community participate in its overall economy and its social aid programmes take care of many of them. Several Jewish community organizations are located in the neighbourhood, such as the Paris Jewish social action centre and a Lubavich centre, which has opened two schools in the area. Thanks to the community associations, Belleville is both a commercial and a cultural centre and this enhances its attractiveness for the Tunisian Jewish community in Paris and entrenches their presence in the area even if most have moved. Thus, Jewish clients who live elsewhere come to shop in local stores. Before religious feasts, as many as 55 per cent of the stores' clients come from other neighbourhoods or from the suburbs.[4] The commercial infrastructure is an extremely important factor in a community's visibility: not only do 'ethnic' stores mark the neighbourhood with their presence, but they also make the community seem larger than it actually is.

On the other half of the Boulevard de Belleville is the Arab city; its restaurants and grocery stores look very much like those of the Jewish sector, except that the butcher shops are no longer kosher but halal. Mosques have replaced the synagogues and Muslim skullcaps the Jewish kippas. The cheap Kabyle hotels of the 1950s have gone; they have been replaced by a profusion of stores mainly centred on food distribution. This shopping area, which spreads from Ménilmontant to the Père Lachaise cemetery, includes bazaars, cafés, restaurants, travel agencies, second-hand clothing stores, import–export offices, grocery stores, butcher shops and fruit and vegetable stores. In addition to these ordinary commercial activities, a centre of Muslim activity has developed near the Couronnes metro station. Two mosques have been opened there, along with several religious bookshops. In this area, meat sold as strictly halal is under very strict control. Kepel (1984: 190ff.) calls this neighbourhood 'Paris's Islamic quarter'. It is controlled by the Tabligh, who are members of the international movement *jama'at al tabligh* (faith and religious practice).

In the Muslim sector, except on market days, far fewer women than men are seen on the streets. The men gather in small tight-knit groups in the central square where Belleville's market stands are set up twice a week. These groups are often extremely dense, with very little space left unoccupied. The presence of North African Muslims is most noticeable during Ramadan, in which the whole neighbourhood becomes involved. Social control reaches its highest point during this period when a Muslim, or a person considered as such, cannot be seen drinking or smoking during the day; if he does, more or less aggressively voiced reprobation will force him to stop. However, Muslims are not the only people concerned with Ramadan: the entire Belleville neighbourhood cannot help but participate in preparations for the feast. Vendors set up shop along the boulevard pavement and sell flat bread, herbs, fruit and sour milk. Shops held by Muslims add special Ramadan products to their usual display. Even Jewish shopkeepers stock up on fruit and drink for the occasion.

North African Muslims and Jews have a lot in common, and this is particularly evident when one looks at their economic activities. Many kosher restaurants employ Muslim waiters, who for a long time made it possible for them to open on the sabbath.[5] The majority of the Jewish bakeries employ Muslims. After emigration, the rules governing the cohabitation of the two communities in North Africa (Lewis, 1986; Memmi, 1974) were reactivated. Tunisian Jews very often speak Arabic, and the memories of Jews and Muslims complement each other within a single North African identity, recognized as such by both groups. They agree to identify the neighbourhood as 'Maghrebian', meaning neither Jewish nor Muslim.

The Asian area was at first limited to the renovated sector of the rue de Belleville; it subsequently rapidly spread to neighbouring streets.[6] Asian businesses are extremely varied in nature and meet most of the Asian community's needs: they include food shops, jewellers, supermarkets, record and video shops, restaurants, bakeries, estate agents, wholesale dealers in fabrics for clothing and leather goods manufacturers. In addition to these businesses, there is a dense network of community services, including doctors, letter writers, leisure clubs, cultural associations, and formal and informal information networks. Although the Asians first settled in Belleville at the end of the 1970s, their presence became significant only in the mid-1980s. One reason for their choice of this area was that the Asian quarter of the thirteenth *arrondissement* was reaching saturation point. The strategy of implantation in Belleville just about matched that applied in the 'Choisy triangle': their arrival coincided with urban modernization programmes (Raulin, 1988). This 'penetration' phase, when Asians began to move into the neighbourhood, mainly into recently built housing, was followed by a 'consolidation' phase with the development of community-oriented businesses. These businesses attracted other Asians to the neighbourhood, and many in turn ended up moving there. Between 1982 and 1990, the Asian population increased by 63 per cent, the highest increase after that of the Turkish population (76 per cent).

The non-Asian shopkeepers feel threatened by the Asian community's vitality and expansionist drive, but so far no collective solution enabling them to ensure their own survival has been devised. There has been little group reaction to the massive implantation of Asian businesses, which is so extensive that Belleville is now considered to be Paris's second 'Chinatown'. Despite their commercial expansionism, there are few Asians in Belleville's other areas, and it is only at the points of contact between areas that they mix with other groups. This strategy of isolation, though not specifically Asian, tends to support the stereotype of a secretive community that keeps to itself and is unwilling to conform to the neighbourhood's social order (Live, 1993). The other groups, which consider themselves much poorer than the Asians, are exasperated by their real or imagined financial power. They are envious of their sense of solidarity, thanks to which Asians are much more successful in the inter-ethnic competition than their partners or rivals. However, the population increase in Belleville has led Asian households to disperse, after an initial period of concentration. Thanks to personal contacts made in their residential context, Asians are perceived as individuals instead of simply members of an ethnic group. As grossly simplified ethnic divisions break down and are replaced by daily exchanges – which involve negotiation – the Asian population is gradually adapting to the common social order. Within this overall commercial structure, various other ethnic groups have opened businesses: there are several Spanish grocery stores and restaurants, one or two African restaurants and an increasing number of Turkish small businesses, mainly 'fast food' outlets (for example, pizza and doner kebab restaurants). Relics of the previous era, the few remaining French-owned shops, are located mainly at the corner of the rue de Belleville and the Boulevard de Belleville. They remain isolated amid the stars of David, Chinese ideograms and Arabic characters and have no influence at all on the atmosphere generated by the dominant groups. The municipality's renovation plans have included attempts to establish new commercial activities aimed at modifying the neighbourhood's image, which the authorities perceive as too 'immigrant'. All new apartment buildings include commercial space, but so far Asians or North Africans lease them all. This demonstrates that both communities are trying hard to maintain their presence in Belleville and that this strategy has won over the municipality's attempt to 'requalify' the neighbourhood.

Public space is thus appropriated by means of easily identifiable markers: buildings, facilities and other public places are marked off as belonging to a specific, almost private, territory. Those who share its 'identity' frequent this territory. These identity signs or markers can be read in shop windows, in the way housing space is occupied, in the playing out of social relationships, or even in people's personal attributes (such as their clothing and personal demeanour). Schematically speaking, the spatial and social morphology of Belleville is a juxtaposition of ethnic strata, alternately dominated by one or another of the ethnic groups. The strata themselves are first the buildings, then the streets, then the shops, cafés and parks, and finally the whole picture is crossed by a transversal stratum represented by community associations and political groups. The way the various groups adjust to this stratified structure determines the Belleville cohabitation model.

COHABITATION MODELS

Now that the framework for our analysis has been established, we can revert to our initial question: how does integration work in Belleville? The restriction of certain ethnic groups to a circumscribed territory, the public display and even the exacerbation of one's specificity, whether religious (Islamic fundamentalism or Jewish orthodoxy) or cultural, are in contradiction with the 'French model of integration'. According to this model, integration is an *individual* process enabling immigrants to participate in the activities of mainstream society on condition they accept its rules and that the society in turn is prepared to integrate the immigrants.[7] This process is based on a strict distinction between private and public spheres. In the private sphere, cultural specificities can be maintained if they do not contradict the fundamental 'values' of the Republic. In the public sphere, however, one must remain 'neutral' or, in other words, one's behaviour must be in conformity with the norms of mainstream society.

What is the situation in Belleville? Here, cultural differences, instead of being downplayed, are emphasized and play an important role in the definition of relations between the various ethnic groups. Far from being neutral, public space is the object of competition for control over it; but instead of being a cause for social disorder, this competition ensures social stability. Ever since the French working class ceased to be the dominant group in the area, no other group has been able to impose its norms or values on the others. The concept of normative behaviour is no longer relevant, and has been replaced by a much more general attitude based on tolerance and respect of proprieties. Social order in Belleville[8] is based first and foremost on a charter of practices devoid of ethnic or cultural references. To use a popular cliché in studies on integration, Belleville's social order is universalist in both spirit and practice.

The coexistence of these groups within a circumscribed area has led to a division of the neighbourhood into small plots. To describe the spatial organization of the groups living in Belleville, the most accurate image is that of a mosaic, 'separate and closed-in worlds which exist side by side but do not mix', to quote R. E. Park (1925). Each urban segment has its own 'local colour' and the atmosphere can differ completely from one street to the next. Each area has its users who feel at home in its atmosphere and contribute, by their presence, to spreading it. These 'microenvironments', in which urban functions, users and specific practices are combined, are undoubtedly 'quasi-communities' (Gans, 1962). The division of space must not be interpreted as a sign of hostility between the different groups. Indeed, it is the only way these groups can use the city while maintaining their own specificity. Without such borders, ethnic groups could not keep the distance necessary for them to be able to live together. At the same time, thanks to these borders, which are constantly shifting, a group can define itself in opposition to the 'others', as Fredrik Barth (1969), whose book has become a work of reference, has pointed out. As competition for space is high, conflicts can only be regulated if compensation is provided to those groups that are not present on the public scene. If one considers the city according to three important aspects – urban, political and symbolic – the sharing of space requires that a considerable number of elements be taken into account. Thus, added to the issue of concrete urban space, there is the neighbourhood's history and collective memory, and in parallel, the political forces and the associations that control the terms of this division: three distinct yet interlinked spheres of action, whose collective actors may differ. If an actor ceases to participate at one level, his participation may increase at another.

THE MYTH AND THE MULTICULTURALS

To create this system, history had to be rewritten and the collective memory condensed into a 'Belleville myth'. The myth has made it possible to create a common area, open to all, and to transcend deeply ingrained cultural specificities. The myth has created the 'imagined community' B. Anderson (1983) described when speaking of nations. Here it is, in a few words. The Belleville myth is based on two assertions: 'Belleville is an old working-class neighbourhood' and 'a neighbourhood where immigrants first settled long ago'. These two assertions are of course based on historical fact, but the latter has been modified, in the spirit of what Roland Barthes (1957) called 'the naturalization of history'. The elements that constitute the Belleville myth are no doubt historically true. But, and it is this sense that a myth has been created, they had neither the impact nor the importance they are believed today to have had. Thus, Belleville is not an old immigrant neighbourhood. Quite the contrary, censuses from the first half of the twentieth century show that Belleville then had the highest proportion of Parisian natives in the city. The immigrant presence in Belleville has never been as strong as it is today. Similarly, although Belleville was a working-class neighbourhood until the 1970s, this was no longer the case at the time the myth crystallized. What is the function of this myth and who perpetrates it?

A myth is defined first and foremost by its aim, which is usually the desire to overcome contradictions. The aim of the Belleville myth is to defuse ethnic conflicts by making them seem outdated. As Claude Levi-Strauss (1958: 231) said:

A myth is always based on events which occurred in the past: 'before the creation of the universe', or 'at the beginning of time', in any case, 'a long time ago'. But the myth's intrinsic value comes from the fact that these events, which took place at a given time, create a permanent structure; this structure determines the past, the present and the future.

By associating the immigrants with the neighbourhood's collective memory, the myth acts as a 'nativity factory'; thus, ethnic conflicts cannot be based on the refusal of one group to accept the other's presence, since they both equally *belong* to the neighbourhood. In other words, using Elias and Scotson's (1965) paradigm, thanks to this myth, immigrants cease to be *outsiders* and can aspire to the more legitimate status of the *established*. Thanks to the contraction operated by the myth, attitudes of intolerance and rejection, which are often observed in situations where local residents emphasize their cultural specificity, become totally irrelevant.

The myth also concerns relations between social classes. By laying emphasis on the neighbourhood's identity as working class, it aims to make up for the social inequalities reflected in the housing conditions. Acceptance of this myth represents, for members of the middle and upper classes, a guarantee of their own integration into the neighbourhood. Even more so, they play a significant role in creating and spreading the myth, in particular through the action of *La Bellevilleuse*, a local residents' association devoted to fighting the neighbourhood renovation programme.

Local residents wishing to weigh upon decisions about the lower Belleville area's renovation programme created the association in 1988. Today, it has 500 members, mainly from the recently settled middle and upper classes. Participation in this neighbourhood association enables them to express, through militant action, their faith in a certain vision of society. Furthermore, they take an active part in local politics and play a crucial role as intermediaries between society as a whole (represented here by the public authorities and the technical services of the City of Paris) and the minority groups. Because of their strong attachment to ethnic, cultural or social 'mixing' or diversity, these new residents may be called 'multicultural'. Their commitment to collective action, aimed at defending the right of immigrants and the working class to remain in Belleville, can be interpreted on two levels.

By insisting on people being rehoused in the same neighbourhood, the 'multiculturals' anticipate changes in Belleville's population: they wish to prevent the too rapid gentrification of the neighbourhood and preserve the atmosphere they came for in the first place. Thus, they have become the advocates of a working-class identity, which is not theirs but for which they feel sympathy. They are themselves often of working-class background, and participation in community action is a manner of 'reparation'. The aim is to promote, at the local level, a social model that has not taken shape at the national level. The commitment of the 'multiculturals' has provided the working class with a new edge in power relations. Indeed, when dealing with the authorities, immigrants and French workers are usually deprived of means of pressure; the 'multiculturals' are thus able to serve as mediators, which is what they did in relation to the neighbourhood renovation programme. On a wider scale, their role as mediators has enabled them to create a more positive image of a social world that so far had been perceived as impoverished and pernicious. Through their joint reaction of protest against the renewal programme and the bureaucratic monster that supports it, the neighbourhood's different groups were able to get together symbolically and, to a certain extent, to come closer operationally. W. de Jong (1989) described a similar process in an old neighbourhood of Rotterdam, 'Het Oude Westen', which resembles Belleville in many respects. There, ethnic conflicts were overcome thanks to associations of local residents committed to preventing the deterioration of their neighbourhood.

The Belleville model can thus be seen as a successful system of regulation of differences: these differences are asserted within separate and structured 'communities' and expressed in 'community areas', which are interlinked without competing one against another. Urban space is identified as belonging to North African Jewish or Muslim immigrants, to Asians and, to a lesser extent, to Africans. Even though they do not have their specific 'turf', the 'native' residents, that is to say the French workers, who represent the neighbourhood's living memory, are a significant component of the Belleville identity. Last, the recently-arrived middle and upper classes, which have the financial means and the extremely valuable ability to circulate with ease in the world of social relationships and contacts, have a specific role to play in the sphere of political and community action. In Belleville, each person has a place, has his or her *own* place within a dynamic system that is constantly changing. Only on this condition can people overcome their objective differences and share a strong local identity. To describe this model, we chose to compare it with a mosaic, a composite image that refers to a surface made up of assembled pieces as well as to the political system of the ancient Ottoman Empire. Belleville can be compared with both: on the one hand, it is made up of juxtaposed, heterogeneous parts and, on the other, the

Ottoman Empire is part of the historical and political background of two of the neighbourhood's main groups. In this respect, the Ottoman Empire, as an attempt to reconcile different cultures within a unified political system, represents a historical precedent, which has yet to be studied in all its implications (Courbage and Fargues, 1992; Valensi, 1986).

The mosaic model owes its existence to historical circumstances in which different population groups going different ways found themselves at the same time in the same place. Many immigrants who managed to improve their social status moved out of the insalubrious buildings, whereas rehabilitation programmes gradually evicted others. The gentrification process has increased in scope and is now reaching out for the last fragments of territory still accessible to immigrants. Belleville is undergoing a gradual transformation, from 'ethnic neighbourhood' to 'urban immigrant centre' (*espace de centralité immigrée*) (Toubon and Messamah, 1991). Even when the members of a community move to another area, they maintain their ties with Belleville, which continues to develop its community-oriented economic, cultural and social activities: the area is thus becoming a centre of attraction for both symbolic and practical reasons. This phenomenon of 'territorial dissociation', which is characteristic of a 'networked' society, has been observed in several ethnic neighbourhoods in Paris, such as the Goutte d'Or (Toubon and Messamah, 1991) and the Choisy triangle (Raulin, 1988). This new function seems to be a new stage of 'transitional area', or rather, to use the term Ernest Burgess (1928) coined, of 'first entry ports', which enable immigrants gradually to adapt to their new society without experiencing a total break with their past way of life. The future of these neighbourhoods remains uncertain; the opinion most commonly held is that they will disappear through acculturation. In our opinion, this is not happening in Belleville. Thanks to new forms of 'distance shopping' practised by both the older and more recent diasporas – immigrants from Southeast Asia, Ashkenazi and Sephardic Jews, Armenians, North Africans, Africans, Turks and others – ethnic territories can remain a permanent aspect of the urban environment. They can perhaps even serve as a basis for the elaboration of a community structure of national scope.

Notes

1. Cf. Hemingway's celebration of Paris in *Paris est une fête*, quoted in Ory (1994).

2. This approach owes a great deal to the pioneer (in France) research work carried out by V. de Rudder, M. Guillon and I. Taboada-Leonetti. They focused on multiethnic cohabitation in several neighbourhoods of Paris (the Choisy neighbourhood in the thirteenth *arrondissement*, the Aligre and Lot Chalon neighbourhoods, and the wealthy neighbourhoods of the sixteenth *arrondissement*). Summing up the team's approach, Taboada-Leonetti (1989) writes: 'Our aim was to carry out empirical studies to show how people manage their differences in an *ad hoc* manner, depending on the issues at stake and the circumstances, and how they produce collective identities which can vary from one situation to the next without necessarily generating social crises, social dysfunction or ethnic identity crises.'

3. Unified Jewish Social Fund: this is the main source of funding supporting the various Jewish cultural, social and community institutions in France.

4. Survey conducted in front of shops in Belleville for a study on economic activity in the lower Belleville area (see Fayman and Simon, 1991).

5. The religious revival, which has affected the Jewish community in France, was also felt in Belleville. Today, most kosher stores close on the Sabbath.

6. A detailed map of Asian businesses in Belleville can be found in Ma Mung and Simon (1990: 99). However, this map dates back to 1985 and the neighbourhood's business infrastructure has changed considerably since then. More recent information is available in Live (1993).

7. This formulation is a condensed synthesis of the definitions of integration as given by two official sources; the Commission de la nationalité (1988) and the Haut conseil à l'intégration (1991).

8. The notion of 'local social order' refers to the one G. Suttles formulated about a slum in Chicago. Even though those who live there have been rejected by mainstream society as 'people with disreputable characteristics', slums are not 'disorganized' (Suttles, 1968). Social order is interpreted here as a system of rules, norms and values making it possible for different social groups, which are interdependent yet reject each other, to live together. In Belleville, where residents belong to very different ethnic or social groups, the neighbourhood stands for a reference. Since all these groups live in the same area, to get along, they must develop a common code of behaviour for the neighbourhood.

Part III

Political Inclusion/ Exclusion at the Neighbourhood Level

9 The Residential Concentration and Political Participation of Immigrants in European Cities

Marco Martiniello

Academic and political debates about the position of immigrants and their offspring in European societies offer various insights according to space and time. What themes are discussed, studied or lead to public policies depends on the national context, the characteristics of the urban setting and the orientations of those in power. In France, the political participation of immigrants and their offspring became an issue for a while in the 1980s, but sank into oblivion when the Beur movement (comprised of young North Africans born in France) ran out of steam. Today, few people openly question the voting behaviour of the French of foreign origin, the phenomenon of immigrant elected MPs or the representation of immigrants and their offspring in the French political system.

Moreover, the use of an ethnic vocabulary continues to pose problems, as evidenced, for instance, in the cool reception Michèle Tribalat (1995) and her team received for their recent survey. For the first time in a large quantitative study carried out in France, she emphasized the need to take into account immigrants' ethnic origins, beyond the ordinary criterion of nationality, to describe more faithfully their integration and assimilation into French society. A taboo had been broken, even though at the end of the day the findings of her team proved the efficiency of the French model of integration, supported by figures. Use of the ethnic variable was enough to heap opprobrium on this piece of research, which was almost faultless from a strictly methodological point of view. For some people, daring to speak of the mobilization of ethnicity in French politics, an area into which Tribalat does not venture, is an infringement of the norms of 'republican political correctness' (Martiniello, 1996b) and an unacceptable questioning of a single and indivisible republican citizenship.

The debate on integration is thus often incorporated into a larger problematic dealing with *les banlieues*, the city and social exclusion. It usually focuses either on social and economic factors or on the law and order dimension. This is to the detriment of the political aspects of exclusion and how they are articulated with social and economic exclusion. The incorporation of migrants and their offspring into a changing labour market has received wide attention, as has the issue of ethnic crime and social dislocation in urban settings. The various forms of political exclusion and/ or of the non-participation of migrant origin populations in the local public sphere and in the political and policy-making processes of cities and underprivileged neighbourhoods are more rarely studied (Geisser, 1997). They may nevertheless be expected to have crucial implications for the development of an active local citizenship and for social integration and solidarity.

In Great Britain, however, the position of ethnic minorities in the political process has, since the 1980s, progressively become a legitimate and recurrent theme in academic literature and political debates (Anwar, 1994; Geddes, 1993; Saggar, 1998; Solomos and Back, 1995). The ethnicization of the British political field at local as well as national levels has become a legitimate object of research and debate. The debate has focused on issues such as the 'black sections' within the Labour Party, the emergence of ethnic minority MPs like Bernie Grant, Diane Abbott and Paul Boateng, or the political power of the citizens of Indo-Pakistani origin in some cities,

A particular historical pattern of migration to each European country has given rise to quite different approaches to the political participation and representation of immigrants and their offspring. However, beyond these differences, a common feature characterizes numerous urban entities throughout Europe – high residential concentrations of immigrant origin populations. In some countries, this high density is in the poorer areas of the inner cities or in areas close to these. In Brussels, for instance, or in the inner cities of Great Britain and some large Dutch cities, the boundaries of these areas tend to be fairly clearly marked by an underground, railway line or river. In France, however, while this type of geographical implantation of immigrant populations also exists, the supposedly most problematic residential concentrations are in the high density housing projects and *banlieues* located much further away from the city centres. One such housing estate, Vaulx-en-Velin near Lyons, provided the cradle of the Beurs' collective action (Bouamama, 1994). The smart areas of big European cities and their rich neighbourhoods, which in English are called suburbs, house the less conventional immigrants, the more or less temporary expatriates. Examples of these are Japanese businessmen and their families in Amsterdam, European civil servants that have settled in the green landscapes of the Brabant Wallon near Brussels, and elite Arabs in the centre of London. Questions of social exclusion or political participation are, of course, of little concern to these luxury immigrants. They are unaffected by post-migratory problems (Martiniello, 1993) because their presence is rarely looked upon as a problem. Different geographical concentrations of immigrant populations in urban spaces that are marked out (at least symbolically) can be accounted for by various mechanisms of segregation and self-segregation. These should be examined with care, but this is not the place to do so.

The question raised in this chapter concerns a possible link between residential concentrations of immigrant populations[1] and their political mobilization and participation. In other words, we want to study the impact of residential concentration on the immigrant population's political integration and/or exclusion. On the one hand, we can ask how residential concentration advances or prevents the mobilization of immigrant ethnicities in the formal political space. On the other hand, we can study the possible link between residential concentration and the representation of immigrant populations in political institutions.

Because the focus of this chapter is exclusively on the participation of immigrants in the formal political environment, namely those who are eligible to vote, it excludes all the other forms of political participation that are at their disposal, at least theoretically. Consequently, the starting question can be more empirically rephrased as what is the link between the residential concentration of populations of immigrant origin and a possible ethnic vote?

The approach is comparative and draws on ongoing empirical research and data published in France, Belgium, the Netherlands and Great Britain. Purely theoretical reflections have been reduced to a minimum. Methodological difficulties will, however, be dealt with because they reduce the scope and depth of the potential comparisons.

The aim is to extend the debate on exclusion and migrants in the cities by taking into account a dimension that is often neglected, though crucial to democracy. This is the inclusion and exclusion of migrants and migrant origin populations in politics, namely in political institutions, in decision-making and agenda setting on public affairs at the local level.

RESIDENTIAL CONCENTRATION AND ETHNIC VOTE

The 'ethnic vote' has been a recurrent theme in US political science for several decades. Since the Voting Right Act of 1965, which created a new electorate by giving black Americans the right to vote, the political behaviour of ethnic and racial minorities has attracted increasing interest among political scientists. However, the existence of a link between political behaviour in general and electoral behaviour in particular on the one hand, and ethnic and racial belonging on the other, has yet to be confirmed by a convincing general theory (Taylor, 1996). The existence of an ethnically or racially motivated vote remains dubious. Nevertheless, with each election, common sense points to the need for each candidate who has entered the lists to win the votes of Jews, Blacks, Hispanics and, more and more frequently, sexual minorities.

Consequently, researchers cannot consider the existence of the ethnic vote as data, whether they work on this or the other side of the Atlantic. Their task consists rather of discovering what factors and circumstances are likely to benefit and explain the development of electoral behaviour that is specific to electors who belong to ethnic categories, in this case electors of immigrant origin.[2] The residential concentrations of ethnic categories undoubtedly belong to these numerous factors (characteristics of the electoral system, mode of division into constituencies, gerry-mandering, existence of social networks based on ethnicity, and types of discrimination suffered by immigrant populations).

Before studying the potential link between residential concentration and the development of an ethnic vote, the latter term should be clearly defined. In a first meaning, 'ethnic vote' refers to the individual vote cast by an elector for one or several candidates of the same ethnic group, or for a party that regroups candidates from that ethnic background. The electors consider such candidates or parties as their automatic repre-sentatives because of their shared ethnic identity or origin. The latter is sufficient to account for the expressed vote whatever the political pro-gramme proposed. In a second sense, we can talk of an 'ethnic vote' when electors from a particular ethnic category unanimously decide to support such and such a candidate for such and such a party whatever his or her ethnic identity. This collective or block voting may be subjected to a certain amount of bargaining between electors and candidates, with the latter promising to give the group some advantage in exchange for their votes. This vote can also result from the subjective awareness of a group that a candidate or party better understands the concerns of an ethnic category and is likely to defend its interests better. This distinction is clearly theoretical. Indeed, it is easy to imagine cases where the vote could simultaneously become ethnic in both meanings described above. It should nevertheless be stressed that a voter with an ethnic background does not necessarily – by nature so to say – express an 'ethnic vote' in the meanings considered above: it may or it may not be the case.

Furthermore, to respect the quantitative methodological option in classical electoral studies and to try to establish the emergence of an ethnic vote in one or other of its meanings, it is necessary to have figures on the political behaviour of voters of foreign origin. However, not every European country records the ethnic and/or national origins of those who appear in its national statistics. In Great Britain, a question about ethnicity was asked in the 1991 census (Ni Brolchain, 1990). In the Netherlands, a list of ethnic groups officially targeted by ethnic minority policies is known and statistical data taking into account ethnicity are available. Moreover, since 1985, legally settled immigrants have been allowed to take part in local elections both as voters and candidates (Rath, 1993). In France and Belgium, for reasons specific to each national context, there are still huge obstacles to taking ethnicity into account in the official statistics. The methodological problems that result from this lack of available data often affect the quantitative assessment of the potential emergence of an ethnic vote. Consequently, assessing the impact of residential concentration on this possible 'ethnic vote' is even more difficult. If data were available on a national scale, we would have to draw comparisons between towns and areas with high or low densities of ethnic categories. Consequently, there may be grounds for pursuing a qualitative approach. It should allow for an in-depth understanding of the mechanisms that command the political behaviour of immigrant populations in areas where they are highly concentrated as well as in other areas. Therefore, at least partly, we could hope to understand the impact of residential concentration on such behaviour and especially on the vote. Finally, another methodological approach being used for the current research consists of combining the quantitative and qualitative aspects and somehow going as far as possible in each approach. In view of these methodological factors and of the incompleteness of the research, the following developments must be considered as simple indications of the possible construction of an 'ethnic vote' in European towns and areas with a high density of immigrants.

In Belgium, voting is compulsory for all citizens who are aged 18 and over. Among this electorate we count several dozens of thousands of Belgians of immigrant origin who have acquired Belgian citizenship as a result of the various reforms of the nationality code that have taken place over the last 15 years. For reasons mentioned earlier, the exact number of those who are sometimes inappropriately called 'the new Belgians' is unknown. However, there seems to be no doubt that their residential concentration is highest in some municipalities and areas of Brussels, the federal capital. For the moment, their voting behaviour has not been subjected to any published large-scale quantitative study. However, this new electorate arouses the interest of political parties insofar as in some municipalities, their votes are liable either to stabilize the majority in power or to provoke its defeat. In this respect, the next local election to be held in the year 2000 may be quite interesting.

For the time being, there is nothing to indicate the existence of a relevant 'ethnic vote' at the local level. During the last municipal elections, a party composed mainly of socially and economically upwardly mobile young citizens of North African-origin called MERCI (European Movement for the Recognition of Citizens, including citizens of immigrant origin) presented a list of candidates to five municipalities in Brussels with large Moroccan immigrant populations. The ethnic identities the candidates shared with part of the electorate did not prevent their bitter defeat. In none of the five municipalities did MERCI exceed 0.8 per cent of the vote. Contrary to what was sometimes feared, 'new Belgians' do not automatically vote for a candidate from their own ethnic background. Of course, candidates of immigrant origin running on the lists of the traditional parties experienced some success in areas with a high density of immigrants. In fact, these candidates often came from a community environment. Consequently, their commitment may have transformed them into desirable leaders for some young immigrant voters: if they worked for this youth at a social level, were they also perhaps in a good position to defend them through their political commitment? The individual electoral choices of some young immigrants have probably given a positive answer to this question.

As far as the 'ethnic vote' in its second meaning is concerned, it is clear that candidates contacted ethnic associations or other candidates to negotiate block voting. One must remember that in Belgian local politics, even a few dozen votes are not to be neglected. However, there are insufficient data available to be able to claim that such and such a candidate was elected thanks to the Belgian-Moroccan vote.

In the French case, the political behaviour of North African immigrants aroused political as well as academic interest as early as the second half of the 1980s. That was when the thesis of the immigrants' 'entry into politics' was first put forward (Withol de Wenden, 1988). The Beurs, in particular, were progressively perceived as new political actors, whose associative practices, party activism and various forms of cultural mediation to which they committed themselves were studied. Discovered by the political world through their 'March of the Beurs', this new potential electorate caught the imagination of the left, who saw it as a means of countering the first signs of a dreaded decline.

Though the media talked several times about the existence of a 'Beur vote', a 'North African vote', or even a 'Jewish vote', for political as well as methodological reasons, no national electoral survey of the French of North African or Jewish origin was ever conducted. Fragmented work is available on various urban situations, but there are no comparisons of areas with high and low densities of immigrants to allow us to assess the impact of residential concentration on the ethnic vote.

Before trying to define the possible reality of an 'ethnic vote' in France, we must first tackle the essential issue of registration on the electoral roll and effective participation in the elections. Contrary to Belgium, voting is not compulsory and this question takes on great relevance. France Plus, an association set up in 1985, had among its objectives precisely to promote the Beurs' registration on the electoral roll. It managed eventually to build up pools of ethnic votes allowing the Beurs to negotiate the presentation or re-presentation of eligible candidates from ethnic categories on the lists of the parties interested in those votes. Clearly, the logic was that of an 'ethnic vote' in the second meaning of this term. Given its organizational deficiency and the weakness of its implantation in deprived urban areas, France Plus had varying luck. It tried on various occasions to win over elected representatives of immigrant origin. The fact remains that its strategy was successful only in specific local contexts in which the immigrant population was concentrated.

As far as the 'ethnic vote' in terms of its first meaning is concerned, there is no study available to prove that a candidate's ethnicity plays any more important a role in explaining the voting behaviour of a North African voter than of any other voter (Kelfaoui, 1996). However, some ethnic political actors turn up in immigrant areas to try and inspire French citizens of foreign origin to adopt an ethnic logic to their voting behaviour. Among other things, they attempt to convince them that because of their common ethnic or religious affiliation, they are uniquely placed to defend their ethnic group in the French political system. Studies have also shown that in the case of Jewish people, the hypothesis of an 'ethnic vote' cannot be rejected outright and that the possibility of communitarian logic at least partly influencing the vote deserves to be studied. This is one of the conclusions of Strudel's (1996) study on the political behaviour of Jews in Sarcelles.

In Great Britain, ethnic minorities have long been considered to vote for the Labour Party. The available data have to a certain extent confirmed this hypothesis. Indeed, the Labour Party, which traditionally presented itself as the party of all the workers, supported the independence of India and has always been opposed to racial discrimination (Layton-Henry, 1992). In this sense, an apparently ethnic vote in its second meaning seems to have always existed in Great Britain. It was mainly based on the class position of colonial immigrants in British society. Besides, the two other big parties, the Conservative Party and the Liberal Democrat Party, have been trying to draw the votes of the minorities for several years. This has sometimes been successful, especially with the economic elite of Indian origin.

The geographical concentration of ethnic minorities has more potential influence over a majority ballot election than over one based on proportional representation. In some constituencies, the potential electoral power of ethnic minorities is quantitatively so important that the ethnic vote in its second meaning can tip a seat from one party to the other. Aware of this situation, some minority activists have tried to exert pressure on the choice of candidate the party puts forward in a particular constituency. However, we cannot say that electors systematically vote for candidates of the same ethnic origin as themselves in areas with either a high or low density of ethnic minorities.

Finally, in the Netherlands, since 1985 there have been numerous discussions on the electoral power of ethnic minorities and many hypotheses have been developed about the ethnic vote. As in the other countries, there is no national level electoral survey that takes ethnicity into account, but exit polls have been used to study the main Dutch cities (Tillie, 1994). In general, the turnout to elections seems to be lower among ethnic minority voters than among non-ethnic minority Dutch citizens. Though national and ethnic origins clearly affect voting patterns, most migrants seem to vote for traditional Dutch parties. The emergence of ethnic parties, which has long been dreaded, has so far not taken place. When there are elections, immigrants as a rule tend to vote for one of the major Dutch parties (Rath, 1993). However, in some areas with a high density of ethnic categories, for instance the Bijlmermeer area in Amsterdam, West Indian activists have recently demanded the right to have a black mayor.[3] According to them, only a black mayor can represent an area that has become largely black. This sort of demand would be impossible in an area with a low residential concentration of ethnic categories.

At the close of this brief review, it clearly appears that there is no hard evidence to suggest that residential concentrations of ethnic categories have a direct effect on the emergence of an 'ethnic vote'. However, given the quantitative deficiency of these categories in the national electorate, the hypothesis of the emergence of a politically relevant ethnic vote only takes on its full meaning in areas with a high density of immigrants and their offspring. It is only once they constitute a quantitatively interesting potential electorate that the parties are likely to approach the immigrant populations, which might then try to mobilize ethnic and community networks in formal politics while taking into account the constraints linked to the structure of political opportunities.

CONCLUSION

In the current state of our knowledge, no general and final answer can be given to the wider question of whether there is a link between the formal political mobilization and participation of immigrant populations and their residential concentration. A few remarks can nevertheless be put forward.

First, that this issue is being raised at all is an indication of an emerging visibility of a larger phenomenon, which in some European countries is, however, often ignored – the multiform ethnicization of the political environment, which benefits from the assertion of extreme right-wing political parties and a nationalist revival. This ethnicization of politics, which is of course subject to highly positive or negative reports, corresponds to a reality that forms the framework of an interrogation into the possible emergence of an 'ethnic vote'. The vote for extreme right-wing parties throughout Europe is an indication of the ethnicization of politics. This could also be analysed in terms of an ethnic vote.

Second, this question only has a meaning if the immigrant population's potential political power is perceived as strong enough to constitute a political stake. A quantitative effect is undoubtedly of some importance and is mainly significant in municipalities with a high concentration of immigrant origin population. In national elections, the electoral power of ethnic categories remains relatively weak in all the countries we studied.

Third, this question comes within the scope of a wider reflection on the notion of representation in today's Western democracies. Insofar as most of them, albeit sometimes reluctantly, accept their multiculturality and multiethnicity, is it now time to re-examine traditional principles of political representation based on ethno-cultural homogeneity. Reflections on multicultural citizenship (Kymlicka, 1995; Martiniello, 1996a and 1997), which in their attempt to revive democracy neither France nor other European countries feel able to mention, is a stake that seems to be suffering quite a lot. Is a political system that systematically excludes or under-represents some groups from formal political institutions because of their alleged culture or ethnicity, really a strong democracy? To answer this question is to try to assess the importance of other dimensions of exclusion than the mere socioeconomic ones and allows us to stress the various facets of exclusion and inequality that undermine the democratic ideal.

Notes

1. The above-mentioned luxury immigrants are not included in this study. This does not mean that their concentration cannot be politicized on principle. For instance, the rich Dutch who settle in the well-off villages north of Antwerp next to the Dutch border, are sometimes rejected by the local population and some political representatives who blame them for using Belgium as a luxury dormitory without taking part in its social and economic life. However, so far those European citizens have shown no intention of getting involved in Belgian politics.
2. The expressions 'ethnic categories' and 'ethnic communities of immigrant origin' were defined in an earlier study (Martiniello, 1992: 85–96).
3. I thank Hassan Bousetta for passing this piece of information on to me.

10 Political Dynamics in the City: Three Case Studies

Hassan Bousetta

This chapter on the collective dynamics, sociopolitical participation and ethnic mobilization of immigrant minorities is based on comparative case studies of Moroccan communities in three small and medium-sized cities in Belgium (Liège), the Netherlands (Utrecht) and France (Lille). Three main ideas inform the design and rationale of this research.

The *first* is that immigrant incorporation is increasingly being shaped by socioeconomic and political dynamics at work locally. In this age of post-industrial transition, inter-ethnic relations are increasingly entangled with broader social and economic phenomena affecting cities. In countries like France, the Netherlands and Belgium, this is reflected in patterns of policy management of ethnic diversity. The policy interventions of these countries' public authorities have gradually begun to address the socio-spatial dislocations confronting urban areas. A significant feature of European governments' policy response to urban decline and immigrant integration has been to decentralize power to local authorities. Whereas migratory flow regulation remains a matter for governmental and European inter-governmental approaches, the integration part of migration policies is often tailored to fit immigrant policy issues emerging in the big cities.

Second, it is important to emphasize that migrant communities are not necessarily at the forefront of the new relationship between economy and society, for which the city has set the stage. From a political sociology point of view, the city has surfaced as a relevant and privileged unit for empirical investigation. For political and social scientists, issues such as the political incorporation of migrants, the enfranchisement of foreigners and immigrant ethnic mobilization provide the basis for a new appraisal of relations between civil and political society. They raise the question of how best immigrant minority groups can organize and participate in local decision-making to defend and preserve their collective interests.

The *third* idea at the heart of this research is its focus on the collective response of one immigrant minority group in three settings and to study the forms and patterns of its collective sociopolitical insertion.

ETHNIC MOBILIZATION AND SOCIOPOLITICAL PARTICIPATION

Immigrant Sociopolitical Participation

Earlier research on postwar immigration showed that immigrants recruited as a labour force of guestworkers quickly confronted the need to organize their collective interests. Initially, they did it within the framework of industrial relations, but their claims quickly moved beyond that arena. Mark Miller (1981) and Catherine Withol de Wenden (1977, 1978, 1988) were among the first to reflect on these realities and to challenge the then dominant Marxist assumptions about the political quiescence of the immigrant labour force (Miller, 1981: 22–9). Both authors suggested that migrants were becoming more than a temporary labour force and were developing new kinds of political mobilizations that did not rely on electoral politics. In the framework of this theoretical and empirical reconsideration, immigrants came to be regarded as political subjects, rather than the political objects they had been seen as until then to sustain class divisions and the conservative needs of the capitalist economy.

Earlier work on the political sociology of immigration reintroduced some basic reflections on the boundaries of the nation-state's political community and on the sustained challenge migration posed to classical conceptions of citizenship and nationality. In most cases, first-generation migrant workers in continental Europe acquired differentiated and inferior citizenship statuses, to which Hammar later attached the label denizenship (Hammar, 1990). As non-nationals, immigrant workers in countries like France, the Netherlands and Belgium were granted access to various social and civil rights, but their political rights were restricted.[1] They were, in effect, excluded from electoral participation. An important exception to this rule occurred when the Dutch, Irish and Scandinavian governments gave foreigners the franchise at the local level. Unlike their counterparts in France, Germany and Belgium, immigrants in these countries were allowed active electoral participation (the right to vote and be elected) at the local level. In terms of political analysis, this was and still is a significant factor because immigrant communities in Belgium, Germany and France have never represented a significant electoral force.[2]

For a number of reasons, the sociopolitical participation of immigrant ethnic minorities is an important and worthwhile subject of study for the political sociology of liberal democratic societies. In recent years, it has become a bit more multicultural, multiethnic and multi-religious. Withol de Wenden and Hargreaves (1993: 2–3) identify three reasons for the continuing significance of immigrant sociopolitical activism. First, are the memories of alternative means of political participation open to disenfranchized immigrant communities, such as strikes, hunger strikes and marches? Second, consultative institutions have been established in many countries where, as foreigners, immigrants are not entitled to full political rights. Third, immigrants have, to varying degrees, been granted access to nationality in their receiving countries. This option, which opens the door to full citizenship, has had particular relevance for the second and third generation, particularly in countries that have traditionally based their naturalization procedures on *jus soli*.[3] A fourth reason for studying the sociopolitical involvement of immigrants is because the binding relationship between nationality and citizenship, at least in its political dimension, has over the last 20 years been seriously thrown into question. Citizenship of the European Union and foreigners' experiences of enfranchisement at the local level are instances of a decoupling of citizenship and nationality, the main consequence of which is to open the door towards granting some political rights to non nationals.

These elements indicate that, over the past 20 years, the situation in northwestern immigrant receiving European countries, such as the Netherlands, Belgium and France, has changed qualitatively. Immigrants and their supporters have gained some important victories. Whereas migrant workers and their families were left with practically no access to mainstream political institutions in the 1970s, most immigrant receiving European countries have now established a number of procedures and institutions to increase their political participation and representation. Though some convergence is observable, the nature and scope of these channels of participation differ from one country to another (Layton Henry, 1990). Nevertheless, there are now a number of formal channels through which immigrants can articulate their political demands.

These institutional developments have influenced methods of theorizing immigrants' political inclusion. Breaking away from culturalist interpretations of immigrants' sociopolitical behaviour, recent literature has paid increasing attention to the role and influence of institutions and policies. It has been argued, for instance, that both the nature and impact of immigrant political participation predominantly depend on the political context they confront (Ireland, 1994). This approach leads to a crucial point for European comparative research, for it holds that most of the variations that can be identified across national boundaries are more dependent on the specificities of the domestic political context than on the deliberate strategic choices of minority groups.

Without going deeper into the complexities of the theoretical debate, a cautious interpretation of the actual role of institutions and policies is called for to avoid turning the proper role of immigrants into that of a passive agent determined by structural political and institutional factors. Any attempt to influence politics and to gain more access to the political process necessarily implies the mobilization of collective actors. The organizational basis of immigrant political action should therefore be taken as a focal point in studying immigrant participatory patterns. Before discussing this in relation to the Moroccan experiences in three cities, a clarification of two related concepts of particular relevance to the *problématique* is proposed in the next section, namely the concepts of ethnic mobilization and of ethnic minority associationism.

Ethnic Mobilization and Ethnic Minority Associationism

As suggested earlier, several channels to political participation are open to ethnic minorities. In the three countries central to this analysis, social scientists have pointed out the importance of the liberalization of foreigners' rights of association to the political participatory opportunities available to immigrant communities (Layton Henry, 1990). The setting up of independent associations has been a major development for immigrant communities denied all the attributes of citizenship of the majority. It has opened a door for them to organize their own sociopolitical interests in institutions independent both of the country of origin and of the host country's various solidarity organizations. Ethnic minority associational life has in many instances provided the organizational basis for new types of identity-driven mobilizations, such as ethnic mobilization. However, and this is the point to emphasize here, ethnic minority associations have a twofold orientation, which allows them to distinguish between their role as conveyors of ethnic solidarity and their role as ethnic political actors. The point is that the study of immigrant minority associational life does not provide the basis for a single conceptual approach in terms of ethnic mobilization. Ethnic minority associations can provide an organizational vessel to some forms of ethnic solidarity without necessarily being the vector of ethnic political mobilizations.

By introducing this distinction, I wish to reinstate a point expressed earlier by ethnic competition scholars who established a theoretical and empirical distinction between the concepts of ethnic solidarity and ethnic mobilization (Olzak, 1983; Olzak and Nagel, 1986). There has been a tendency in the English-speaking literature to subsume all forms of immigrant collective action under the category of ethnic mobilization. Positing an immigrant ethnic mobilization needs a priori definition of what is ethnically defined in their mobilization, as well as a conceptual framework that allows one to account for forms of immigrant mobilization that are not organized solely along ethnic lines. As John Rex's Barthian perspective on ethnic mobilization suggests, this should depend above all on a situational definition of the projects in which ethnic groups engage (Barth, 1969; Rex, 1991, 1994). In other words, the meaning of ethnic political mobilization does not rest on the cultural values and norms of the group's membership, but on a process, which includes boundary drawing, in which ethnicity serves as an instrumental resource for collective action. This conception of ethnic mobilization is of interest because it provides one with a pivotal concept on which to build a broader conception of multicultural society. For Rex, ethnic mobilization in a multicultural society is a valuable strategy of collective action, which immigrant ethnic minorities should pursue to defend and preserve their collective interests (Rex, 1985, 1991, 1994). He does not see ethnic mobilization as being at odds with the definition of the idea of equal citizenship of all individuals of the liberal democratic tradition. As he put it (Rex, 1994: 15), 'In fact, one of the goals of ethnic mobilization is precisely the achievement of this kind of equal citizenship and it may well be that ethnically mobilized groups will act together to achieve such an end both with other ethnic groups in a similar position and with indigenous peers.'

With this clarification, we can now turn to the role of immigrant ethnic associations in relation to their communities and to the political process. Ethnic associations have received unequal interest from academics. In France, they have formed the subject of numerous works; in other countries, such as the Netherlands, they have been almost ignored in social science research.[4] A brief international overview of studies of immigrant ethnic associational life shows a great variety of interests and approaches, which cannot be encompassed within a single *problématique*. Though social science researchers tend to view their roles and functions quite positively, ethnic associations have been analysed in different countries at different times for different analytical purposes. In an international comparative study, S. Jenkins and her co-authors looked at ethnic associations from the point of view of the satisfaction they provide to fellow co-ethnics. They suggested that their role be reconsidered for inclusion as policy actors in the delivery of social services (Jenkins et al., 1988). The role and functions of ethnic associations have also received consideration in Rex's classic community study of Sparkbrook (Rex, 1973). Another study by Rex, Joly and Wilpert (1987) looked at the functions of ethnic associations from an international comparative perspective and viewed them as a non-transitional phenomenon offering a range of identity options to immigrant populations. Schoeneberg (1983) provided an interesting and comprehensive assessment of the role and functions of ethnic associations in Germany. He sought to establish the relationship between organizational participation in ethnic associations, direct contact with majority group members and cultural assimilation. From his research, he concluded that these relationships are complex and depend largely on the nature of the organizations, though they can be assumed to have a general positive effect.

THREE LOCAL CASE STUDIES[5]

Liège

In 1996, the Moroccan community of Liège numbered 5270 individuals, most of who had come as immigrant workers or student migrants. This community included numerous organizations displaying diverse profiles. Moroccan ethnic associations in Liège are structured along a number of well-established cleavages, including gender, age, ideological orientation towards the country of origin, ideological orientation towards the country of residence, religion or secularism and regional identities (Berbers versus non-Berbers). Though the Moroccan community's formal organizational structure in Liège does not reveal much variation in comparison with the two other cities, one can contend that this community is weakly mobilized in the formal political field. It has also failed to establish a coherent political movement in the face of deteriorating socioeconomic conditions. A good illustration of this is the absence of any significant involvement in electoral politics by Moroccans of Belgian nationality.[6] The relationship between the Moroccan community in Liège and local political parties is a chapter that still has to be written. Another indication is that Moroccan ethnic associations are clearly under-represented in local inter-organizational networks mobilized around immigration/integration issues. A range of multiethnic and Belgian solidarity organizations, such as human rights associations and antiracist groups, dominate the mobilized actors. The ideological fragmentation of these organizations may partly explain the Moroccans' under-representation. Many solidarity organizations are either affiliated to a specific segment of Belgium's rather pillar-like society, such as the Christian or socialist movement, or are close to alternative political parties such as Ecolo, the green party in French-speaking Belgium. To explain this situation, it is necessary to go beyond normative judgements about the capacity of leaders to articulate the demands of their community. More interestingly, the point is to analyse the interaction between the internal and institutional factors that shaped the sociopolitical trajectory of the Moroccan community in Liège. The most important obstacles that Moroccans, like other smaller ethnic and religious minorities, have repeatedly confronted in Liège is a shared consensus among the political elite of the majority about the normative meaning of integration. So far, the dominant assimilationist ideological framework has impeded the emergence of alternative ways of representing ethnic minorities either in the formal political process or in the implementation of public policies. To some extent, one could contend that this has resulted in the reproduction of immigrant's powerlessness through a systematic non-politicization and non-specific decision-making. In comparison with the three other case studies, the absence of a specifically local policy theorizing on integration issues is evident.

In 1973, Liège had, however, experienced a pioneering initiative with the establishment of a consultative institution. This consultative council, the CCILg (Conseil consultatif des Immigrés de la Ville de Liège), was for a long time the only formal institution where immigrant minority communities could articulate their political demands. Like many peer consultative bodies, the CCILg has steadily confronted a number of difficulties in its communication with the local council and has never managed to increase its power within local politics (see Martiniello, 1992). The CCILg stopped its work in 1991 and the new municipal authorities, elected in 1994, have tentatively begun to develop a policy of *interculturalism*. This new policy framework has for the first time sought to stimulate a few associative projects promoting 'intercultural encounters'. However, the relationship between local authorities on the one hand, and multiculturalist and ethnic activists on the other, have suffered from the enduring lack of communication between the local council and voluntary associations. An illustration of this was given recently by a confrontational mobilization against the local authorities and Department of Intercultural Relations on the issue of the voluntary sector's representation in the newly established regional centres of integration, a new institution promoted by the Walloon government.

The lack of consistent and coherent avenues of political participation did not, however, lead to political quiescence. The public political sphere's lack of investment is counterbalanced by vigorous activity within the community's institutions and associations. In fact, the context in which Moroccan sociopolitical action takes place in Liège emerges from a historical outlook towards its institution building. In the earlier phases of Moroccan settlement in Liège, collective structuration took on two main orientations, in opposition to one another. The two dominant organizational forms were initially developed by Islamic groups under Moroccan government control[7] and by secular leftist groups. The former's objective was to establish Islamic associations committed to setting up and managing mosques. Political issues in the homeland, though, largely informed the political activities of the secularists of the left. However, these types of organizations, which included the Liège section of the National Union of Moroccan Students (UNEM) and Solidarité Arabe, have gradually focused their activities on local issues. Members of the Moroccan secularist left wing have for instance been involved in consultative politics at the city level in Liège within the CCILg and at the level of the French-speaking community within the CCPOE (Conseil consultatif pour les Populations d'origine étrangère).

A number of Moroccan Islamic organizations have in the past struggled for autonomy against Moroccan consular representatives and have fed a number of conflicts that have resulted in the creation of new mosques.[8] These conflicts involved mixed issues of identity, ideology and theology. It is apparent from these internal debates, however, that the sociopolitical interests and attitudes of Moroccan Muslims are fragmented and not amenable to a single strategy of ethnic mobilization. Empirical studies of Islamic institution building reveal considerable dissent among the membership of Islamic associations over the issue of publicizing Islam. Whereas some streams have pleaded for a more visible positioning of Islamic identities in the public sphere, others have opposed and mobilized to keep their religious space immune from public concern. The El Itissam mosque has undoubtedly gone furthest in the first strategy, while the El Mouahidin mosque has traditionally opted for the second one. The El Iman mosque, a stronghold of Moroccan consular agents and of the friendship societies of Moroccan merchants and workers (*amicales*), has on the other hand relied on forms of ethnic lobbying based on individual networks among the local political elite. These *amicales* have also had two representatives elected after the CCILg's elections of 1984.

Islamic associations in Liège enter the public political arena not only over local matters, such as a request for Islamic cemeteries[9] and the organization of educational activities, but over national issues such as the representation of Islam according to the Belgian law of 1974 (see Panafit, 1997). The Islamic association El Itissam is at the forefront of this claim and has developed a strategy of vertical integration (at both national and regional levels) with Brussels-based Islamic groups. Unlike the secular left wing, Islamic groups have not participated in regular political relays within the local political arena and have only managed to find occasional access to the policy process on issues of direct concern to them.

Lille

The 6260 Moroccans in Lille represent the most important group of non-nationals. Apart from a small minority who acquired French citizenship, first-generation Moroccan immigrants have had no access whatsoever to the electoral process. Their status as non-nationals has denied them access to the most formal political arena. The first significant developments in terms of electoral political participation appeared with the political emergence of the second generation. In Lille, the most recent municipal elections confirmed the slow and uneasy emergence of second-generation individuals in the political arena. In 1989, three candidates from North African youth organizations were put forward by the socialist party. One of them, a co-founder of Les Craignos, was elected and appointed the mayor's delegate for 'citizenship and human rights'. In 1995, several North African candidates ran again for a seat in the local council. Among them, two well-known figures in second-generation North African associational life and a social worker of Moroccan origin have been successful.[10]

Before the second generation started to organize politically and to set up its associations in Lille, first-generation Moroccans had been less quiescent than Beur historiography has sometimes tended to suggest. In Lille, as in other European cities, the Moroccan government became involved early on in setting up collective infrastructures for Moroccan migrants. Setting up a federation of *amicales* in the north was here again the Moroccan regime's pivotal instrument for strategy of control. The role of Moroccan diplomats in this process of community organization and control was never clearer than in the 1986 conflict when Moroccan miners of the northern French coalfield opposed the Charbonnages de France. After a long strike led by a group of Moroccan miners from the French trade union CGT (Confédération générale du Travail), 3600 Moroccan miners were unfairly dismissed after an agreement was reached between the Moroccan embassy and their employer, the Charbonnages de France (for more details, see Sanguinetti 1991: 75–8). Although many Moroccan miners were forced to return to Morocco, the struggle for their social and economic benefits is still going on today. In 1987, the former Moroccan leaders of the CGT who remained in France founded an independent association (Association des Mineurs Marocains du Nord) and joined the national federation of the Association des Travailleurs marocains en France (ATMF).

Parallel with the first-generation community organizations the second generation, most often headed by young Algerians, has emerged in the sociopolitical field at both local and national levels. As Bouamama recalls, the mobilization of the second generation and the setting up of associations started to become a central issue in Lille with the first nation-wide 'Marches des Beurs' of 1983 (Bouamama, 1989). Texture and Les Craignos are two important associations that were founded in this period. The setting up of a large number of smaller associations, most often youth associations involved at a neighbourhood level, has recently followed their pioneering work in the city of Lille. While Les Craignos has set up a federation of neighbourhoods youth associations, the Fédération des Associations des Jeunes de Quartier (FAJQ), Texture has supported the foundation of a multiethnic immigrant women's association called Femmes d'ici et d'ailleurs.

In Lille, as in Liège and Utrecht, in recent years there has been a strong development of Islamic associations. The Lille Sud mosque is at the forefront of the mobilization of North African Muslims in the north. Its activities are strikingly similar to those of the El Itissam association in Liège. Vertical integration with regional Islamic associations and Paris-based federations, mobilization on educational matters, and the provision of services and activities to the second generation are some of the issues with which the Lille Sud mosque is engaged.

There are two interesting points about the nature of North African political incorporation.

First, there seems to be a strong generational divide between first- and second-generation collective action. Whereas the first generation relied mostly on ethnic mobilization within trade unions, independent associations and mosques, the second generation tends more towards universalistic political inclusion. This has given rise to some interesting debates among members of North African associations in Lille. Texture has promoted the idea of intergenerational solidarity within the migrant population and has sought to distance itself from narrow forms of ethnic mobilization. In 1989, for instance, it sponsored an electoral list purportedly composed of an aggregate of candidates from migrant communities and socially excluded populations. The mobilizations of France Plus and Espace Intégration are further examples of ethnic mobilizations not necessarily fitting the nature and profile of the organizations in question. In Lille and in the north of France more generally, these two organizations have developed a discursive strategy of republican integration (namely assimilation) into French society, while at the same time activating ethnic boundaries as a basis for political bargaining. This apparent contradiction has been widely discussed in the French literature; it is what Vincent Geisser (1997) tentatively identified as the emergence of a 'republican ethnicity'. Unlike Texture, which has deliberately avoided grounding sociopolitical activism in ethnic identifications, the latter are interesting examples of ethnic mobilization being embedded in discursive strategic use of an assimilationist vocabulary.

Second, the so-called town policy (*la politique de la ville*), which has been implemented as a partnership between national government, regions and municipalities, has provided a number of professional opportunities to individuals formerly involved in immigrant associational life. This policy has created and sustained a demand for leadership within impoverished immigrant neighbourhoods. One can speak here of the institutional production of an immigrant associational life of proximity. The seamy side of the story, however, is that it has increased control over the practices and ideologies of second-generation activists, while weakening the autonomous political action of civil society (Bouamama, 1989).

Utrecht

The Moroccan population in Utrecht consists of 13,595 individuals. Unlike their counterparts in Lille and Liège, Moroccans in Utrecht have been enfranchized for local elections since 1986. The Moroccan community has also been identified as a specific target group for the national minority policy implemented since 1983. At the Utrecht city level, integration has been under constant consideration for at least two decades. In 1973, a consultative council was created in Utrecht to advise local authorities on community relations issues (Feirabend and Rath, 1996). The *amicales* responded very early on to the opening up of this avenue of participation. In Utrecht, as in several other Dutch cities, the *amicales*, with the support of Moroccan diplomats and through their networks of personal contacts within the Moroccan communities, have been acknowledged as legitimate representatives of the political interests of this population,[11] though for a very short period. After 1976, the *amicales* were vigorously challenged by the creation of a nationwide independent organization of Moroccan workers, the KMAN (van der Valk, 1996). Most activists involved in establishing left-wing Moroccan associations in Utrecht have had some initial involvement with the KMAN. This was so for the founders of two very influential associations in Utrecht – AMMU and the KMANU, breakaways from the KMAN. Once the *amicales* had lost their influence in Utrecht (and in the Netherlands in general), AMMU played an important role as policy adviser to the local council and has come to be the most central actor in Utrecht's Moroccan community. AMMU has also stimulated the creation of separate ethnic associations for Moroccan women and for Moroccan youth (PMJU).

The activities of left-wing Moroccan activists in Utrecht raise important questions about the co-optation of elites. The minority policy in Utrecht (and more generally in the Netherlands) has created and sustained an impressive number of social work, multicultural and antiracist institutions and agencies. This has created numerous opportunities for elites, both as professionals and as leaders of ethnic communities.

Minority representation of these institutions by an elite clearly creates a number of non-political opportunities to voice immigrant claims within the mainstream. However, Moroccans have also pursued strategies that challenge the integrationist approach of Utrecht's Moroccan leaders of the secularist left. Among these are forms of ethnic mobilization around regional identities in the cultural field. Rifan Berbers are currently the most active in this area. Their strategy of institution building has steadily confronted the opposition of Moroccan left-wing associations. Ethno-religious mobilization within Islamic associations is another strategy pursued by Moroccans in Utrecht.[12] As Feirabend and Rath (1996) point out, Utrecht is more reluctant than other Dutch cities to create a space for Islamic institutions within local sociopolitical life. This development is reflected in the decision to stop funding the educational activities provided by the El Dawa mosque,[13] the biggest mosque in Utrecht.

Over the last year or so, the city of Utrecht has completely reconsidered its policy options in relation to immigrant minority communities. Publication of research the local council commissioned from the University of Utrecht was at the source of a new assessment of the *problématique*. The Burgers Report called for a shift from a minority policy towards corrective measures focused on socioeconomic differences (Burgers et al.,

1996). The ensuing debate between the municipality and representatives of ethnic minorities led to the definition of a new policy hinged on the operationalization of the concept of 'interculturalization' – a far cry, however, from the intercultural approach of the city of Liège.

One element of this policy, besides its attempt to combat a dualization of urban life along ethnic lines, is a new partnership between ethnic minority self-organization and the municipality. The framework for this relationship had already been defined in a policy report of 1989. In the programme the municipality recently issued, the role of self-organization is identified as a bridge between societal and internal community dynamics. The concept of 'interculturalization' is a central idea in this policy framework seeking to develop a proactive approach to the forming of a social coalition within society (*maatschappelijke coalitievorming*). This reflects an attempt to avoid the separate development of ethnic communities, which was allegedly produced by the earlier minority policy. Indeed, the city of Utrecht's new policy implicitly gives a positive answer to the following questions: Has the minority policy led to the isolation of immigrant minority communities from the mainstream? And was the old policy framework disruptive in terms of social cohesion?

CONCLUSION

This comparative overview of three case studies has taught us some important lessons about patterns and forms of immigrant political incorporation. We have observed sociopolitical participation in mainstream political institutions, ethnic mobilization and less politically significant internal community dynamics. The minority response the Moroccan communities exemplified revealed the importance of ethnic mobilization within independent ethnic and religious associations, the deployment of civic, youth, gender and neighbourhood mobilization, as well as the involvement of minority candidates in mainstream party politics.

The Islamic groups and associations have shown us that their form of ethnic mobilization may not be temporary. In all three cities, Islamic organizations proved their capacity to attract massive audiences within Moroccan communities and one could contend that the impact of Islamic ethnic mobilization is, in political terms, still in its infancy. Although some Islamic associations of the older generation are resisting Islam being brought into the public sphere, the opposite phenomenon has been growing in significance within Moroccan communities since the mid-1980s.

Though one can, of course, identify more secularized attitudes among the second and third generations, the ethnic mobilization of Islamic associations should not be seen as dependent on cultural and religious values and norms. Islam provides an identity option, the significance of which will depend in the long run on the projects pursued by this youth and by the place open to them within their societies. On the other hand, the secularist left-wing movement of Moroccan workers and students that dominated the stage during the 1970s and 1980s has in the three cities lost its capacity to engage in mass contentious collective action. We have also seen appearing the mobilization of youth, gender, generational and locational identities, which proves that minority communities are internally segmented along a number of consequential divides. These factors of internal division should be seen as being a problem intrinsically, even though they preclude the possibility of uniting resources and energies. Of course, a common immigrant political agenda cross-cutting internal and external ethnic boundaries is, under such circumstances, close to utopia.

In the three case studies, we have seen external institutional forces constrain integrationist forms of political incorporation. We have also seen that local authorities have a number of policy options at hand to deal with the sociopolitical demands of immigrant minority communities. The local authorities of the three cities under review adopted policies of sustained communication with ethnic and multiethnic minority associations (Utrecht, Lille), funding to ethnic and multiethnic associations (Lille, Liège, Utrecht), consultative politics (Liège, Utrecht), and enfranchisement for local elections (Utrecht).[14] The efficiency of these policies partly depends on their cumulation and coordination. However, as the Dutch case study reveals, a consistent, coordinated, multicultural approach still manifests serious difficulties.

This latter indication points out that both the institutional political strategy of incorporation and the minority response have not had far-reaching effects on the collective position of minority communities in the three societies. In other words, while the nature of immigrant's inclusion has diversified, the impact of immigrants' mobilization on a wide number of issues of collective importance has remained extremely weak. The collective position of Moroccans in areas such as education, employment or housing in the three countries, remains an issue of serious concern and the same holds true for the legal position of Moroccan women. Although Miller (1981) was partly right in saying immigrants and their offspring are neither voiceless nor powerless, the reality seems to fall short of his optimistic view of foreign workers as an 'emerging political force'. One must conclude that the social, political and economic emancipation of ethnic minority groups is still heavily dependent on the implementation of liberal political agendas from the majorities. The experience that Moroccans share with other ethnic minorities in northwest Europe leads to another more general conclusion. Although their demographic share is massively increasing within European urban populations, this has not yet been reflected in the most formal political institutions in which, collectively, they remain under-represented.

Notes

1. One should, however, call for cautious use of the classical Marshallian distinction of citizenship rights in three spheres: civic, social and political (Marshall, 1950). In many circumstances, political activities are not dependent on the possession of formal political rights. The civil and social rights open to immigrants play in many cases as a legal juridical protection to their extra-parliamentary political activities (see also Miller, 1981: 15–20).

2. On this particular point, the situation for foreign communities in continental Europe is substantially different from that in Britain, where foreign residents who are citizens of Commonwealth countries are fully enfranchized.

3. Withol de Wenden and Hargreaves (1993: 2) rightly note that this option has always been more than a theoretical possibility for foreign residents even in countries implementing *jus sanguinis*-types of naturalization regulations.

4. There are some notable exceptions to the rule, including among others de Graaf (1986); de Graaf, Penninx, Stoové (1988) and Van der Valk (1996).

5. Use is made in this research of a qualitative methodology based on the selection of three urban sites of empirical work in three different countries. The three urban contexts were chosen in the three countries with the largest Moroccan emigrant communities. Among the 1.1 million Moroccan emigrants settled in Europe, almost half are permanent residents in France, Belgium and the Netherlands. I have selected three cities that attracted significant numbers of immigrant workers in the period of massive immigration from the Mediteranean (1959–74). It should also be mentioned that they are university cities, which is a relevant consideration given that the migration of Moroccan students towards European universities has played an important role in the sociopolitical organization of these communities.

6. In Begium, the most formal aspects of political participation (the right to vote and to stand as a candidate) are dependent on the possession of Belgian nationality.

7. Historically, the first attempts to create collective infrastructures for Moroccan workers came from the government of the country of origin. These resulted in the establishment of a European-wide network of *amicales* (friendship

societies of Moroccan merchants and workers). Their role consisted of organizing political control over the Moroccan communities. The very undemocratic activities of the *amicales* supported by Moroccan embassies and consulates have, in many middle sized European cities, triggered the same sort of fierce conflicts that were being activated in the same period in bigger cities like Amsterdam, Brussels and Paris (van der Valk, 1996).

8. The mosque of El Mouahidin early on refused to make any reference to the 'the Commander of the Faithfuls', King Hassan II of Morocco, during the traditional Friday speech (Saïdi and Aghion, 1987).

9. Liège is one of the few Belgian cities with an Islamic cemetery within a Belgian one. The high demand for burial in this cemetery can no longer be handled, thus the request for a new Islamic cemetery in the region of Liège.

10. Farid Sellani, a young Algerian, running on the list of former and re-elected Mayor Pierre Mauroy, has been appointed the delegate to support the 'association's projects'.

11. One of Utrecht's first *amicale* activist, and later co-founder of the controversial Union of Moroccan Mosques in the Netherlands (UMMON), recently reflected on this period in a chapter of a book in which the leader of the Dutch right-wing party VVD held conversations with minority leaders (see, Bolkestein, 1997: 45–65).

12. There are six mosques in Utrecht, which can be classified in three groups: (1) the mosques controlled by the coalition of Moroccan consular agents, the *amicales* and the Union of Moroccan Mosques of the Netherlands (UMMON), (2) the El Dawa mosque of the Worldwide Islamic League and (3) a group of smaller independent and neighbourhood mosques.

13. In the Municipal Department for Welfare's 1997 programme, this decision is justified as follows: 'The project has been funded for two years (. . .) Although it answers a need, we are not ready to extend the subsidies. There is no more funding for 1997. It is important that we do not provide structural funding to educational activities organized by people who are not independent of religious organizations' (rough translation of *Ontwerp Welzijnsprogramma*, 1997, City of Utrecht, Department of Welfare).

14. Although the enfranchisement of foreigners is a prerogative of national authorities, local decision-makers can influence political participation through, for instance, policies of information in the languages of minorities.

11 Rethinking the Politics of Race: Participation, Representation and Identity in Birmingham

John Solomos and Les Back

One of the most interesting features of contemporary race relations in Britain is the question of the changing relationship between minority communities and political institutions. By political institutions we refer to a wide range of structures, including political parties, local and central government and community based organizations. It is therefore of some interest in the context of this particular book to reflect on these developments and their impact on the political inclusion and exclusion of minority communities in urban political life. In developing the key arguments of this chapter we shall draw on a project conducted in Birmingham during the period from 1989 to 1993 on race, politics and social change in Birmingham,[1] although we shall also refer to other related research to contextualize our arguments.

Putting it briefly, the research we conducted in Birmingham was concerned with three intertwined processes. First, the historical context that has shaped the political understandings of race within British political culture and institutions. Second, the mechanisms ethnic minorities have used to mobilize themselves politically. Third, there are the responses of political parties and institutions to racial and ethnic questions. In tackling all three processes, we have sought to utilize the case study of Birmingham to illustrate how constructions of race need to be located within particular discursive contexts.[2] This, in turn, ties up with wider theoretical and conceptual dilemmas that lie at the heart of a number of debates about the processes that can encourage or inhibit the social and political inclusion of minority communities in contemporary European societies.

In this chapter we want to take the opportunity to reflect back upon some of the broader issues raised by our research and relate them to another key question: namely, the place of racialized minorities in the changing political environment of contemporary Britain. Any rounded analysis of this issue needs to include the political dimension as one of its main concerns, as can be seen from developments in a wide variety of societies in recent years. In particular, the growing political influence of racist movements, combined with attempts to mobilize antiracist movements, has given added weight to the need to understand the dynamics of racialized political processes at both macro and micro levels.

CONTEXTUALIZING THE RESEARCH

Our research in Birmingham focused specifically on the changing dynamics of race, politics and social change (Solomos and Back, 1995). This issue has, surprisingly, received little or no attention within the main body of research on race, politics and ethnicity in Britain. This is partly because there have been few theoretically informed studies of political mobilization and activism that have sought to explore the role of race in shaping political identities, party politics and political representation in the context of British society. Most studies have analysed political processes from a very narrow perspective, which has meant in practice ignoring the wider social and cultural environment within which ideas about race have been formed. Or they have lacked an in-depth analysis of how political actors and institutions have attempted in practice to come to terms with the racialization of political life in the current situation. It is to remedy this imbalance that we have conducted research that combines an interdisciplinary theoretical perspective with an ethnographic analysis of the everyday processes that help to mould political debates about race and ethnicity in contemporary societies.

We wanted specifically to gain access to those actors within the local state who were in positions of influence, to those political actors seeking to gain such positions and to black and white politicians who were in one way or another involved in the political process. Such access had problems. For example, at the beginning of our research one of the key areas we wanted to explore was the impact of the growing number of black politicians on the political system. However, in approaching this issue we were concerned to locate the phenomenon of black politicians within the wider structures and processes of local politics within the city and the national politics of race. We were not only concerned to interview the 21 black Labour councillors who were in office when we started the research, but we wanted to know how these politicians were positioned within patterns of political patronage. For this reason, we decided to interview as many of the elected representatives as possible, drawing our sample from all political parties. This decision immediately meant that we had to deal with some important ethical and practical dilemmas inherent in our research.

In addition to targeting the councillors we also decided to interview the key council officials ranging from those people working within the established race relations structures, to chief officers for all the major departments that serviced the key committees within the council structure. We also decided that we would talk to as many people as possible who were active within mainstream and community politics. The intention here was to get an idea of how the city council was viewed from within the wider community. Given this range of objectives, we inevitably had to confront rather different methodological dilemmas from those faced by researchers with more limited research agendas.

It is on the basis of this research that we sought to explore the key processes that have shaped the racialization of politics in Birmingham during the past two decades. We have discussed the substance of this research at length in our book on *Race, Politics and Social Change*. In this chapter, we want to take this account as the basis and look at the question of the impact of growing participation by minority communities in political institutions during the 1980s and 1990s.

It was during this period that the minority political presence became a major feature of Birmingham's political culture, as indeed it did in other urban localities. Yet, we still know relatively little about why this transformation took place at this time and what the consequences are likely to be for the racialization of social and political relations in Birmingham and other localities. Although the focus of our research was on Birmingham, it is important to note that similar processes have been noted in other cities and towns. Indeed, even in the short period since we conducted this research, we are struck by the way in which the key issues we have looked at have come to the fore of political debate in a wide variety of national and local environments. The period leading up the 1997 general election is a case in point. During the period leading up to the election, debates about the representation of minority communities in local and national politics came to the surface in a number of localities and, in many ways, they remain unresolved. These include Birmingham, where there was intense but ultimately unsuccessful pressure on the Labour Party to select at least one minority candidate in a winnable seat. Similar controversies took place in a wide range of localities such as Manchester, Tower Hamlets, Bradford, Glasgow and Leicester. Such controversies have been particularly intense within the Labour Party, which has so far been the main vehicle for minority representation in political life. In the Tower Hamlets constituency of Bethnal Green, the controversy became particularly intense as the Labour Party sought to find a 'suitable' minority candidate, at the cost of many aspiring politicians within the local Bangladeshi community (*East*, 21 February 1997).[3] There are now nine black or Asian MPs in the House of Commons, out of a total of 659.

THE CHANGING CONTEXT OF RACIAL POLITICS

To understand the pronounced political changes in the role of minority communities in Britain over the past two decades, we need to examine fundamental aspects of what is happening within particular political processes at both the local and national levels. In our research in Birmingham, we focused on: (i) the analysis of the changing terms of political discourses about race in a particular political environment; (ii) an account of the reasons why we have seen the development of a new politics of race in the past two decades; and (iii) an evaluation of the impact of increasing black participation and involvement in mainstream party politics and political institutions. By exploring all three dimensions together in the particular environment of Birmingham, we wanted to provide an analysis that explored the new context of racial politics.

A key point to remember is that our research was carried out at a point when there was intense debate about the role of political mobilization and participation within minority communities. In the late 1980s and early 1990s, there was a vigorous public debate about the changing balance between civil society and the state, particularly in relation to the need to redefine citizenship rights to take account of minority communities' claims to specific religious and cultural identities (Asad, 1990; Parekh, 1991). Part of this debate was reflected in a questioning by both the left and right about what it really means to call Britain a *multiracial* or *multicultural* society. It was also reflected in a questioning of the possibility of achieving such a society in any meaningful sense through the policies and initiatives that successive governments have pursued. It also led to vigorous debates about how far social exclusion and discrimination characterize the economic and social positions of racialized minorities.

It would be wrong, however, to see the contemporary politics of race simply through the prism of the language and actions of white politicians and activists. This would at best provide a partial view of the politics of race, and at worst ignore the role that minority politicians have played in the construction of a racialized politics. Yet what is clear from research about national and local politics is that a key voice in contemporary debates about race is that of black and ethnic minority politicians who are increasingly involved in mainstream politics. This is why we talk of the emergence of a 'new black politics' within localities such as Birmingham. By this, we are referring not only to the growing number of black and minority politicians within local political institutions, but the wider social and cultural impact of black political mobilization.

In addition, it would be misleading to see the growing number of black and ethnic minority politicians and activists as sharing a common political ideology about either racial or wider social and economic questions. It is quite the contrary. Apart from black and minority political participation being increasingly a feature of all the main political parties, it is also evident that there is little prospect of black politicians coalescing around a shared set of values and policies. Indeed, in terms of everyday politics, it is clear that political identities are not formed simply on the basis of 'race', 'ethnicity' or other singular identities. It is equally important to take class, religion, gender and ideology into account when analysing black politicians' political ideologies and actions.

This becomes more evident when one looks at the debates surrounding the Rushdie affair and the role of religious identities in political life. Such debates have linked up with a growing preoccupation in academic studies of this field with questions of culture and identity (Grossberg et al, 1992; Rutherford, 1990). In the context of the changing dynamics of race relations in Britain, one reflection of this concern has been the growing literature on the relationship between racial, religious and gender identities (Anthias and Yuval-Davis, 1992; Brah, 1996; Grewal et al, 1989; James, 1992; James and Harris, 1993). It is also interesting to note that many radical writers in this field have increasingly begun to point to the need to analyse the dynamics of racial and ethnic identities in Britain and other European societies (Gilroy, 1991; Hall, 1991; Rattansi, 1992). In addition, a number of writers have started to question whether the use of a general category like *black* to describe all racial minorities in British society has the effect of simplifying the complex ethnic, cultural and religious identities that characterize minority communities.

An interesting attempt to conceptualize the changing politics of race and identity by taking account of the role of new forms of political identity and social movements is to be found in Hall and Held (1989). Taking as their starting point the need to broaden out the conception of citizenship to make it less class reductionist, they argue (1989: 176) that:

> A contemporary 'politics of citizenship' must take into account the role that the social movements have played in expanding the claims to rights and entitlements to new areas. (This means addressing) questions of membership posed by feminism, the black and ethnic movements, ecology and vulnerable minorities like children. But it must also come to terms with the problems posed by 'difference' in a deeper sense: for example, the diverse communities to which we belong, the complex interplay of identity and identification in modern society and the differentiated ways in which people now participate in social life. The diversity of arenas in which citizenship is being claimed and contested today is essential to any modern conception of it because it is the very logic of modern society itself.

This attempt to broaden conceptions of citizenship to include a plurality of 'differences' has led in recent years to a veritable explosion of writings on and around this issue. Such studies have done much to highlight the political dilemmas we face in developing a new politics that can deal with the politics of multiculturalism and ethnicity. They have also served to highlight the contingent and constantly changing forms of racialized politics that have emerged and taken root in recent years.

But there are clear dangers in the emerging focus politics of identity and difference. As Homi Bhabha has warned, part of the problem with this focus is that there is a constant danger of constructing notions of difference in fixed and unchanging terms. 'The representation of difference must not be hastily read as the reflection of *pre-given* ethnic or cultural traits set in the fixed tablet of tradition.' But while he rejects such *pre-given* notions of difference, it is also clear that Bhabha is articulating his own vision through the language of difference. He goes on to argue: 'The social articulation of difference, from the minority perspective, is a complex, ongoing negotiation that seeks to authorize cultural hybridities that emerge in moments of historical transformation' (Bhabha, 1994: 2).

It is important to note here that Bhabha is both criticizing a fixed and unchanging conception of 'ethnic and cultural traits' and articulating an alternative perspective on the 'social articulation of difference'. But, although Bhabha's critique of fixed notions of difference is highly pertinent in the present environment, we should not lose sight of the continuing, and in some senses growing, influence of essentialist and absolutist definitions of 'ethnic and cultural' difference. Whether one looks at the political language used by racist movements, or certain political movements within racialized minority communities, there is a clear tendency to rely on fixed and unchanging notions of community, culture and identity. At the level of practical politics, the emergence of forms of political fundamentalism within Muslim and Hindu communities in Britain is perhaps the most widely discussed example of this trend (Bhatt, 1997). But, it is by no means the only one.

What these trends suggest is that there is a clear need for an understanding of how it is that political identities around race and ethnicity are constantly formed and re-formed. We need to explore the complex dynamics through which such political identities are influenced in one way or another by other forms of identity based on categories such as religion, gender, ethnicity and locality.

MINORITY REPRESENTATION IN POLITICAL INSTITUTIONS

A key concern of our study was to address the question of the origins and impact of minority representation within the political system. Claims to increased representation of minorities within political institutions and parties are made of course for a variety of ideological and strategic reasons. In exploring the politics of race and social change, one of the issues we faced throughout our research was the question of how to conceptualize processes of political representation in a context in which race and ethnicity have become an important influence on patterns of political mobilization, whether locally or nationally. A key theme in the discourses of black and minority activists was summarized by the question that was often posed to us: Who Represents Us? This was a question we confronted at all stages of our research and, in one way or another, it is at the heart of the attempts made by black communities from the 1970s onwards to gain greater access to political institutions, whether through the Labour Party or the Conservative Party. Yet, it is also clear that, simple as it is, in its wake this question raises a whole array of issues about the politics of representation in political systems that are becoming increasingly multicultural.

A central concern of much of the political mobilization by minorities within the Labour Party over the past decade, for example, has been the need to increase the number of black and minority political representatives. As we have shown in the case of Birmingham, they have to a large extent been successful in achieving this objective if we look simply at the number of local politicians who are from minority backgrounds (Solomos and Back, 1995). But this is clearly not the whole story, particularly if one is concerned not simply with numerical equality but with more complex issues such as political power and influence. It is quite clear, for example, if we look at the internal dynamics of local political institutions in Birmingham that the growth of minority representation cannot be simply read as an indication of 'empowerment'.

It is important to produce an account of the changing politics of race that gives due weight to the growing presence of black and minority politicians within the political system. This should be done without making assumptions about what this phenomenon means in terms of the social and political position of racialized minorities at a wider level. A whole array of political, social and cultural processes and issues have facilitated the construction of a particular politics of race in major urban conurbations such as Birmingham over the past two decades. But nuanced accounts of these processes have been largely absent from explanations of the politics of race in British society, in contrast with the wealth of detailed research on the urban politics of race in the United States (Smith and Feagin, 1995). But, there is a need to develop this kind of analysis if we are going to provide a dynamic account of the complex ways in which race impacts on political institutions and on everyday political processes within political parties. This explains our focus on the micro and macro political processes. It was precisely this that allowed us both to listen to the voices of political actors and to account for the role of institutional processes in shaping the possibilities for change and reform.

An important dimension of political representation emerging in cities like Birmingham is the diversity of views and interests the minority politicians see themselves as representing. A key theme that emerged from our minority politicians is that, though they bring a distinctive voice into political life and culture, it is by no means univocal. For example, a councillor of south Asian origin (interview: March 1990) commented:

> Some people would say that black is a political colour and will cover anybody who is not white. Others, like the Asian community, are more reserved and say we are not black, we don't have a black skin. But my opinion is that, call it whatever you want to, the problems we face whether Asians or West Indians are similar: that is racism. We should all stick together under one name.

The development of a strong inclusive black caucus within the Labour Group was not realized during this period, and the prospect of such a political development does not seem imminent. With one exception, all the councillors to whom we spoke expressed dissatisfaction with the degree of influence they had in the political process, often claiming that if they could act as a united caucus they would be able to apply much greater pressure for change. Over half the black and minority politicians we interviewed said that they would want an effective and united 'black caucus', but they were aware that the nature of local Labour politics militates against this, particularly with regard to the way political identities are constructed and through patterns of political patronage. But, it was also clear that internal diversity among the group of black and minority councillors contributed to this situation.

In the context of our research, there were no clear patterns with regard to the relationship between ethnicity and lines of political support among black and minority councillors. Rather, what emerged was that issues of ethnicity and religion always needed to be understood in relation to other factors such as ideology, personal interest and factional affiliation. There was no mechanistic relationship between, say, Kashmiri Muslim councillors and a particular political aim and agenda. The political machinations of the Labour Group were infinitely more complex than can be captured by any simple model of ethnic mobilization. Having said this, there were some clear features of local minority politics, which created a situation where the development of a unified 'black caucus' proved difficult to establish.

Minority politicians thus constantly have to position themselves in relation to the wider power bases within the Labour Group. A black councillor who joined the council in the mid-1980s reflects on his own illusions (interview: June 1990) about how to organize politically in this context. With an academic background and interest in policy creation, he initially thought the logical step was to write a strategy document and circulate it among his black colleagues:

I wrote a paper – I put all the ideas of what blacks should be doing [in it] and all the policies we should be pushing. Can you imagine it now? I mean I did all that. And circulated it to the black councillors. It's important – that kind of naivety – again you can see having a kind of academic background is dangerous, because I thought that writing a paper was a sensible thing to do, if you write a paper as a basis for the meeting. ... We had the meeting on a Friday night and on the Monday morning I call for a meeting with the group officers. I realized that they were calling me before them because obviously someone had given them a copy of the paper. I was very bitter about it, very bitter that they were calling me to account because I was trying to organize. ... I realized then that there were nine black councillors there [in the Council House]. Labour's majority was such that if nine black councillors voted against Labour they'd lose. I think I was stupid enough to actually put this in the statement. Admittedly, I didn't circulate the paper to anyone other than the black councillors, but what I didn't know was the treachery of [some of the black councillors].

In this kind of context, where black and ethnic minority politicians are vying for positions of political favour, incidents like this provoke intense personal conflict. The patterns of personal antagonism among the councillors themselves are thus central to the question of why a united caucus has not developed. Intense feelings of betrayal leave a powerful legacy in the everyday political encounters that take place. This is often coupled with a questioning of the authenticity of particular councillors and the sincerity of their commitment to representing the interests of minority communities.

Councillors we interviewed did express some sense of division on crude African-Caribbean and south Asian lines. Some councillors as a way of explaining why these two racialized groups do not share political interests invoke this division. One commented (interview: August 1990), for example:

If I suggested that we have a black group in the Labour Group, you know a caucus group, I would have been thoroughly stoned for that idea by the people. But you see we're a very significant group on the Labour Group, if you take the African-Caribbeans, Indian Asians and Pakistani Asians, but there is so much fear within and I hate to say this because there's so much racism between the black groups. The Asian group is not very comfortable with the African-Caribbean group. I know there is friction amongst some members of the Asian group and I think that's really sad because we're not able to organize.

The divisions should not be over generalized, because we also found politicians who were very much opposed to exploiting the notion of African-Asian differences. However, it would be irresponsible not discuss the importance of these distinctions in prohibiting meaningful alliances.

For example, one African-Caribbean political activist argued (interview: March 1992):

> The only thing about the Asians is that they are only black when they need West Indian support – I know we are all prejudiced. ... I hate West Indians too, but I hate them because they are so stupid and they don't see that it is the Asians who are getting rich, while we stay in the same place ... they are the people who are making the money – not us. The Asians take our business and we let them, and the same thing is happening in politics, the same thing is happening here. We have mass recruitment and it is the Asians who are taking it for themselves. There used to be an understanding in my [ward], because it is a mixed ward, that the chair would be white one year, black the next year and Asian the next. Now they are trying to take all the posts and the management committee. It is the same thing again, the same thing all over again. The people who are in charge of race relations, they are all Asians, and when things are going out from the city, they are leaked, so it is the Asians who make the best of it.

These crass narratives of intercommunal hostility provide a backdrop to political life and the lack of dialogue among minority politicians. The important point to stress here is that minority politicians themselves can use racial discourses against rivals. The Asian Mafia discourse is clearly present in the following quotation (interview: March 1991) from this politician:

> I was talking to an Indian friend of mine the other day and he said that the problem with Indian councillors in Birmingham is that they still think they are back in India. He told me in India when someone gets elected they all get a little something, it is like a tribute system, whereby people pay to get things done, you know, councillor [a south Asian politician] gets a little bit of money here and a little bit of money there, and this was an Indian man who was telling me that – an Indian man was saying that about the Indian councillors in Birmingham.

This quotation bears all the hallmarks of the racialized codes present in white political discourse, in particular the conflation of the notion 'Indian' with south Asian as racially marked collectivities. Interestingly enough, the politician being referred to in this account has no connections with India at all.

These discourses are not only utilized across racial divides. They are equally frequently used in disputes between south Asian politicians where accusations of corruption and membership irregularities may be used strategically for personal ends. Equally, there are important divisions within south Asian groups. The issue of caste can be crucial, for example, in providing the basis for mobilizing supporters and ensuring a strong basis of support.

In the aftermath of the May 1992 local elections, Labour did very poorly in Birmingham, losing 11 seats and narrowing its majority in Council House to five votes. Many Labour strongholds had their majorities dramatically cut, including the seat of the leader of the council, Dick Knowles, whose majority in Sparkbrook fell from 3000 to 442. The result of these losses meant that the hegemony of Labour's right-wing leadership on the city council was severely disrupted. Beyond this, 64 per cent of the seats lost by Labour belonged to politicians aligned to the right-wing faction of the Labour Group. The seven minority candidates who contested the election were all re-elected and four of them had majorities of over a thousand. This turn in electoral fortunes created an environment where the local leadership had to respond to the shifts in the Labour Group's political make-up. The number of minority councillors rose temporarily to 21. With the position of the leadership in question, the minority councillors were in a highly influential position with the potential to exercise influence in determining the local political agenda.

It was in this context that it was suggested that a gathering of the minority councillors should take place to discuss strategy. This suggestion had been made in previous years, but given the new circumstances a number of councillors who had supported the right were interested in the possibility of an inclusive black alliance. However, a senior black politician in an informal meeting discredited this proposal, and it did not take place. In the votes that took place at the AGM of the Labour Group it was clear that a small number of minority councillors had struck an alliance with the leadership in return for some key political posts. This is important because it demonstrates the complexity of these negotiations. Given that the Labour majority was only five, it meant that if the small numbers of minority councillors acted in concert they could wield substantial influence. Rather than open this caucus up to a wider inclusive group, five south Asian Muslim councillors were able to station themselves in a strong position without sharing their influence. As a result, this group of councillors, who had recently been poorly treated by the leadership, voted steadfastly with the controlling group, even backing long-time rivals. In opposition to this, a rival Muslim caucus supported the left on a number of key votes. The important point we want to emphasize here is that in the context of a situation where a formerly strong controlling caucus was weakened, minority councillors were in a stronger position to bargain for influential positions. While these realignments yielded important gains for some black councillors, they did not herald the emergence of a caucus that could have potentially pushed for much larger-scale change.

PROSPECTS FOR CHANGE

Do the transformations we have analysed make a difference? On the basis of our research in Birmingham, it seems clear that they make a noticeable, though perhaps not decisive, difference. What then are the likely routes of development as we look forward to the next century? These are the key questions that underlie many contemporary debates about race and ethnicity. But, we are aware that there is a need to be careful about making easy predictions and we have eschewed the temptation to make glib generalizations. From our perspective, it is vital that research should focus on the ways in which particular avenues of change are possible as a result of specific political, cultural, social and economic contexts. This means that there is an urgent need to move beyond abstract generalities and examine in greater detail developments in cities and towns such as Birmingham, if we are to comprehend the changing forms of minority participation in politics and their impact on political institutions.

It is also clear that we need to know more about changing political identities within minority communities. This issue has led to many debates in recent years. Stuart Hall has captured an important element of this process when he writes of the need to understand the complex 'new ethnicities' that are being formed at the present time and of the need to go beyond the innocent notion of the essential 'black subject' (Hall, 1988: 28). He has argued that there is a need to look more closely at the diverse cultural identities that compose the category 'black', pointing to the shifts and tensions surrounding the construction of blackness as an organizing category that referenced common experiences of racism and marginaliz-ation. Tariq Modood, writing from a very different position, has also been vociferous in recent years in arguing that the political notion of 'black' has had damaging consequences for 'Asians'. Modood argues that the racial dualism of 'black' and 'white' is not appropriate to the complex ethnic and racial identities that characterize British society, and that it is necessary to establish a viable ethnic pluralism (*Guardian*, 22 May 1989). He rejects the assertion that he is promoting a divisive retreat in to absolute racial particularity. 'The choice, then, is not between a separatist Asian ethnicity and unity of the racially oppressed; the choice is between a political realism which accords dignity to ethnic groups on their own terms and a coercive ideological fantasy' (Modood, 1988: 403). From this perspective, the whole notion of a 'black politics' has to be replaced by a perspective that privileges the different routes taken by various ethnic groups in terms of social mobility and political mobilization.

Such arguments have unfortunately remained at a level of abstraction where they do not address the changing terms of minority political participation in everyday political processes. It is noticeable that, although both Hall and Modood place a strong emphasis on the emergence of new and complex forms of ethnic identity, they tell us very little about the role of political actors in shaping everyday struggles and mobilizations. Though we would not want to impose a coercive racial ontology, it is important not to lose sight of the political conditions that have led to the construction of specific political identities. As we have shown in some detail, the articulation of new forms of minority political mobilization within the Labour Party, and to some extent the Conservative Party, cannot be understood simply through the notion of specific types of 'Asian' and 'African-Caribbean' politics. While Hall and Modood may be right to question simplistic notions of a unitary and essential model for identity, we still need to understand how the notion of 'black' can serve as an organizing category in contemporary political life. Conceptions of 'blackness' remain an important organizing theme within political life. The politicians to whom we talked in the course of our research have demonstrated other alternatives to this, while at the same time recognizing that the communities from which they come are subject to discrimination and racism. Thus, while it is necessary to question essentialist and simplistic notions of blackness, it is important to retain a political and analytical notion of blackness as a way of describing points of convergence and volatile alliances. As a number of commentators have pointed out, the contemporary political situation requires a conceptual language that can cope with the possibility of 'division within unity' (Werbner, 1991). The notion of a new black politics provides an analytical category to describe political implosion as well as nascent transcultural alliances.

CONCLUSIONS

The focus of our research in Birmingham was on the changing dynamics of racialized politics. It is also clear that the question of political participation is at the heart of contemporary debates in various countries about the role of migrant and long-established minority communities. In countries all over western Europe, the question of political mobilizations by minority communities has been at the heart of many of the recent controversies and debates about immigration and racism. In countries as diverse as Belgium, the Netherlands, France and Germany, there is evidence of various kinds of political and social mobilization by minorities. This has taken a number of forms. On the one hand, we have seen evidence of growing involvement and interest in the institutions of mainstream politics and attempts to gain access to political representation. On the other hand, there is strong evidence that minorities are also seeking to exert political influence through the development of ethnically or religiously based organizations and movements. This is particularly the case where minorities are largely excluded and marginalized from mainstream party politics.

Quite apart from these forms of political involvement, it has become clear that the politicization of race has taken on quite divergent forms in different societies. There is a wide body of research across the major west European societies that suggests that questions about immigration have come to occupy an important role in political debate at both the local and national levels. Migrant communities have sought to exercise political influence both through mainstream politics and through the formation of voluntary associations concerned with specific social and political issues. In other words, they have sought to mobilize politically to ensure that their interests are not marginalized as a result of political exclusion. These mobilizations have led to pressure on political parties and institutions to respond to the social, cultural and religious demands of migrant communities.

The reasons for this pressure are of course by no means uniform and one has to bear in mind the diverse political cultures and institutions at work. But, it is clear that what we are looking at is a process that encompasses a range of societies, albeit in different ways. In a context in which patterns of migration, settlement and the development of ethnic communities have substantially transformed the social and political structures of these societies, the meaning of citizenship and national identity is being rapidly transformed. As Castles and Miller have shown in their study of international migration, current trends point to the globalization of patterns of migration: 'The age of migration has already changed the world and many of its societies. Most highly-developed countries and many less-developed ones have become far more culturally diverse than they were even a generation a go. A large proportion, indeed the majority, of nation states must face up to the reality of ethnic pluralism' (Castles and Miller, 1993: 271). Yet, what is also clear is that how different societies respond to this challenge varies enormously according to the wider social and political context (Wrench and Solomos, 1993). Indeed, there are clear examples of the ways in which responses vary within nation states, according to political values, locality and region. Moreover, it is evident that there are competing ideologies both about the meanings of multiculturalism and ethnic pluralism and the political strategies necessary to achieve greater equality for minority communities. At the same time, it is also evident that political mobilization among minority communities has taken on new forms in recent years. One example of this is the growing number of black political representatives who have been elected at both the local and national levels. But, it is also reflected in the changing forms of political discourses about race and ethnicity that have been articulated at all levels of the political system.

The issues we have addressed in this chapter link up in one way or another with some of the key political dilemmas about race and ethnicity that confront us at the present time. There can be little doubt, for example, that in virtually all advanced industrial societies a key area of public debate is the question of the social and political rights of minorities. Whether one looks at the media, official reports or the agendas of major research centres, the question of the political impact of racialized minority communities has come to the fore of the political agenda, and is likely to grow in importance in the future. At the same time, it is also clear that attempts by minorities to mobilize politically on the basis of ethnic and religious identities have led to widespread concern about the present and future position of minorities in many Western democratic societies.

Notes

1. The Economic and Social Research Council financed the project during the period from 1989 to 1992. In the period after the completion of the research we have kept in touch with the main political actors involved and have also attempted to develop an analysis that includes developments in other cities.

2. We have attempted to develop the theoretical basis of this argument further in our book on *Racism and Society*, where we use examples from political institutions as well as other social relations.

3. Interestingly enough, the candidate eventually selected was a young black woman, but not from the largest minority community in the area, namely Bangladeshis.

12 Symbolic Politics of Multiculturalism: How German Cities Campaign against Racism

Sigrid Baringhorst

Germany's political class is facing increasing political apathy and public discontent (von Beyme, 1994). Political scandals, clientelism and corruption, as well as a seeming incapacity for political reform and innovation, have placed its reputation in question. The economic and ecological consequences of accelerated modernization have strengthened the demand for intervention in public governance. However, the more complex the social reality becomes, the more difficult it seems to be to find, agree on and implement adequate measures of political intervention.

Governments and major political parties react to their failing political legitimacy with ever more sophisticated strategies of symbolic politics. Diminishing political achievements are compensated for by professionally staged political rituals and spectacles. It is a picture with which we are all familiar: ritualized demonstrations of granting or denying respect; pictures demonstrating the power of elites and portraying the activities and skills of ruling politicians; and impressive speeches to reassure voters that everything is under control.

Official ceremonies and demonstrations of authority use the same criteria for selecting information as the modern mass media in that they are performed according to their general news value. In other words, the features emphasized are those such as the prominence of the actors, the novelty and sensationalism of the events, the emotionality of the content, conflict orientation, and the personalization and simplification of complex structures. While empirical evidence of the flight into symbolic politics is usually drawn from the national political stage, in this chapter there is a shift in the level of analysis from the national media and politics to the urban political arena. In local politics there are more opportunities for political participation, public meetings and face-to-face encounters not structured and manipulated by powerful media or party political organization. But, as my argument will show, even at the local level, public space – interpreted as a realm of public discourse and rational reasoning (Jürgen Habermas) – is on the defensive and threatened by new forms of spectacular public dramatization.

The empirical evidence refers mainly to the public campaigning strategies local authorities – often in cooperation with urban local initiatives – have developed in the 1990s to raise public awareness of racial violence and the social exclusion of migrants and asylum seekers. Some institutional and programmatic characteristics of German approaches to municipal minority politics are outlined. The local strategies of the symbolic politics of multiculturalism are highlighted and analysed with reference to political iconography, social meaning and the potential political consequences of staging multiculturalism as a new type of local public spectacle. The findings are interpreted on the one hand in the light of a crisis of regulatory municipal politics and, on the other, in the light of the increased individualization, hedonistic utilitarianism and expressive solidarism of the actors.

A POPULIST NATIONAL CLIMATE AND THE URBAN POLITICS OF MULTICULTURALISM

Of the country's 81.8 million inhabitants, 7.2 million are legally defined as foreigners. Turks, who number 2,014,000, form the largest migrant community, followed by the 798,000 people from former Yugoslavia. About 586,000 are from Italy; 360,000 from Greece; 316,000 from Bosnia and Herzegovina; 277,000 from Poland; 184,000 from Croatia; 132,000 from Spain; 125,000 from Portugal; 109,000 from Romania; and 107,000 from Iran.[1] In addition, there are about 100,000 Sinti and Romany, 50,000 Serbs and a group of 100,000 coloured Germans who have to be regarded as ethnic or racial minorities (Kappler and Reichart, 1996: 75ff.).

As the overwhelming majority of foreigners came as labour migrants recruited in the 1960s and early 1970s, as part of family unification or as refugees, the settlement structures mirror the former dividing line between east and west Germany. While the average percentage of foreign migrants in major cities of the old *Bundesländer* amounts to 16.0 per cent, the equivalent factor for the new *Bundesländer* is only 1.5 per cent. The highest percentage of foreigners is in Frankfurt/M, with 29.0 per cent, followed by Stuttgart with 23.6 per cent, and Munich with 22.7 per cent (see Ausländerbeauftragter des Senats der Freien und Hansestadt Hamburg, 1995; Beauftragte der Bundesregierung für die Belange der Ausländer 1995: 32).

Although the number of foreigners was extremely low in east Germany, it was there especially that the repercussions of German unification caused a hitherto unknown wave of racial hatred and violence in 1992 and 1993. But, it is not only in east Germany that migrants are seen as aliens and competitors for scarce societal resources. Although there has been significant social advancement among migrant communities in the last 20 years (Ministerium für Arbeit, Gesundheit und Soziales des Landes Nordrhein-Westfalen, 1994), unemployment and general working conditions are still comparatively bad (Gerster, 1996). In many major cities, as for instance in Munich, Stuttgart, Cologne, Hanover and Saarbrücken, the unemployment rate among foreigners is twice as high as among the indigenous German population and in some places even higher.

For a long time, urban integration policy consisted of the special welfare and advisory services the three main German welfare organizations offered. They acted as subsidiary state agents (in accordance with the principle of subsidiarity) in the implementation of social policy – Caritas (on behalf of the Catholic Church), *Diakonisches Werk* (on behalf of the Protestant Church) and *Arbeiterwohlfahrt* (on behalf of the labour movement). Migrant communities were divided by national origins and accordingly assigned to one of the local branches of these rather paternalistic welfare organizations (Puskeppeleit and Thränhardt, 1990; Thränhardt, 1987). The legal construction of these internal divisions on national grounds has recently been changed and migrants are now free to choose from which of the welfare organizations they wish to seek help.

In the 1990s, under pressure from a growing number of self-help ethnic organizations and challenged by increasing racial violence, the German authorities began to realize that a *laissez-faire* policy and ignorance of the increasing multicultural fragmentation of the urban population (with its intendent economic, social and cultural consequences) were becoming counterproductive. However, institutional reforms undertaken so far have been very limited: they have been concentrated mainly on the introduction of *Ausländerbeauftragte* commissioners to deal with matters relating to foreigners (Kulbach, 1996; Schmitt, 1996). Most of these commissioners form part of a small staff in the Lord Mayor's Office with cross-sectoral responsibilities. Jörg Noorman's comment about Frankfurt's Department of Multicultural Affairs, which was established in 1989, also applies to the *Ausländerbeauftragte* commissioners in other local authorities. Though they were set up to collaborate closely with all the local government and administration agencies to promote social integration and harmony, when they start to call for real changes they encounter the energetic opposition of most municipal departments. None of these are eager to be 'coordinated' by the foreign minorities' new advocates, which is how they are usually perceived (Noorman, 1994).

In the absence of any national anti-discrimination legislation, some commissioners have recently started to introduce equal opportunity initiatives to increase the number of migrant employees in municipal administrations (see, for instance, Ausländerbeauftragte des Landes Bremen, 1995). In general, the scope for action varies greatly according to the size of the community, party political majorities and other contextual local conditions.

Given the range and difficulty of their tasks, the numbers of commissioners and their fiscal budgets are generally extremely low. A major city like Hamburg, which along with Berlin and Bremen is considered to be a federal state politically, has about 1.7 million inhabitants, of which 266,237 are foreigners, representing 15.62 per cent of the overall population. In 1995, the *Ausländerbeauftragte* of the city had an operative budget, that is a budget not including running costs for personnel, of 184,000 Deutschmarks. Of this, 130,000 Deutschmarks have been spent on public relations, bills for interpreters and solicitors, and 4000 Deutschmarks for *Repräsentationsaufwendungen* (representation costs). In addition, the *Ausländerbeauftragte* in question had 6.5 regular posts at his disposal. These were a scientific director, a public relations expert, a lawyer, two social workers and a secretary (Ausländerbeauftragter des Senats der Freien und Hansestadt Hamburg, 1995: 57).[2]

MULTICULTURALISM AND MUNICIPAL PUBLIC RELATIONS

The previous conservative government denied that Germany had become an immigrant country and thus saw no need to encourage multicultural integration. It is not surprising that neither the interior minister nor the federal commissioner on matters relating to foreigners gave local authorities any concrete directives on developing multicultural policies. However, increases in racial violence since 1989 have prompted some federal initiatives to support local authority policies to combat racism and promote ethnic and religious tolerance. These efforts were particularly directed towards the new federal states, not only because the wave of arson attacks on hostels for asylum seekers started from east Germany, but also because of the lack of experience and of agencies to deal with ethnic and racial conflicts.

As the legal and fiscal framework of local and regional actions could only be altered at the federal level, non-federal actors would mainly concentrate on communicative means of influencing the 'public climate of opinion'. The communication programme's objectives were defined as:

- enhancing tolerance and openness;
- changes of attitudes (prejudices), values and actions (aggression); and
- strengthening pluralism and diversity (see Ausländerbeauftragter des Senats der Freien und Hansestadt Hamburg, 1995: 13).

The following target groups were singled out for specified attention: commissioners, political decision makers, public opinion leaders, organizations involved in initiatives, the media, the 'active', 'passive' and 'rejecting' public, foreigners, open-minded youth, hostile youth, and students (Ausländerbeauftragter des Senats der Freien und Hansestadt Hamburg, 1995: 29). Different communication strategies were recommended for different target groups. These included workshops for TV, radio and press, action weeks, brochures, poster competitions and twin partnerships (Ausländerbeauftragter des Senats der Freien und Hansestadt Hamburg, 1995: 86ff.).

In fact, many local administrations have meanwhile developed various communicative and persuasive measures to influence public opinion. An analysis of the annual reports of municipal commissioners from 30 major towns in east and West Germany (including cities with more than 300,000 inhabitants) reveals that local authorities give high priority to political communication skills. These consist of organizing conferences, workshops and training initiatives for social workers, employees in welfare and self-help organizations or in the municipality, teachers and representatives of the local media. These mainly educational initiatives cover a wide range of topics. They include the cultural and religious traditions of minority groups; political legislation on immigration, citizenship, asylum policies and the Schengen agreement; general information on the causes of racial violence and on means of solving racial and ethnic conflicts; and discrimination and equal opportunity in the mass media. Though all these initiatives are essential for the dissemination of adequate basic information and for creating local experts in the field of ethnic relations, they are usually confined to a fairly small group of those aware of the problems and already backing multiculturalism and antiracism.

Apart from educational measures, many local authorities – especially those run by social democratic governments or red–green coalitions – put a strong emphasis on more visible and effective means of reaching not only the already aware 'active' public, but also the so-called 'passive' public or silent majority.

Launching all-party resolutions is one of these measures, usually taken after a racial incident has occurred in a city. These resolutions serve a predominantly symbolic function of assuring the public of political awareness at the top, of demonstrating solidarity with those affected by major racist incidents and, more generally, of stressing the limits of tolerance of urban communities. Confirming only the most basic political norms of non-violence and human dignity, the political messages are mostly indisputable. Motions that might challenge the political consensus, like demands for dual citizenship, criticism of federal asylum legislation, or the suspension of repatriation measures for certain groups of asylum seekers are seldom included in municipal resolutions designed to reach a consensus among all political representatives.

Generally, official declarations have an inclusive as well as exclusive dimension: the municipality presents itself as the public conscience shocked by improper behaviour. It condemns the disgraceful action and asks for severe punishment of the culprits as well as social exclusion of potential racist supporters from the urban community. At the same time, tolerant, law-abiding residents are confirmed in their liberal values and invited to support the municipality in its efforts to promote the allegedly friendly and cosmopolitan climate of the city.

These ritually repeated confessions and resolutions are visualized in solid symbols and slogans of urban collective identity: *Ihre Stadt läßt sie nicht allein* (your city won't leave you alone) states the comforting headline of one brochure from Stuttgart's magistracy. The picture underneath is typical of a widespread iconography of multiculturalism: two people shaking hands, one passing a flower to the other, both smiling. The gesture of touching hands has become an icon for multicultural friendship in city campaigns: sometimes many hands are stretched out, as in an appeal by the city of Wiesbaden. Sometimes you see only one hand stretched out and held up, as in an Augsburg initiative, which is similar to the emblem of the French SOS racism movement, adopted by a less successful antiracism campaign of the German unions with the slogan

Mach meinen Kumpel nicht an! (Don't attack my mate!). On some campaign posters, people form a circle and then hold each other by their hands. Or, many hands hold a globe, signifying the unity of mankind and our dependence on universal collaboration for human survival.

In the 1990s, many cities launched professionally designed advertising campaigns to improve their image and to promote intercultural understanding. *Menschen in Mainz* (people in Mainz) reads the slogan of an official campaign of the city of Mainz. The multicultural composition of urban dwellers is visualized mainly by replacing one or two letters in every line with photographs portraying faces of different ages, sexes, professional statuses and national and ethnic origins. Faces are smiling right into the camera or the observer's eyes. *Mainz: Multikulturell seit 2000 Jahren* (Mainz: Multicultural for 2000 years) – a line in tiny letters printed vertically at the bottom right of the poster – puts the message into historical perspective and confirms to the recipient the alleged continuity of German multiculturalism.

Some campaign messages are even more symbolically explicit: TOLERANZ: *Frankfurt gegen Fremdenhaß* (TOLERANCE: Frankfurt against xenophobia) or MENSCHLICHKEIT: *Frankfurt gegen Fremdenhass* (HUMANITY: Frankfurt against xenophobia). The design of the posters of this campaign launched by the lord mayor of Frankfurt, together with the leader of the city council and the political parties of the council, reminds us of official street signs indicating the beginning and end of a city's territory. Only the colour has changed from black writing on a yellow background to black on red. In a play on words, the word 'Frankfurt' is replaced by highly abstract and consensus norms that demarcate the city's territory not by geographical but by moral criteria: *Frankfurt gegen Fremdenhaß* – the alliteration renders the slogan easy to remember; the appeal is plain and simple; it is something with which no democratic member of the community could publicly disagree.

MULTICULTURALISM AS PUBLIC SPECTACLE

Apart from resolutions and advertising campaigns, the most significant symbolic event is the annual intercultural week, which takes place in every major German town. The *Woche der Brüderlichkeit* (week of brotherhood) was originally started by the two Christian churches as an annual event to demonstrate solidarity between Christians and Jews. In the 1980s, an equivalent week of solidarity between Christians and migrant communities was launched under the motto *Woche der ausländ-ischen Mitbürger*, literally translated as 'week of foreign fellow citizens'. Though Christian organizations, especially welfare ones, still play an important role in organizing the week, over the years the whole event has become more secular. The paternalistic and excluding words *ausländische Mitbürger* have been replaced with *Interkulturelle Woche* (intercultural week), indicating the strong emphasis given to the cultural dimension of solidarity with migrant communities.

Intercultural weeks take place all over Germany at the same time of year, usually late September. In some cities, commissioners for matters relating to foreigners have become the central agents for planning and coordinating various local initiatives associated with the annual event by offering numerous cultural contributions. In other cities, like Wiesbaden, the city council has commissioned a special committee '*für Bürgerbeteil-igung und Völkerverständigung*' (for citizen participation and the under-standing of peoples) to organize the week in cooperation with the local Council of Foreign Citizens. In other cities, mainly those without institutionalized departments of multicultural affairs, like Mönchenglad-bach, the Council of Foreign Citizens does the main preparatory work.

Local administrators are frequently supported by a conference of inter-cultural collaboration, a group of active representatives of ethnic or wel-fare organizations. The local authority often manages public relations for the events by issuing and distributing information brochures and posters, by launching press releases, and by collecting press articles on the events, which are then published in a brochure. Often, all initiatives are bundled under a common slogan, chosen by each city to give the many local events a common topic and to differentiate them from similar events in other towns.

Generally, the topics chosen are unspecific so that all kind of cultural events can be included. The annual slogans contain similar messages of tolerance as the campaigns discussed above. Kiel, for instance, the capital of the Bundesland Schleswig-Holstein, has organized the intercultural week since 1993. The common motto of all events is always '*Vielfalt in Kiel*' (Diversity in Kiel). Each year it is combined with a particular slogan such as: '*Vielfalt in Kiel: Bunt und Gleichberechtigt!*' (colourful and with equal rights) in 1993; '*Gleiche Rechte Rechte gleich!*' (equal rights rights equal) in 1994; '*Miteinander Füreinander*' (together and for one another) in 1995; and '*Gemeinsam Zukunft gestalten*' (shape the future together) in 1996. The motto of the 1997 intercultural week was '*150 Kulturen: Unsere Stadt*' (150 cultures: our city).

The messages indicate a minimalist moral, the lowest common denominator of an increasingly heterogeneous urban population, namely tolerance, pluralism and a Christian ethos of solidarity and care. During each week, there are about 30 to 60 single events taking place in major cities. There are exhibitions, public lectures, workshops, dramas, pantomime performances, lotteries, special church services, concerts, films, dancing and sports events.

There is a lot of goodwill on both sides. Foreigners show their willingness to integrate by living up to German expectations of the exotic but friendly other; Germans demonstrate their willingness to integrate foreigners into the wider urban community by attending the events and even by taking part in their organization.

Their social effect reaches beyond mobilizing those directly involved in or attending the events. For one week the local cultural agenda is set not by the indigenous residents but by those generally excluded from public and political urban life. Local journalists are generally willing to report extensively and positively on the events. At the same time, opening speeches by political leaders, often the lord mayor is the patron of the programme, publicly stress the need for integration and tolerance and thus remind the community of essential common Christian and democratic values. Often, the opening speeches are given in the city hall. A territory politically owned by the German majority for a day or night changes into a multicultural festival arena. Notwithstanding the contribution of intercultural weeks towards strengthening local civil society and towards creating a desirable politics of recognition of ethnic and cultural differences among urban residents, from a social theory perspective, however, they do raise some critical comments.

First, they foster a strong tendency to essentialize and ethnicize collective identities. Ethnic differences are often reduced to differences in traditional dances and costumes that are hardly relevant to the social interactions of everyday life.

Second, intercultural weeks and events are becoming increasingly commercialized, with a growing dependency on financial support from private companies. Their logos are often presented on brochures, posters and information sheets. Apart from that, intercultural events often resemble an ethnic niche market, a huge and open one-world shopping event.

Furthermore, urban intercultural events are being turned into more and more spectacular urban mega events. Organizers need money from sponsors to be able to invite prominent speakers or musicians. If a well-known VIP is unavailable, then bands and other attractions have to be increased to provide sufficient incentive to lure an audience away from all the other local suppliers of cultural attractions that persistently court it, especially the ever increasing number of TV channels and programmes. Organizers of intercultural weeks and other multicultural city events react to this challenge by making the events increasingly professional and festive. City festivals like the Hamburg 'Festival for Friends '97' are organized and staged by hired marketing companies to satisfy the tastes of a generation accustomed to spectacular sports events, media consumption and cosmopolitan cultural gestures. Interrupted only by a religious service and two speeches by members of the European Parliament, the main stage of the Hamburg festival offered a public spectacle. This consisted of 'action, fun and show', a 'world of dance and music', 'gospels from the Ghana Catholic Society Choir', 'songs from the Musical Cats', 'hip hop' and 'street dancing' as well as 'international rock on stage'. The musical performances were offset by a variety of trendy sports attractions, such as football, baseball, figure skating, ice-hockey, street soccer, beach volleyball, basketball, bike-dual-slalom, street tennis and circus performances.

The marketing company's emblem on the brochure accompanying the event was even bigger than Hamburg's coat of arms. Among the 24 logos of sponsoring organizations, the difference between public or private, political or non-political organizations is completely blurred. The circle of stars from the European Commission is placed at the same level as Adidas or Coca-Cola; the signet of the archdiocese of Hamburg is hardly distinguishable from the logos of insurance companies and skate sellers.

MULTICULTURALISM AND THE POLITICS OF SYMBOLIC EVENTS

How can we explain the astonishing importance of spectacular festivals and campaigns in urban strategies to fight for multicultural tolerance? The trend towards spectacular urban politics can be examined from two analytical perspectives: on the one hand, structural changes in urban and national policies can be seen to influence local political decision-making in such a way that persuasive and symbolic strategies gain ever more importance as the only available choice. On the other hand, symbolic politics, staged as public festivals and spectacular fun events, appeal to an increasingly fragmented urban population and offer new opportunities for collective identity formation, especially for younger residents.

The growing trend towards the symbolic politics of multiculturalism has to be seen against a background of structural changes in the development of urbanization. According to Hartmut Häußermann and Wolfgang Siebel, we now live in a period of 'de-urbanization' characterized by new challenges – diminishing job opportunities, high rates of unemployment, low levels of net investment, and increasing poverty and homelessness (Häußermann and Siebel, 1993: 12). Crises on the world market and increased international competition have reached the cities and promoted a structural crisis that is far from being solved. Problems of governance at the national level are reflected at the local level. The demand for political intervention, especially welfare and ecological intervention, is high, but the constant cuts in national and local authority budgets are reducing opportunities for remedial action. However, the costs of symbolic politics are usually low compared with the expected gains. This is particularly true of the symbolic politics of multiculturalism.

For a start, an image of ethnic and racial harmony improves a city's reputation as a whole and, in particular, that of its ruling political factions. The political outcomes of social policies are usually invisible to the wider public. Visibility is often negative, with rising poverty, homelessness, unemployment, drug addiction or urban violence damaging valuable reputations in the competition for new investors. Paying social benefits or offering shelter to the poor and needy is neither spectacular nor a public expense generally approved of in times of accelerated deregulation.

Confronted with these challenges, passing all-party resolutions to promote multicultural coexistence, launching tolerance campaigns and organizing intercultural weeks and multicultural city festivals are comparatively cheap ways of presenting a city to the public in a cosmopolitan and futuristic light. Spectacular events are mostly one-off occurrences, which, unlike investments in social networks, don't incur the long-term expenses of employing administrative personnel, office rents and maintenance. Once the campaign is over, the participatory self-help organizations are not expected to claim any further support.

Furthermore, multicultural campaigns and festivals are not run solely for the benefit of minorities. Most voters show little interest in backing or giving special support to residents of run-down council estates or members of disadvantaged communities. In contrast with more polarizing strategies, like affirmative action or redistributive policies, symbolic events like multicultural festivals or city image campaigns are generally thought of as socially inclusive. Although multicultural campaigns and city events are still neither generously financed nor enthusiastically supported, especially by the extremely conservative opponents of multiculturalism, most local governments of major cities welcome ostentatious signs of tolerance for ethnic and cultural differences.

COLLECTIVE IDENTITY FORMATION AND TRANSFORMATION OF URBAN SOLIDARITY

The success of the politics of symbolic events should not be explained only with respect to structural urban changes and the instrumental reasoning of ruling urban elites. Symbolic politics can only succeed if it meets the needs of the target groups it addresses. And, for the majority of participants, multicultural city festivals, concerts and sports events are attractive cultural political offerings in a number of different respects.

They correspond with utilitarian action strategies as well as with the expressive needs of a highly individualized heterogeneous audience. Attending multicultural events is cost effective because there is usually no entrance fee. Moreover, cultural pleasures are offered not only cheaply but also with a kind of moral blessing. Participating in multicultural events, for instance listening to rap, hip-hop, rock or folk music, can be conceived of as being more than just indulging in hedonistic pleasure. It becomes a form of public confession or political statement, a demonstrative action of solidarity that combines self-related with solidarity action motives. At a time when the society's moral resources seem to be even more scarce than its material resources, taking part in public solidarity events represents a cost-effective way of easing a guilty conscience about one's political inertia and passivity. It may even enhance one's social reputation in one's family or circles of friends.

Apart from utilitarian considerations, urban festivals of multiculturalism can be seen as an important means of urban collective identity formation. Neo-Durkheimian scholars have described mass events like coronations, presidential inaugurations, national remembrance days and even the ritual of general elections as contributions to national collective identity formation. The same applies to local symbolic events like intercultural weeks, carnivals, concerts or other festivals. They are signs of a new form of post-traditional expressive solidarism, an 'event solidarity' (Schulze, 1994: 340), characterized by a synthesis of fun and morality. The secret of the success of symbolic solidarity events is that they mobilize self-reflective instrumental motives, the need for aesthetic self-representation and moral action motives like empathy, tolerance and solidarity.

Multicultural parades and festivals satisfy an expressive need for distinction and offer opportunities for individual participation in new forms of community building. The inward-oriented search for identity succeeds only through the outward-oriented view of others. Urban multicultural festivals, like other big symbolic events, serve as codes of inclusion (Giesen, 1991), which create a community of like-minded, mostly German, participants built around the lowest common moral denominator of tolerance and non-violence.

But, the moral and political values are often less important than the spectacular aesthetic form of public mobilization. David Kertzer has analysed the social function of rituals in modern societies. He stressed their contribution to community building, not on the basis of common values and shared convictions, but on the basis of common procedures and actions. As he said, 'what is important in ritual is our common participation and emotional involvement, not the specific rationalizations by which we account for the rites ... rituals can promote social solidarity without implying that people share the same values, or even the same interpretation of the ritual' (Kertzer, 1988: 67, 69).

Despite the social function of community building and expressive solidarity mobilization, the potential effects on the explicit aim of multicultural campaigns and festivals, namely to contribute to a culture of tolerance and to combat racism, should not be neglected. In this respect, however, hopes should not be exaggerated: a recent study on the effects of tolerance campaigns carried out by Georg Ruhrmann questions the political effectiveness of tolerance campaigns. Seemingly, those who address tolerance appeals judge campaign messages more on aesthetic than on moral grounds. Less tolerant respondents might well judge tolerance campaigns positively if they like their aesthetic format, while tolerant respondents may disapprove of solidarity campaigns if they dislike their aesthetic and formal presentation. Thus, the aesthetic values, or, as Gerhard Schulze has called it, the event value, of symbolic political means tends to outweigh the political and moral values. Through strategies of public dramatization, complex political, economic or social structures are rendered easy to understand and to evaluate. But, at the same time, political criticism is more and more replaced by aesthetic judgements on the attractiveness and entertainment value of politics.

Notes

1. Among the other groups of foreigners are 58,000 from the former Soviet Union; 57,000 from Hungary; 82,000 from Morocco; 26,000 from Tunisia;

22,000 from Ghana; 17,000 from Brazil; 59,000 from Afghanistan; 33,000 from China; 35,000 from India; 55,000 from Lebanon; 37,000 from Pakistan; 55,000 from Sri Lanka; and 96,000 from Vietnam. Among the less visible and hardly discriminated against foreign minorities are 184,000 Austrians; 116,000 British; 113,000 Dutch; 99,000 French and 108,000 citizens of the United States (see Kappler and Reichart, 1996: 75).

2. Since 1996, he has even had to do without one of these posts.

Part IV

Law and Order, Security and Justice

13 Migration and the Politics of Security

Jef Huysmans

Not many people will deny that a multitude of security claims circulate in relation to migration in western European societies today. There will be disagreement over whether this is a good or a bad thing, whether it is legitimate to speak about migration in terms of security, whether migration really is a security problem. In this chapter, I do not want to engage head on with some of these debates. Rather, I would like to phrase another question. What does it imply to utter 'security' in the migration area? What is involved in defining migration as a security question? As I have done in other articles and other people have done in relation to other security questions, I could begin by explaining that security is not really an objective given but a social construction. In other words, a security question is always a result of a social process of securitization. Then, I could repeat the analysis of how politicizing migration as a security question organizes social relations *vis-à-vis* migration differently from an economic or human rights approach. The conclusion would resemble more or less the following quote:

> To put migration on the security agenda, or to speak of the migrant as a security problem, is not simply to describe a given reality. In speaking of the migrant as a security problem, he/she becomes an actor in a security drama. This is a drama in which selves and others are constructed in a dialectic of inclusion and exclusion and in which this dialectic appears as a struggle for survival. In this drama, there is always a risk that the interaction between the natives and the migrant turns to violence. ... This does not mean that, once migration is put on the security agenda, violence between the natives and the aliens is unavoidable. It only means that the risk is there and that in certain contexts it might be relatively high. There are good arguments for saying that in the present western European context that risk is relatively high.
>
> (Huysmans, 1995: 63)

179

Instead of repetition, I would like to use this chapter to introduce another cut into the question of what is implied in claiming security *vis-à-vis* migration by emphasizing that security is a technique of government of the population. I will also indicate how this technique differs from the technique of security that relates to the rationality of war. As a result, some of the complexities of what is involved in security policies should be rendered visible more explicitly. If individuals walking a city argue that they feel insecure, this generally means that they fear that they might become subjects of physical harm – of robbery, or killing. Although this is a personal state of the mind, or state of the body, a public claim of insecurity often also implies an (implicit) request upon the state or the relevant political authority to do something about it. Security is a good, or one of the key values that a political authority has to distribute and to guarantee. It could be argued that security claims have a strong capacity for turning local experiences into key questions for political authorities. If a claim of public insecurity can be established, political authorities feel an imperative to act, which also creates a possibility for them to affirm their authority and their concern with the public interest. However, security is not simply an utterance requesting a political authority to act. It is first and foremost a specific technique of political action, that is a particular method of doing an activity. It is a knowledge practice that structures the interplay of social practices in a specific way. Power knowledge is never simply an instrument externally given to a political agent for manipulating the practices of other agencies. Its significance develops internal to social practices; it is a work of action upon action. Of course, agents can dwell upon this technique in their instrumental action, but the technique is not bound to an individual agent. Thus, as a technique, security is not just an instrument of a political authority but the authority is also a function of the technique that articulates a specific mode of ruling society, including definitions of the relationship between a political authority and society. The tools that are deployed in relation to a technique, such as policing, identity control and military operations will be called technologies.

One way of researching this technique is to explore its micro-physics, that is the work it does and the technologies it implies in various specific localities, such as in detention centres, military exercises, or urban planning in the context of the integration of migrants. The deployment of technologies, including the use of scientific knowledge to obtain practical purposes (for example statistics) and the effects it has is the key entrance point for a microphysics of security. For the subject of this book, the study of these technologies is probably what one is primarily interested in:

which technologies are used in relation to the presence of migration in cities? However, this is not the only way to explore the technique of security. The work of the technologies is only intelligible within a more general picture of the power relations within which they operate and which they constitute. This is the question about the rationality of the technologies, which makes their micro-work intelligible at the macro level. It is more a political theory of security than a study of the technology of security as such. In this chapter I will concentrate on a specific rationality of governance within which security emerges, namely government of the population. I will also indicate that this understanding of security adds an extra dimension to most of the security analyses of migration.

SECURITY: A TECHNIQUE OF GOVERNMENT OF THE POPULATION

To explain the emergence of the technique of security, I will rely on Foucault's interpretation of the development of the question of government.[1] Foucault's general research problem is '[H]ow did a certain (critical, historical, political) analysis of the state, its institutions and its mechanisms of power appear in the West?' (Foucault, 1997: 75, my translation). More specifically, he looks at how the general question of government – 'how to be ruled, how strictly, by whom, to what end, by what method' (Foucault, 1991: 88) – emerged in the sixteenth century and how it has developed since then.

Under the general question of government, Foucault contrasts the art of government with the question of sovereignty to draw two contrasting rationalities of governance. The rationality of sovereignty developed in relation to the problem of the Prince. For the Prince, the central question of governance is how to survive and how to establish a relationship with the principality that supports his sovereignty. Because the Prince relates to the principality as an external and transcendent body, he continuously faces the question of how to confirm his power and to guarantee his survival *vis-à-vis* his principality. The problem of power is thus one of justifying a discontinuity between the power of the Prince and the other powers in the principality, such as the power of the Church, rather than one of giving form to a continuity of power constituting a continuous and internal relation between Prince and principality. The question of power is posed differently in the art of government. While the Prince is posited in an external relationship to his principality, government emerges from within society and refers to a multifarious practice, including government of the self, government of the family, government of the state. Its problem is not one of justifying power in a relation of transcendence, but one of explaining the continuity of power within society and its government. The power of government has not to be justified in opposition to challenging powers.

Rather, the rationality of government requires an explanation of how to conceive the government of the self, the family and the state as three dimensions of a continuous form of power. The rationality of sovereignty and of the art of government also posits a different finality. Sovereignty aims at a confirmation of itself: a continuation of sovereignty by assuring that subjects obey the law. (Foucault, 1991: 94–5) The finality of sovereignty is thus a continuous assertion of itself. The art of government, on the other hand, defines a finality outside itself. Government is not for the sake of government, but for optimizing men's relation to various things such as health, hygiene and wealth (Foucault, 1991: 91–5). Government is 'a right manner of disposing things so as to lead ... to an end which is 'convenient' for each of the things that are to be governed' (Foucault, 1991: 95). The general object, which brings together these various objects of government, is 'life'. Government is a government of life (Foucault, 1991: 91–5). Here, another crucial difference between sovereignty and the art of government enters the picture. Sovereignty rules by law and force and finally by the sword. The bottom line of the exercise of power is the Prince's right to kill. Sovereignty is thus a rule by death. The art of government, in contrast, exercises power not through the sword but through the promotion of life. It makes life; it stimulates its continuation, for example through health policy and improvement of wealth (Foucault, 1997: 213–14). It rules through advancing life by optimizing different aspects of it. '*On pourrait dire qu'au vieux droit de faire mourir ou de laisser vivre s'est substitué un pouvoir de faire vivre ou de rejeter dans la mort*' (Foucault, 1976: 181).

It is important to remark that the art of government does not approach the question of life via a management of individual bodies.[2] Rather, it works upon and through a multiplicity which is called the population: 'a global mass affected by a whole of processes that are proper to life' (Foucault, 1997: 216). It is not an aggregate of individuals but a collective of people who derive their collectivity from being embedded in processes of life, processes proper to living. The emergence of the population category creates a new field of visibility, of policies and of power relations. Moreover, the population is also the ground upon which government will act. It, thus, defines both the ends of government and the plane upon and through which government works (Foucault, 1991: 99–100). In the government of life, every thing governed is approached in terms of its functionality for the population. Politics takes the form of bio-politics (*bio-politique*) (Foucault, 1976: 182–5). For example, unlike sovereign rule, the question of territory is only relevant in so far as it fulfils a function for the optimization of fertility, demographic composition and health policy. The protection of territory is not an end in itself. It is in relation to the emergence of bio-politics in the Classical Age that migration, together with birth rate, life span, public health and housing, came into view as particular objects of political practice and economic observation (Foucault, 1976: 184). Migration is one of those forces that have to be governed to optimize the life of the population. One could easily argue that demographic concerns and considerations about the quality of life in cities uttered in relation to migration express a bio-political approach.

At the micro level, the dynamics of life are constantly changing and are rather unpredictable. For example, in specific households, the composition of the population, the level of hygiene can change relatively quickly. Government does not aim to optimize individual lives or small communities, but searches to establish a stable, balanced development of the population as a whole. Its object is a global entity and dynamics it experiences. Individual bodies as such are not that important for a steady development of the population. The practice of government of the population thus requires a particular technology that makes it possible to identify the global mass as having its characteristic dynamics, which constitute the population. This is the technology of statistics and probability calculation. It is a particularly powerful technology for rendering visible dynamics in their globality rather than through their representation in the life of individual bodies. The invention of the statistical average with regard to identifying social dynamics has played an important role in the development of bio-politics. The combination of statistics and probability calculations has provided a key instrument for the government of life whose aim is to assure a certain equilibrium in and a balanced development of the population (Foucault, 1997: 218–19).

Why this relatively long explanation of the art of government? Because it is within the development of the government of population that a specific technique of security emerges in Western societies: 'guaranteeing the citizen against old age and misfortune, redistributing resources, . . .

security comes now to signify not the old military notion which referred to the occupation of territory, but that modern idea which enfolds in itself the lives of each and all' (Defert, 1991: 232). It opens up an opportunity for 'the state to introduce itself as an intimate, regular presence in the existence of its citizens'. (Defert, 1991: 232). Demographic institutions, the regulation of integration of migrants and the social security system are among the apparatuses of security that have emerged in relation to the government of population. These apparatuses 'seek to establish a kind of homeostasis not through individual dressing, but through the global equilibrium' (Foucault, 1997: 222). Security is here much closer to the concept of stability than to the military concept of defence. Its major aim is to establish a global equilibrium in the different dynamics of the population. It focuses on dangers that are internal to the system, that is dangers intrinsic to developments in the population (Dumm, 1996: 131; Foucault, 1976: 182–3; Foucault, 1997: 222). Calculating migration pressure and thresholds of tolerance, for example, are a security policy in this sense. They make it possible to identify dangers migration and immigrants could pose to a balanced development of the population, often expressed in terms of social cohesion. This method of security has three general traits:

It deals in series of possible and probable events; it evaluates through calculations of comparative cost; it prescribes not by absolute binary demarcation between the permitted and the forbidden, but by the specification of an optimal mean within a tolerable brand of variation (Gordon, 1991: 20). This technique of security differs from the method deployed in the context of defence, or the rule of sovereignty, which works on the basis of binary opposites between friend and enemy or citizen and criminal. The three traits also show that the concept of the internal enemy does not belong to the technique of securing the development of the population. An internal enemy is defined within the context of sovereignty in which territorial integrity opposes an inside from an outside. The internal enemy is a function of the quest for sovereignty rather than a danger intrinsic to the dynamic of the population. Security and enemy construction, internal or external, signify here explicitly within the Clausewitzian matrix of war and a particular understanding of Hobbes (Huysmans, 1995; Wæver, 1995). Different from the society of security (Gordon, 1991: 20) developed in relation to the art of government, security policy then concentrates on managing relationships of enmity and amity. Its major problem is how to neutralize enemies. While the society of security governs for the purpose of optimizing life by making life, security as defence rules through the power to kill. This raises an interesting question: do we have two very different security techniques in our society, each bound up with a different understanding of politics and power, or, is there more to it than a pure contrast? This tension is rendered visible in a very interesting – analytically speaking – but also in a worrying – normatively speaking – way in the field of migration in present-day western Europe.

SECURITY AND THE EXTERNALIZATION OF DANGER

Although security talk in the migration area today implies the construction of migration and migrants as inimical forces, it is not the only and probably not even the primordial form of regulating migration by means of a security technique. In daily policy migration is not an object of war but first of all an object of government of the population. It is a problem for securing a continuation and optimal development of the population, but this does not necessarily imply that it is a threat. Migration policy today embodies to a considerable extent the assumption that migration negatively affects the quality of life of the population and therefore has to be severely regulated. The policy rests on calculations of costs and benefits of immigrants and asylum seekers for the local economy, on evaluations of the probable impact upon the quality of life in cities and on an examination of the possible impact upon the demographic evolution of the population. Although it often results in representing migration as a negative, disturbing phenomenon, its danger emerges from inside population dynamics. It is seen as a part of these dynamics, although a problematic part. The policy searches to remedy the detrimental effects upon the life of the population by strictly regulating and restricting population movement across borders, by integrating immigrants into the domestic society and by stimulating them to leave the country. A wide range of technologies, including identity control, assignment of housing and welfare applications, are at work to optimize population dynamics and the quality of life through the most efficient means. These security apparatuses do not construct immigrants as outsiders in the strict sense of the word because they are to a considerable extent approached as an intrinsic element of population dynamics. In that sense, they enter the multifarious regulations of men's relationship to different things, such as wealth, public health and birth rate. The government of migration does not primarily rely on a bipolar opposition between insiders and outsiders, but develops knowledge based on probability calculation and a search for optimal means to improve the quality of life.

The formulation of thresholds of tolerance is a good example of how security technology works in the migration area, and especially in urban areas. But, also the criminalization of migration can operate within the contours of this security policy. Particular migrants are constructed into a costly category of the population due to them having a higher probability of committing a crime. In a sense, this is not that different from defining optimal urban planning or optimal demographic trends. It is embedded in a political economic approach where one tries to assure an optimal development of the governed population through the most efficient means.

The technologies of government play a primordial role in integrating security claims of citizens into a security question that concerns the wider community. Individual fears are transformed into a problem of the population and receive political intelligibility from being embedded in the general dynamics of life, for example, through statistical representations of crime, or risks for public health. The microphysics of security technology is crucial. It may even be argued that rather than public security claims, the professional deployment of security technologies are the central issue in the process of securitization.

The presence of security policy in the migration area is not limited to the role of security apparatuses managing population dynamics. Besides a bio-political governance, immigrants and refugees are also politicized as a threat to public order. The representation of violent unrest in big cities often plays a triggering role. Also, the subtler criminalization of categories of immigrants – which also operates as bio-politics – can transform the question from a problem of optimal management of the population into a problematic of the rule of law. Here bio-politics slips into sovereign politics in which rule by means of differentiation between the forbidden and the permitted displaces 'the specification of an optimal mean within a tolerable brandwith of variation' (Gordon, 1991: 20). Furthermore, some argue that immigration has also been dragged into governance through enemy construction. In this logic, immigrants are represented as a hostile community threatening to destroy the harmonious community of natives. Thus, there is to a certain extent an overdetermination of bio-politics and rule of law by a rationality of war in the present politicization of migration questions. An interesting question here is what role the historical image, or the symbolic value, of cities and the representations of violence in cities play in mobilizing expectations of war, especially when they are overdetermined by a fear of Islam emerging within the complex and powerful symbolic structure of Orientalism.[3]

Consequently, in western Europe today, migration is not simply a problem that is intrinsically related to the dynamics of life. The bio-politics of migration slips into other understandings of security in which the externalization of dangers – implying exclusion and/or enemy construction – and ruling by the sword, that is, through the capacity (symbolically) to kill, displaces the managerial problematic of government of the population. This risk of slippage from bio-politics to a politics of war and/or a politics of rule of law can be observed in many places today. For example, the Europeanization of migration policy has experienced a slippage from socioeconomic regulations in the internal market, that is a regulation through a distribution of economic costs and benefits, into a security regulation operating in a Clausewitzian matrix of war that manages the distribution of externalized threats. The problematization of the control of external borders of the EU in relation to the abolishment of internal border control has played a significant role in the spillover of an economic into a security project (Bigo, 1996; Ceyhan, 1997; den Boer, 1994; Huysmans, 1997). But also, more local security claims, most explicitly visible in extreme right-wing practices, articulate this externalization of fear.

In the complex play of slippage and displacement of different security techniques, which is very visible in the securitization of migration, the question arises of how one can have a policy of death in a society that highly acclaims a politics of life. This is a rule in the name of sovereignty, and especially a rule within the Clausewitzian war matrix. In other words, how can one have a policy ruled by the capacity to kill within a political context that is also ruled by an imperative to 'create' life? One possible answer is racism, more specifically, the appropriation of racism by the state (Foucault, 1997: 234).

Racism introduces a split in the domain of life between those who can live and should be made to live optimally and those who have to die. It thus fragments the biological field into groups that are worthy of life and others that are not. Furthermore, racism also symbolizes the 'killing' of the other as a strategy of survival: eliminating the inferior races becomes part and parcel of a strategy of optimizing one's own race (Bauman, 1989; Bauman, 1992; Canetti, 1992; Foucault, 1997: 227–8). Racism has a capacity to transform a politics of life into governance through war from within the biological field – that is, war signifying primarily in a biological sense rather than in a military or political sense (Foucault,

1997: 227–8).[4] Probably a similar account can be given of nationalism. Like racism, it fragments the species and externalizes dangers, but it does it in cultural terms rather than biological, somatic ones. Historically, there has been a close relation between nationalism and racism (Miles, 1989). This opens a box of questions of how these two are related in the present problematization of migration and how powerful they are for introducing a governance articulating a rationality of war in a field largely dominated by a government based on the rationality of life and bio-politics.

This leads us to a more general question about the meaning of the security technique in the contemporary political field, and especially, in the politicization of migration. Given the importance of a politics of life aimed at an optimization of the population, a securitization of migration is slightly more complex than the identification and governance of a relationship of enmity between migrants and the indigenous population. It also suggests that the dynamics of inclusion and exclusion that are at work in security policies cannot be reduced to a simple in-group/out-group differentiation.[5]

The politicization of migration articulates a complex play of slippages between different rationalities of governance, implying an overlay between different techniques of security. In this chapter, I have tried to indicate some elements of this slippage by differentiating between a politics of life and a politics of death, as it is articulated in rationalities of sovereignty and war. However, the most interesting question does not concern the difference as such between techniques of security and rationalities of governance, but the way they have overdetermined one another – or, in other words, their interdependence. This would require detailed analyses of the microphysics of technologies of governance in the migration area (examples of which one can find in some other chapters in this book). It would open up interesting questions such as: What role does violence in suburbs play in the transformation of migration policy into a question of the internal enemy? What is the impact of the growth in knowledge that largely reduces explanations of social relations to a cultural terminology?

Notes

1. I rely on the following works for the analysis below: Donzelot, 1993;. Dumm, 1996; Foucault, 1976, 1989, 1991 and 1997; Gordon, 1991; and Szakolczai, 1992.

2. Power does not work upon and through an individual's body, as if it were a discipline (Foucault, 1975), which is the other form of the policy of life (Foucault, 1976: 182–3). It also implies a particular knowledge (*savoir*): political economy, but this is not part of this chapter. Ewald has shown at length how probability calculation played a crucial role in the genealogy of the social security system (Ewald, 1996: part II). That does not mean that questions of sovereignty or enmity are irrelevant or that there is no relationship between them and bio-politics. It means that one has to explore how other uses of security relate to the question of government. For example, how do questions of security and sovereignty in international relations appear and how have they been rearticulated in relation to the development of the art of government? These questions become very visible when one takes a closer look at the securitization of migration in present-day western Europe.

3. For an interesting and critical discussion about the construction of a fear of Islam in France, see J. Cesari (1997a and 1997b); on the question of the role of cities and especially suburbs in the construction of fear, see Henri Rey (1996).

4. The intensive use of medical metaphors in national security and military discourses suggests that the difference between or within the technique of security does not necessarily represent a radical separation.

5. The problematic nature of this easy inclusion–exclusion interpretation is also a result of the way the category 'migrant' itself operates in west European societies. Migrants will always to a certain extent remain liminal, that is be both inside and outside a society (Sayad, 1991). It could therefore be argued that it is not just the slippage within the security technique that is responsible for the complexity of the inclusion/exclusion dynamics and their mediation. It is also the signification of the 'migrant' as a stranger in Bauman's sense (Bauman, 1990, 1991), that is not a foreigner but an inside/outsider.

14 Migration, Crime and the City: Contexts of Social Exclusion

Simon Holdaway

THE PERSISTENCE OF QUESTIONS ABOUT RACE AND CRIME

One of the most contentious questions facing contemporary social science is the nature of the relationship, if any, between race and crime. Political parties, groups and individuals on the far right frequently allege that immigration and the settlement of ethnic minority groups lead to higher crime levels in receiving countries. Some argue that their rhetoric has permeated the minds of large sections of national populations, mostly disseminated by the media and through political speeches (Hall et al., 1978; Hargreaves, 1996; van Dijk, 1991). This acceptance of an exclusionary rhetoric has criminalized and marginalized ethnic groups *per se*.

In Europe generally, and the states of the European Union in particular, social scientists have to some extent therefore been concerned to rebut claims of an intrinsic relationship between groups of people identified by their membership of a 'race' and their tendency to commit crime. There are sound reasons for an engagement with the 'race and crime' question, not least because its backcloth is formed by the twentieth-century spectre of Nazism and mass destruction.

Taking this context into account, the atmosphere of research about race and crime is often highly charged. In England, for example, allegations about immigrants' criminogenic behaviour have often created a polarized debate. For some commentators, the problem is not crime but a pervasive, systemic racism, enacted by police, those who impose the sentences and others within the criminal justice system. Statistics of reported offences are rejected completely, the subject of 'empiricist haggling', as Paul Gilroy put it (Gilroy, 1982 and 1983). The reply from the opposite corner of the academic boxing ring is that criminal justice statistics demonstrate a higher level of offending among some minority ethnic groups than among the ethnic majority (Waddington, 1984 and 1986).

Apart from the political and sociological rhetoricians, however, there is also a measured (literally) group of researchers who occupy the middle ground. They base their analyses on methods of inquiry that remove research adequately from the limitations of political preference, or so they assume (Tonry, 1997). Within this diverse group there is recognition that in all major European cities, the position of migrants, including their patterns of crime and victimization, are important research subjects, pertinent to policy reform.

In this chapter, I discuss some of the statistical evidence about migrants and crime. This is not, however, my sole or primary interest. 'Race' is a social construct and I argue that, if we are to understand migration and crime adequately, we need to begin from this conceptualization, which many researchers have inadvertently forgotten. I do not dissolve 'race' and 'crime' away as epiphenomena, as the contrivance of an economic system (Miles, 1982). I also do not wholly accept the 'new racism' type of analysis in which 'race' is conceptualized as a discourse, an illusive yet powerful construction. We need research that describes and analyses processes of social exclusion, the processes of racialization that affect migrants.

RESEARCHING 'RACE' AND CRIME IN EUROPEAN CITIES

Any research that involves collecting data about crime levels in Europe will encounter significant difficulties. Even in European Union countries, there are no consistent definitions of crime or of migrant status. Defining equivalent crime categories in different societies is not easy. The police record the available statistics and we know that they are a significant under count. Official statistics are shaped by victims' commonsense definitions of crime; their need to report crime; their level of trust in the police; police prejudice; and discriminatory policies and practices. It is possible to fall back on victim survey data to calculate levels of offending, but they are of limited use for an analysis of crime committed by offenders from particular ethnic groups because few victims can identify the ethnicity of their assailant. These difficulties are compounded when one attempts to analyse official or other crime statistics at the neighbourhood level. The geographical areas to which official statistics refer are not always suitable for the study of crime or victimization patterns in neighbourhoods. Available statistics more frequently relate to areas defined by administrative rather than research based criteria.

In some societies, the ethnicity of offenders is not recorded in official statistics. In Germany, for example, it is forbidden to collect race-based statistics. Ethical questions are raised in arguments against the collection of racially categorized statistics. It is said that 'race' is reified as a categorization of populations and given credibility; that discrimination and criminalization are encouraged; and that there is a tendency to focus on offending but not on victimization.

Where the ethnic origin of offenders categorizes crime statistics they are usually aggregated, which makes the analysis of particular ethnic groups or of particular offending patterns difficult. In Britain, many groups committed to 'antiracism' have resisted a refinement of ethnic categories. The adjective 'black' has defined all people whose skin is not white. When crime and victimization statistics are disaggregated, however, one finds significant differences within and between ethnic groups.

In England and Wales there seem to be significant differences, for example, between crime rates for Afro-Caribbean and Asian youth. We do not know, however, if there are different rates of offending within the category 'Asian'. There is recent evidence to suggest that people of south Asian, Bangladeshi and Pakistani origin have different experiences of racially motivated crime and different crime reporting habits (Modood et al., 1997: 259–89). There might also be different patterns of offending between these groups. There are differences within and between groups of men and women (women commit far fewer crimes than men do). There are differences between generations (there are higher levels and different types of offence patterns for initial, then first- and second-generation migrants). There are differences between legal and illegal migrants. In some societies, like the Netherlands, subgroups of illegal immigrants find their way into drugs offences. Also, neighbourhoods differ (police policies of stop and search are different in different geographical areas). And, there are differences between offence categories (organized crime and trading in drugs and women are very different offences from the more usual crimes of theft and burglary). The basic point is that diversity is found whenever relevant data are analysed in detail, which is nothing to do with the adoption of postmodern fashions by criminologists and everything to do with research attention to a social world that is ambiguous, changing and demanding of empirical inquiry.

This leads to a fundamental point about the conceptualization of 'race'. Virtually all social scientists agree that it is a social construct. A crucial task for social scientists is therefore to describe and analyse the social processes that reconstruct and sustain racialized relationships. Very little research attention has been given to the mundane processes that racialize relationships between members of different minority and majority ethnic groups (Holdaway, 1997). Further, there has been a neglect of related processes that lead to particular forms of social exclusion.

The crime data criminologists spend so much time unravelling are the outcomes of complex social processes, to which little or no research attention is given. Their favoured, statistical method of regression analysis, which filters out extraneous variables to leave the scum of 'race', is valuable, but it fragments the social world into discrete variables, related to each other by a numerical expression. This distorts the ways in which complex social processes racialize relationships (Holdaway, 1997). The same criticisms could be made about the concept of social exclusion within a good deal of European research (Room, 1995). There seems to be little interest in mundane social processes that lead to the marginalization and exclusion of particular social groups.

The concept of 'racialization' is central to my argument, based on the notion that race is a social construct. Mundane social processes sustain racialized relations. We should describe and analyse social processes that lead to relationships and phenomena being connoted with and denoted by the meaning 'race'.

QUANTITATIVE STUDIES: THE EVIDENCE

The initial research framing criminological and sociological interest in immigration and crime was undertaken in the USA. Although the data analysed were patchy, it was apparent that, for some offences, 'American-born children of immigrants had higher crime rates than did American-born children of American-born parents' (Tonry, 1997: 21; see also National Commission on Law Observance and Enforcement, 1931).

Explanations of this finding have mostly been based on a version of anomie theory. Immigrants' actual standards of living or opportunities to improve their standard of living were enhanced by immigration, but the expectations of their offspring could not be fulfilled. They perceived themselves to be members of economically poor households, with frustrated opportunities in education, the labour market and other institutional spheres. Crime was one means of realizing some of the material benefits they lacked. Ideas about children being between two cultures, of relative deprivation and so on were embedded in US criminological thought and have survived transportation to Europe (Shaw and McKay, 1942).

There are many reasons to question this explanation of immigration and offending. First, in some European societies, it has been found that subsequent generations of youths from some ethnic minority groups, notably those from south Asia, have consistently lower crime rates than 'home-born youths' (Junger-Tas, 1997; Smith, 1997). There are also differences in recorded offending rates between different south Asian groups, which do not correlate with indices of deprivation.

Second, insufficient attention is given to the ways in which cultural features of particular immigrant groups might affect their adaptation to a host society and subsequent involvement in crime. This does not imply a pristine cultural heritage passed from generation to generation. It does beg us to understand how processes of racialization mould different cultures. In the Netherlands, for example, Turks and Moroccans have different self-reported and recorded crime levels (the former much lower than the latter) but similar experiences as guestworkers (Junger-Tas, 1997). These differences may partly be related to age structures and to the class composition of different groups, but the sustaining of cultural processes that militate against criminal behaviour cannot be dismissed.

Third, the framework of the social and criminal justice policy the immigrants enter is likely to have a lasting effect on an immigrant's offending patterns. The more inclusive social policies of Sweden, for example, though not greatly reducing crime rates of some migrant groups, do seem to have a relative effect (Martens, 1997). Attention should also be paid to the occupational and organizational cultures of agencies that implement social and criminal justice policy. In England, for example, the occupational culture of the police rank and file enhances racialized prejudice against black youths that can lead to discrimination (Holdaway, 1996 and 1997; Holdaway and Barron, 1997).

Fourth, the US thesis of higher crime rates for 'home-born' immigrants is based on an inadequate theory of action. The reasons why people migrate, the different perceptions they have of their experience of migration are crucial aspects of a study of crime and victimization at the neighbourhood level. Migrants who are determined to succeed economically may have a different relationship with offending than those who are less motivated by their sense of economic wellbeing. Illegal and legal migrants might have different crime trajectories (Leman, 1997). The meaning of migration to migrants is an all too often ignored aspect of criminological research.

Finally, we have to remember that many migrants are not poor. Migrants from Hong Kong, Japan and other societies do not always begin their period of settlement from a position of poverty. These migrants can communicate frequently with relatives at 'home' and in other countries; they are able to travel to meet their ethnic peers and can join ethnic associations. Their relationship to criminal behaviour is likely to be very different from that of less established migrants.

CONTEXTS OF RACIALIZATION

I now want to consider in slightly more detail three key related contexts of relevance to migrants' experience of offending and victimization.

Policy

First, I deal with the policy context of migration, by which I mean the range of social and criminal justice policies germane to the inclusion or exclusion of migrant people as citizens of a society. This context is important because it is part of the structural framework within which members of particular ethnic groups perceive and create a style of life.

The extent to which migrants can gain access to a public sector of welfare is consistent with the existence of opportunity structures supporting legality and inclusion. The experience of Sweden, with its social security and welfare provisions for migrants, is evidence of the relatively significant effect this can have on offending rates (Martens, 1997).

Many migrants need access to welfare services and the labour market. At the neighbourhood level, state and voluntary associations can be of considerable assistance – helping members of minority groups understand the range and type of services available, by advocacy and by offering other types of support. More informal networks for migrants perform similar functions. The presence of accessible opportunity structures is central to sustaining inclusionary relationships in any society.

These associations and networks may have a somewhat tenuous relevance for vulnerable youth, not least those who experience high levels of unemployment and a deficit of financial and cultural capital to invest in the enactment of citizenship (Hagan, 1994). Voluntary associations and networks might also be as or more concerned with the provision of services other than those offered by statutory bodies, reinforcing an ethnic boundary between minority and majority communities and sustaining a class of secondary citizenship. The extent to which voluntary sector organizations assist migrants vulnerable to offending, however, seems to be important. Burgers and Engbersen's study of migrants in Rotterdam, for example, suggests that without a strong support structure to lead them into formal institutions, Moroccan migrants turn to crime. Consequently, they have a higher rate of offending than Turks and other minority ethnic groups, especially for drugs related offences (Burgers and Engbersen, 1996).

The voluntary sector alone cannot provide migrants with enough help to gain access to welfare and related services. In many cities, state welfare provision is dispersed and managed at area or more local levels, which could be of particular benefit to migrant groups. Policy is often distinct from practice, however, and we need to know much more about how welfare services are delivered to migrants in face to face contexts (Barrett and Fudge, 1981). The occupational culture of welfare organizations can enhance or detract from perceptions of inclusion within a society and within a neighbourhood.

Furthermore, opportunity structures for access to the labour market are equally central, not least because we know that employment provides an important means of gaining the financial capital required to prevent material exclusion and marginalization within a society (Modood et al., 1997). We also know that unemployment is related to offending, albeit in complex ways (Field, 1991). It is noticeable, however, that one of the distinct differences, certainly in England, is the recorded rates of offending between Afro-Caribbean and Asian youth. It may be that the existence of opportunity structures within the Asian population that cater for entry into a specific, ethnic labour market forms part of an explanation of why Asian youths have a lower recorded rate of offending than do black youths.

The more precise ways in which ethnic labour market networks affect processes of negative racialization and alienation, however, is not known. Clearly, the experience of deprivation, including unemployment, does not lead straightforwardly to the consideration of illegality among all or the majority of minority ethnic groups (Field, 1984; Gaskell and Smith, 1981 and 1985). Opportunities to enter an ethnic labour market might nevertheless provide a sense of security and inclusion, which, with other factors, provides the capital and perception of present and future security that helps to prevent offending.

These points are also of relevance to levels of crime victimization. When neighbourhoods are identified as both areas of residence and work for a particular ethnic minority, levels of racially motivated crime may be higher than those experienced in areas of less concentration. Levels of victimization in a number of other spheres can also increase. Employment in cheap labour markets can lead to high levels of factory accidents and poor work conditions that breach employment law. Public perceptions among members of other minorities and/or the majority population of an ethnic group seeking separation and exclusion may be reinforced. Participation in political and other institutions that signal an inclusive citizenship may be discouraged; aspects of ghettoization may be forthcoming. Processes of recapitalization within an ethnic labour market can thereby contribute to the strengthening of ethnic boundaries, with beneficial effects on levels of offending but a lessening of opportunities to engage in institutions that assist inclusive citizenship, and an apparent increase in different forms of victimization.

Policing

In many European countries relationships between the police and migrants have been a repeated source of conflict and concern. Police have been criticized by ethnic minority groups for their inadequate action against the perpetrators of racialized attacks and harassment; their general failure to protect migrants; the over-policing of areas of migrant settlement; and their aggressive tactics. These are very general claims that mask differences within and between societies and there is not room in this chapter to untangle the complex evidence available.

Without finely grained descriptions and analyses of relationships between migrants and police, especially at the neighbourhood level, we will not understand the perceptions, interactions and beliefs on which such relationships are based. I therefore want to identify and discuss briefly some of the factors that might lead to the negative racialization of relationships between police and migrants. I do not have a zero sum game in mind here. The implicit acceptance of such a game has distracted too much criminological attention away from the interplay of categorization and group identification that should be central to an analysis (Jenkins, 1994; Mason, 1992 and 1994). My concern is to identify contexts within which social processes of racialization, inclusion and exclusion are constructed and reconstructed.

In some European societies, the police have a statutory responsibility to trace and prosecute illegal immigrants, which places them in a precarious relationship with some migrant groups. In this context, migrants' routine relationships with the police might become tainted or pervaded by suspicion. The level of trust placed in mundane relationships with the police is consequentially reduced.

As far as the police are concerned, urban populations with large numbers of migrants can come under permanent suspicion, debased by their stereotypical criminalization as illegal immigrants. Special police units with the function of dealing with illegal immigrants are of particular importance here because they build their own momentum, divorcing their members from concern with the routine policing of an area. In a moment of insensitivity, the members of such squads can, however, destroy the difficult task of building good police relationships with migrant groups.

Routine policing, however, is central to sustaining confident relationships between the police and migrant groups. Comparative research findings are not available, but in England we know that, although all levels are high, black and Asian people generally have lower levels of support for the police than the majority ethnic population (Joint Consultative Committee, 1990; Skogan, 1990b). This does not mean that relationships between police and migrants are always tense. It does mean that they can be soured easily, not least by insensitive officers who are unaware of the hesitant or negative ways in which migrants perceive their actions or who are deliberately brusque (Holdaway, 1996).

A clear emphasis on peacekeeping within police patrols will enhance relations with migrant groups. There are a variety of strategies that constabularies can employ at the local level to work as partners with a host of statutory and voluntary organizations to create neighbourhoods with low levels of disorder and crime. These include target hardening, community watch action, the improvement of leisure facilities for youths, and job creation schemes. Much of this work can prevent the physical and social decline of neighbourhoods which, in the US context, Wesley Skogan has argued is critical to the retention of acceptably peaceable neighbourhoods (Skogan, 1990a and 1990b).

Preventative policing policies require implementation. Patrol officers need to perceive them as valuable and to relate them to their routine work. When implemented, however, policy is refracted through the assumptions, beliefs and related actions that constitute the police occupational culture. The effects of the occupational culture are legion. These include inappropriate use of stop and arrest powers; the use of offensive, racist language during encounters with ethnic minorities; and the creation and sustaining of stories by ethnic minorities about how offenders and victims of racist crimes are dealt with. There are many other traits that affect migrants' views of the police and their perceptions of inclusion within a framework of public safety afforded to other citizens (Holdaway, 1997). Events, reports, rumours, allegations and more are thus woven into a reality of formal relationships between police and migrant groups. They become the manifestation, the reality of police policy, not an aberration. Similarly, the occupational culture feeds on traditions and stories about ethnic minorities, including their response to police action, perhaps their criminal attributes and the nature of the areas in which they live (Shearing and Ericson, 1991). Racial stereotypes can be strengthened in the interplay between the police and minority ethnic worlds.

All this leads me to re-emphasize the need to understand what social processes enhance particular perceptions of the police among ethnic minority groups. The interplay between police and migrant perceptions and actions can contribute to marginalization, sustaining a changing but nevertheless distrustful and at times exclusionary relationship. We must remind ourselves constantly that the different ethnic groups, and groups within them, have different perceptions of and relationships with the police.

The Structure and Culture of Migrant Groups

New migrants are often able to relate to established city-based migrant communities, which provide a framework for their lifestyle and openings to the labour market. Some migrants move across borders precisely to commit crime. Others are dazzled by the material benefits they find in societies that are more economically secure than their own and commit opportunity crimes. Although these types of offenders might affect public perceptions of whole communities, here I want to focus briefly on offending within more settled communities.

In their study of illegal migrants in Rotterdam, Burgers and Engbersen concede that immigration laws and formal opportunities to enter labour market and welfare institutions are very important. However, they argue that it is necessary also to take into account structures and related cultures of settled migrant groups when considering patterns of migrant offending (Burgers and Engbersen, 1996). As far as illegal migrants are concerned, ease of access to the informal economy is important. The extent to which workers in voluntary and statutory agencies have found ways of using formal rules of welfare provision to the advantage of illegal migrants and the extent to which opportunities exist to enter settled criminal markets, particularly the drugs market, are also important. The relative positions of Turkish and Moroccan migrants are discussed in Burger's study.

Further, a considerable body of research has revealed the importance of parenting patterns in creating disorderly, sometimes offending, behaviour in children (Shaw and Riley, 1985). Though this is not linked directly with the US culture of poverty and family pathology literature (Moynihan, 1965), we should take note of how relationships between parents and carers in some migrant groups differ considerably. US research in this area has shown that lone parents are bound to find it more difficult to control their children than a parent with adequate financial resources does, or one with ready, regular assistance from other people. This applies particularly to women on whom the task of parenthood is likely to fall, who are under pressure to find an adequate income for their family and who cannot rely on consistent support from a partner. A lone parent living in poverty will find it more difficult to retain an interest in a child's leisure habits and relations with peers, which research has revealed are relevant to the taking of opportunities to offend (Shaw and Riley, 1985). The tight, supportive structures of some south Asian communities in England and Hindustanis and Asians from Surinam in the Netherlands might illustrate this point. No research has been conducted on how notions of masculinity and support between men within different ethnic groups are related to ideas about appropriate behaviour, including offending. Given that men commit by far the greatest numbers of crimes, such research might have potential.

Other beliefs and related values are obviously also important for our understanding of offending behaviour. Leman's study of migrants in Brussels includes recognition of the way in which religion is influential in the lives of Polish and Filipino people (Leman, 1997). He also mentions the value of peers within the Turkish and Chinese communities, who provide financial and other support for the improvement of educational and economic levels of performance.

RESEARCHING MIGRATION AND CRIME

Many of the questions I have posed about migrant groups and offending are also relevant to majority ethnic groups. We should not place minority groups in a hermetically sealed ethnic tradition, preserved across generations. Ethnic cultures are multifaceted, dynamic and diverse. Their relationships with societally more dominant cultures are complex, being a shifting response to racialized and other categorizations and to group membership (Barth, 1969b). Members of migrant groups have diverse orientations to ethnic cultures, as Ken Pryce's study of Afro-Caribbean people in Bristol, England demonstrated (Pryce, 1979). The ways in which ideas and action are related within ethnic cultures are also complex, requiring a highly sensitive researcher to tease them out.

My fundamental response to published criminological and sociological research is that insufficient attention has been paid to how racialized relations are constructed and reconstructed within mundane settings. Taking my cue from Ulf Hannertz's ethnographic research, I would like to see the development of neighbourhood studies in which attention is given to the ways in which migrants perceive and respond to their society. It is also helpful to look at their relationship with what they identify as an ethnic culture, including their perceptions of aspects of offending (Hannertz, 1969). Some of these studies could use a life-history approach; participatory and observational methods could also be fruitful. Whatever the method used, a theory of action would be central.

Within the EU, a programme of comparative research about one or two ethnic minority groups, with similar periods of settlement in a small number of neighbourhoods in different European cities, could be the subject of research. The range of employment and welfare institutions within a society, as well as its immigration laws, might determine why a particular society is chosen.

Small teams of researchers would employ a range of qualitative methods to describe and analyse how migrants perceive the opportunities that have been and continue to be available to them to become citizens of their society. The scope of this research would extend beyond nationality laws to include opportunities to participate in and the benefits realized from a range of institutions. An analysis of the ways in which migrants, not least migrant youth, who are particularly vulnerable to offending, have responded to these opportunities would be central.

Simultaneous research could be undertaken in one or two key agencies, including welfare and criminal justice ones, to document and analyse how their personnel interact with migrants (Smith, 1997). Processes of racialization, inclusion and exclusion would be documented and analysed. The proposal is ambitious, but it would probably give us a clearer understanding of the opportunities to offend facing some migrants and, crucially, to do so from an understanding of what Alfred Schutz called the 'life world', the mundane world perceived and to which we respond (Schutz, 1967).

I emphasize this research perspective because my expectation is that the comparative research proposed would identify common and distinct features of different migrant groups living in different societies, as well as similarities and differences within and between ethnic minority groups living in each society. It may be possible to identify phenomenal and essential processes of racialization and, probably of more importance, of social exclusion and inclusion within a number of European societies. This aspect of the research would not only be relevant to policy reform, but would also ensure that the social science was 'grounded' in the terra firma of migrants' mundane lives in European cities. Not least, it would endeavour to remain faithful to a central tenet of the study of race and ethnic relations, namely that 'races' and 'crimes' are socially constructed.

15 The Judicial System and the Social Construction of Migrants' Criminality: The Case of Milan

Fabio Quassoli

Europe is facing a political 'backlash' against migrants. New right-wing parties, governments and the media are concerned about the presence and impact of migrants in these societies. Debates in European polities are evolving over the question of regulation and criteria for inclusion and exclusion. At stake are migrants' rights to cross the borders of any European country, to have access to citizenship and to benefit from the welfare provisions allocated by each state (Baldwin-Edwards and Schain, 1994; Cesarani and Fulbrook, 1996; Martiniello, 1994). European governments are following common guidelines – such as those that are set out in the Schengen agreement – to regulate migrant flows along two lines. First, they are adopting stronger and more coordinated border patrols to prevent the entry of new migrants from countries outside the European Union and to make legal procedures for deportation and expulsion easier to implement. Second, they are increasing police and administrative controls over migrants already inside the European Union. Access to regularization through residence and work permits (which allows migrants to benefit from civic, political and social citizenship rights and to enter the formal labour market) is more and more linked to and constrained by a migrant's criminal record. Migrant criminality has now become a basis for inclusion or exclusion from EU countries. The link between increasing migration waves and crime rates is at the core of current political debates (Agozino, 1997; Brion, 1997; Palidda, 1994, 1995 and 1997; Sayad, 1997). Migration has come to be seen as the main source of insecurity in European societies and is a prominent political and social concern. Public opinion and political and institutional actors have framed every issue related to immigration as an internal or international security problem. The presence of an increasing number of migrants in Europe and the prospect of future waves of mass migration from Third World countries are usually deemed to produce a sharp and dangerous increase in crime rates. The media, institutional agencies (public and private) and social scientists are providing statistical evidence that shows a clear explosion of migrants' crime rates. Not surprisingly, migrant criminality – its causes and impact – has become one of the hottest political issues in Europe (AUT-AUT, 1996).

It is crucial to understand and analyse the processes by which migrants and crime come to be perceived as part of the same equation. In this chapter, I aim to explore how migrant criminality, as a socially constructed phenomenon, is produced. In a brief analytical framework, I study how the process of migrant criminality construction takes place and focus on a specific layer in this process, the judicial system. By exploring the role of the criminal court in Milan, I aim to highlight some of the relevant aspects that shape the category of migrants as criminals in Italian society.

THEORETICAL FRAMEWORK

I am not interested in analysing the 'real' or 'objective' dimension of the problem – whatever meaning we attribute it – or in providing an explanation for migrant criminality. I do not focus on understanding whether migrants' deviant or criminal behaviour can be better explained by individual variables, different types of social organization, or relative deprivation (Segre, 1993). I do not focus on the distribution of power among different social groups or classes (Hagan and Peterson, 1995), cultural influences, or any other set of variables (Pfohl, 1985). I also do not discuss all the factors that could potentially bias the quantitative data in official statistics, which are generally considered the starting point of any scientific analysis of criminality.

Instead, I assume that the above variables play a role in the identification, recognition, and description of migrant criminality by any of the major actors participating in the construction of the category. Ultimately, these actors take into consideration these variables and therefore these variables influence the relevant institutional and political decisions taken in the social construction of migrant criminality. I aim to describe here the process by which migrant criminality is constructed in multiple and often related social contexts as an 'objective social fact' and a source of social insecurity (Hall et al., 1978). My starting point is that 'migrant criminality', as a social fact and an objective phenomenon, exists insofar as social actors use the category to recognize, classify, describe, address and explain social reality. Thus, we cannot separate the objective reality of migrant criminality on the one hand, and the set of procedures and methods that allow us to recognize, describe and explain it on the other. These include police investigations (Manning, 1977; Sacks, 1972), rules used by prosecutors and judges to evaluate criminal cases (Sudnow, 1965) and the assumptions and techniques social scientists use to interpret official data (Taylor, 1982). They also include scientific analyses to demonstrate how the administration of justice is biased by social prejudice and racial, ethnic or power relationship (Blumstein et al., 1983). We can sum up the approach I want to put forward, in four steps.

1. Identifying the institutional/organizational actors involved in the social construction of the phenomenon and isolating the main institutional, organizational and communicative social contexts in which discourses and representations of migrants as deviants, delinquents and criminals take place.[1]
2. Analysing the standard working procedures of each organizational context (point 1) to understand why and to what extent migrant criminality is a relevant symbolic element in everyday activities and part of a shared commonsense knowledge (Hall et al., 1978).
3. Analysing the multiple types of relationships among the social actors participating in the social construction of migrant criminality. The everyday practices and routines of members of different organizations are embedded in a network of formal and informal agreements through which the actors continually negotiate, redefine and reproduce both the characteristics of the relevant fact with which they are dealing and their current status relationships. This process involves formal rules, rules to help define the characteristics of the working environment and to produce good and acceptable evidence, commonsense theories, reciprocal images and systems of expectation. Moreover, the reciprocal influence and communication exists even in the absence of a direct relationship between two or more actors. This kind of interorganizational interaction generally takes place through the role played by the mass media, which allows indirect communication apart from any direct relationship among them.
4. Finally, we have to consider the domain of commonsense knowledge about social reality and how it is produced. In each social setting, people involved in everyday organizational routines develop a common

background of knowledge, images, categories, shared understandings, rules of interpretation and commonsense theories that they introduce into the communication processes in which they are involved (Cicourel, 1973; Heritage, 1984; Mehan and Wood, 1975). Dealing with crime inevitably involves evaluating information from a variety of institutional sources that can support different and contradictory interpretations of the relevant facts. It produces, through a formal and highly regulated process of negotiation, an objective account upon which one elaborates a strategy of action. The decision to arrest somebody, to describe in a particular way the social reality of a neighbourhood, and the elaboration of new legal proposals all lead to the production of public documents as sources of authoritative information that will be used in other decision-making processes or organizational settings.

In this chapter, I consider the second and fourth points, focusing on one of the institutional actors involved in the social construction of migrant criminality, namely the judicial system. More precisely, I show the common institutional practices and cognitive frameworks by which migrants as criminals are recognized, evaluated, investigated and treated by the judicial system, and the commonsense cognitive framework that dominates judges, prosecutors and lawyers.[2]

THE PROBLEM

I limit my analyses to two types of criminal cases that constitute the bulk of allegations of migrant crimes for prosecutors, judges and lawyers. They both derive from red-handed arrest (*arresto in flagranza*). On the one hand, I study minor crimes like theft, aggravated theft, pick pocketing, and shoplifting. On the other hand, I study drug dealing. These two type of crimes – predatory crimes and drug dealing – involve two different branches of the Italian judicial system. Predatory crimes – except for robberies – are reviewed by the local magistrates' court (*Pretura Penale*). Drug selling, in contrast, is reviewed by the criminal court (*Tribunale Penale*). Furthermore, I only focus on cases reviewed under a special type of trial: the summary trial (*Processo per direttissima*).[3]

The crime and the defendant's penal responsibility are evaluated by the three main actors involved – the prosecutor, the judge and the lawyer – at four different moments:

1. the confirmation of the arrest by the prosecutor and the decision about the count of indictment,
2. the validation hearing,
3. the decision about precautionary measures, and
4. the trial (summary trial).

In each single phase, legal general indications have to be implemented and translated into practical rules, procedures and expectation systems. A decision in a judicial setting involves three related processes:

1. to get to a plausible definition of the facts reconstructing what happened, using reflexively a contingent corpus of knowledge, rules and theories that interplay with the practical courses of action under evaluation;
2. to show, by undertaking the above process, the actor's own professional competence in managing the everyday contingencies of work (Sudnow, 1965); and
3. to redefine constantly and through a decision-making process apparently oriented toward an external object, the different types of relationships among the actors and the professional community involved in the decision-making process (Wieder, 1974).

Pastore's work on the normative production of migrant criminality in Italy brings to the fore the vulnerability of migrants as prosecuted foreigners, which becomes an essential element in assessing the fairness of the process (Pastore, 1995). First, we have to take into consideration the lack of residence permits and, more generally, the fragile legal position concerning the rights of migrants facing criminal allegations. Second, we need to take into account migrants' precarious socioeconomic conditions in terms of housing, job, family and social networks. As I show later, both elements play a role in the standard treatment of criminal cases involving migrants. However, in this chapter, I want to focus on how these elements, which can be summarized through the social type of 'irregular, marginal and socially excluded' migrant criminal, are used in the treatment of criminal cases.

This is not, of course, the only 'social type' invoked by prosecutors, judges and lawyers. Nevertheless, it includes the elements that are most frequently manipulated and invoked to make sense of the involvement of migrants in criminal activities and to justify the legal measures taken against them.

The strong association between a migrant's legal status and living conditions on the one hand, and his or her inclination to get involved in criminal activities on the other, permeates everyday activities in the criminal courts. This association tends to assume and reproduce the classical division between labouring and dangerous classes (Chevalier, 1976). The crucial variable used to evaluate a migrant's normal or deviant behaviour is employment, or more precisely, a regular job. Equating normality with formal employment plays a crucial role in the evaluation of a defendant's personality and the circumstances under which the crime takes place. Thus, a migrant's legal position and degree of integration in the formal or informal labour market determine his or her position *vis-à-vis* the courts.

Let us now look at the role of this 'social type' in the criminal court of Milan in cases of petty larceny, theft and drug dealing involving foreign defendants. I focus on two steps of the crime cases: decisions about precautionary measures and decisions about probation.

Validation of an Arrest and the Decision about Security Measures

The validation of an arrest itself does not involve any actual and careful evaluation of the circumstances under which police officers decide to arrest a suspect. The validation is the mere fulfilment of simple formal procedures. Judges limit themselves to checking that the time passed from the time of the arrest to the request of a validation hearing does not exceed 24 hours. Usually, any arrest is validated on this formal ground.

The foreign, irregular, socially excluded, criminal migrant as a category of practice enters the process and starts playing a relevant role when, after the validation hearing, the prosecutor requests precautionary measures. On precautionary measures, the Italian penal code states that, if there is clear evidence of a defendant's guilt, three risks have to be taken into account. These are the risk of escape, the risk of the defendant committing other crimes before the trail, and the risk of the defendant interfering with police investigations.

Therefore, we should focus on the organizational operations and activities that use (and are based on) the penal code as an official classification scheme (Atkinson, 1978; Cicourel, 1968; Sudnow, 1965; Taylor, 1982). Precautionary measures have to be set before the trial, when the only judicially valid act is the validation of the arrest, which is decided, as we mentioned above, on a strictly formal basis. Up to this moment of the criminal procedure, the defendant is presumed innocent by law. Nevertheless, a set of factors are put together to make a decision regarding precautionary measures. This problem resembles the classic case studied by Sudnow (1965). We have general legal categories that have to be interpreted in each case with an evaluation of the defendant's personality and the circumstances under which the crime was committed. What is relevant here is not the penal code *per se*, but how prosecutors, judges and defenders use and manipulate the formal rules to accomplish their practical tasks.

Using evidence collected during fieldwork, we can highlight some basic factors in typical descriptions of the defendants the police provided to the prosecutor. Let us look at some excerpts from my interviews:

It is a controversial matter. There are more or less two different orientations. On the one hand, you can find some lower court judges who usually decide against precautionary measures if the defendant has not got any previous offences. On the other hand, you can find other judges who put the defendant under precautionary custody only because he is a migrant, with no clear name and address and without a residence permit. They think that irregularity does not allow the defendant any alternative source of income than crime ... so they assume that the defendant is very likely to commit other offences.

(Judge from local magistrate's court)

We have many problems with homeless people. If you do not take precautionary measure against a drug addict, with no permanent residence and without a job, as soon as you set him free he will commit a new crime. He does not have any other alternative. We have the same problem with people from the Third World. Between 55 and 70 per cent of people arrested from the Third World have no permanent residence or regular job. They are living in Italy illegally, searching for something on which to survive. They are beggars; sometimes they sell smuggled tobacco. They always find their way out. These factors do not leave you any room for alternative measures to precautionary custody in prison. We are supposed to evaluate the seriousness of the crime, but we also have to consider the defendant's character and way of life.

(Judge from the local magistrate's court)

To be honest, I think we do not discriminate on any basis. We do not have any kind of prejudice. However, if you do not have any document, any permanent residence, any job, how can I control you before the trial unless I put you under precautionary custody in prison? I cannot put you under custody in your house. How can I order the police to control you if you do not have a permanent residence? You can tell me that your brother lives in Bologna, but if I trust you, you are going to hide and after one or two days, you are going to start selling drugs again. You can start selling drugs under an alias. I cannot follow you and control you if your name and address are not clearly established.

(Judge from the criminal court)

The first two elements that prosecutors and judges take into consideration are the identification of the defendant and the evaluation of his or her legal position. Defendants have not always been correctly identified The standard description relies on an absence of identification documents, identity card, passport, residence permit or other official document that would allow the authorities to check the real name and address of the person arrested. Sometimes, later during a trial, a lawyer will suggest that a defendant should present documentation to establish his or her identity and the defendant will produce a regular residence permit and passport. However, unless defendants happen to have these documents on their person when they are arrested, they appear in police and prosecutor's reports as unidentified. As one prosecutor put it:

Another big problem is identification because we never know for sure their identity. They are like ghosts. Moreover, some organizations produce false documents and sell them to undocumented migrants. If the migrants clandestinely enter across Italian borders, they do not have any document (passport); therefore, they are persons whose identity is unknown and impossible to verify. The first time the police check him he gives a false name and address, the second, third and fourth times the same thing happens. I have prosecuted persons who ended up with 20 different names and addresses. We can only rely on fingerprints, so we know that the same person has given 20 different names and addresses to the police, but we do not know his real name and address. This state of affairs has plenty of consequences. We risk putting on trial and convicting a person under a false name that can be absolutely made up or belong to another person.

(Prosecutor from the attorney's office at the local magistrate's court)

The first information the police and prosecutor provide to establish the defendants' relevant 'sociological' characteristics concerns their legal status. The real problem is how to check their real names and addresses. The standaid 'solution' is to consider the defendant's identity to be uncertain, by definition. Two cases come to the fore. First, there are foreign defendants who have no regular document when arrested and so are considered 'illegal' migrants. Second, there are foreigners who have regular documents with them when arrested, but who are nevertheless considered to be incorrectly identified, implying that their documents could be false but that it would be a waste of time and money to check the legality of the documents through consulates or Interpol. In any case, a defendant's identity cannot be known for sure until the police have checked his or her fingerprints and have communicated the results to the prosecutor.

The next step involves the judge's evaluation of the chances of the defendant committing new crimes. To reach and justify this decision, the judge usually looks at the defendant's lifestyle and infers the chances of reoffending from the existence of alternative sources of income. The judge verifies the presence of official documents that prove that the defendant has a regular job. Information about legal status and job situation is linked because a migrant can only have a regular job if he has a residence permit. In the next step, the judge considers the economic deprivation that characterized the defendant's social situation. For the judge, economic deprivation through the lack of a regular job or income leaves the defendant with no alternative other than to get involved in criminal activities.

The link between reliable identification, job and residence generates the alleged social background that explains the crime and the core of the evaluation of the defendant's future behaviour.

In applying the penal code, interpretative procedures and formal characteristics of practical reasoning (Garfinkel and Sacks, 1970) are fully at work. The actors have to provide accounts of any decision taken to carry out working routines in institutionalized contexts. They use their 'commonsense knowledge of social structure' (Cicourel, 1973) to create adequate and persuasive accounts for all practical purposes. Any decision on how to classify a piece of evidence is impossible without a previous understanding of what is happening and without projecting this background knowledge onto the data we think are relevant to confirm it. Moreover, practical reasoning is only possible if we can rely on ad hoc considerations representing invariant properties of practical reasoning. Rules recorded in legal codes cannot explain the behaviour of those who operate in the court of justice. Prosecutors, judges and lawyers invoke them *ex post facto* as rhetorical devices to justify the decision taken and the adoption of ad hoc procedures in organizational contexts that define actors' goals.

Probation

I will now shift to decisions about probation and extenuating or aggravating circumstances. In terms of precautionary measures, both local magistrates' courts and criminal courts exhibit the above-mentioned pattern. However, when decisions about probation are at stake, we can see divergent patterns in the way typical crimes and responsibilities are assessed.[4]

Context bound considerations involving evaluating the seriousness of the crime generate two social categories of 'foreign, irregular, socially excluded, criminal migrant'. In the criminal court, this categorization works in the same direction we describe above. Prosecutors and judges cannot make a positive prognosis even if the defendant had not committed previous crimes, for he cannot demonstrate his real identity and alternative sources of income. Moreover, given the difficulty of establishing his real identity, his lack of records has to be taken for granted because he could have committed crimes under different names – and an accurate control through police records can be incompatible with the schedule of the trial.

Instead, at local magistrates' courts, where the accused are prosecuted for minor predatory crimes, the same elements that lead to a negative evaluation of precautionary measures are often used to reduce the conviction or for a favourable decision about probation. The crime is assimilated as an act committed out of necessity because of economic and social deprivation. Probation is given even after more than two recurrences of the same crime. Drug selling is considered a more socially dangerous activity than shoplifting, pick pocketing or stealing. Consequently, the same social conditions invoked to define an act as committed under necessity to grant probation constitute the basis for negating probation in another court. There is no direct relationship between the two contexts as each of the courts is totally independent of the other – and, in many cases, prosecutors and judges working in the criminal court are unaware of practices in the local magistrates' court.

Some of my colleagues think that if we cannot get the real name and address of the defendant we cannot say that he is not going to commit other offences. I do not agree with them. I think that, on the same grounds, without clear identification we cannot say that he is going to commit other crimes. This consideration has a relevant impact on the decision about probation or about any other alternatives to prison. Some of the legal alternatives available are not enforceable in the case of a convicted migrant. He is not going to ask to be put under the supervision of the social services. He does not even know that he has this option. Nobody informs him about it. He does not have relatives, or a good lawyer. As a consequence, many of the norms are not actually available or applied in the case of migrants.

(Judge from local magistrates' court)

You do an overall evaluation. You consider his way of living, as established by law. You verify if he has a residence, a source of income, some documents, if he did not commit previous crimes, or if committed minor ones, I think he deserves to be put on probation. However, it is more difficult when you face a defendant with ten previous crimes, some of them committed in the last few months. You cannot believe that if you put this person on probation he will not commit other crime. It is a case by case evaluation.

(Judge from local magistrates' court)

Every time we can put someone on probation, when the law allows us to do it, we do it. But we have to be able to formulate a positive prognosis about the defendant's future behaviour. In many cases, we prosecute defendants with no clear name and address, documents that can tell us that the persons has not been prosecuted many times under a different name ... we face a person without a stable job, without permanent residence within the territory of the Italian state. Sometimes they end up having clean records but this is irrelevant. I could show you piles and piles of sentences of the same person under a different name. Upon this basis, we are not going to put anyone on probation.

(Judge from the criminal court)

When a judge is called to make a decision on precautionary measures or on probation, he finds himself in a situation where the penal code does not provide precise rules to link an abstract rule to practical cases. Behaviour, actions, situations and personalities cannot be evaluated with codified definitions. There is no rule that automatically translates what is established in the penal code into what is actually decided. In fact, 'the rules of translation' have to be found elsewhere: in the consideration of crimes as typical or atypical, in consideration of typical or atypical circumstances. However, 'typical' offenders, circumstances and crimes are not legal categories. As categories of practice, they are put together using sociologically relevant information that produces 'normal crimes' and 'normal offenders' (Sudnow, 1965). The latter are symbolic constructions of a particular society; they concern the most common crimes and the offenders, and are a reflection of the actors' knowledge of the social structure.

The normality of crimes and criminals, in this case of 'normal' crime committed by 'normal irregular, economically deprived, migrant criminal' defines a category of practice that is constantly invoked to recognize each occurrence as party of the category. Each new occurrence confirms the category in a process of circular determination.[5]

CONCLUSION

To conclude, I would like to address briefly three related aspects. First, the social category of 'irregular, marginal, criminal migrant' represents only one of the cognitive and organizational devices used by social actors involved in the administration of justice to do their work and to deal with what is called 'migrant criminality'. Ethnic peculiarities, cultural variables and personal characteristics all play a role in the definition of migrants as criminals. More important, these categorization devices often interplay with each other and complicate the social categories that judges, prosecutors and lawyers use to account for both the defendant's behaviour and personality – as particular examples of the overall phenomenon of migrants' criminality – and to evaluate the defendant's attitude during the trial. A typical example of an alternative social category that recently became commonsensical regards people from Albania. Police officers, prosecutors and judges describe them as culturally, socially and economically 'crime-driven' people who choose to immigrate with a clear criminal project in mind. This criminal project would have its roots in Albanian traditional cultural traits, as well as in the recent economic, social and political crisis of the country that has pushed thousands of Albanians towards Italy in the last few years.

Second, I want to highlight the similarities between the social category of 'irregular, marginal, criminal migrant' used as a strategic device in courts and the typical description provided by the mass media, particularly the press. Research recently conducted in Milan (Maneri, 1995 and 1997) shows how during the 1990s there was a shift in the newspapers from news about racist attacks on migrants towards a social representation of migrants as criminals or potential criminals. This change of focus in the press was accomplished after some feature articles published in the early 1990s drew attention to a drop in the migrants' standard of living and their marginalization in the metropolitan areas of northern Italy. Here we can see again at work the usual category of migrants as irregular and desperate individuals without any alternative but to become involved in criminal activities.

Finally, I would like to make a remark about social scientists' use of official data to assess migrant criminality. As I mentioned above, magistrates are involved in an everyday explanatory process that uses and reproduces social categories. They have to build up a plausible story. Newspapers headlines, police descriptions, prosecutors and judges all provide explanatory theories about crime, the circumstances under which it takes place, the defendants' personalities and the social environment from which they come. These explanatory theories are seldom used as theories about crime. They constitute a cognitive linkage through which reality is perceived, defined and constructed. In many cases, they are rather similar to scientific theories on deviance and crime based on official data on criminal statistics. Thus, on the one hand, we have commonsense theories used to support the decision-making process in criminal procedures, as well as police departments that provide crime records collected in official data. On the other hand, we have scientific theories originating from, or verified or falsified through, an analysis of the empirical evidence provided by official data that incorporate, as constitutive elements, the same theories they are supposed to verify. As a matter of fact, statistical data, as a mathematical elaboration of the set of individual crime records, cannot be separated from the system of organized activities and the commonsense practical reasoning within which they were brought into existence (Atkinson, 1978; Cicourel, 1968).

For these reasons, it is crucial to consider and analyse the overall process of production, reproduction and circulation of shared social meanings of migrant criminality. This is done by taking into consideration multiple and specialized social actors such as the media, different types of political actors (political parties and associations), as well as other branches of the public bureaucracy.

Notes

1. In Milan, nine main social actors can be identified. They are the national and local governments, the national and local political system, the state and local police apparatus, the judicial system, the national and local bureaucracies, the mass media, the neighbourhood associations, moral 'entrepreneurs' active at the local level, and scholars that from different disciplinary background work on migrant crime.

2. I draw on the same ethnographic research – involving participant observation and semi-structured interviews with judges, public attorneys, lawyers and interpreters – as I did in the criminal courts of Milan in 1997.

3. Under the Italian procedural penal code, a summary trial can be requested by the prosecutor when the defendant has been arrested red-handed and the prosecutor believes that there is no need for further investigation, proof or evidence to prosecute the accused.

4. I do not consider the impact of an effective defence lawyer or the role played by interpreters during the different phases of criminal procedures against non-Italian speakers. The court usually appoints the lawyer and the most common strategy is based on plea-bargaining to get a reduced conviction. The arrest report provided by the police represents the single piece of evidence and most of the defenders consider impossible to show evidence against it.

5. Likewise, the social condition, recidivism and legal status of the defendants cannot be inferred with a high degree of reliability from the crime files. In the majority of cases, the information available – both for judges and for prosecutors – is insufficient to establish the defendant's legal status and migratory history. The same can be said for their crime careers.

16 Mediation: From Dispute Resolution to Social Integration[1]

Jean-Pierre Bonafe-Schmitt

Since the late 1970s, mediation has been developing in all fields of social life, including the professional and familial areas and in neighbourhood and government services (Bonafe-Schmitt, 1992). What are the reasons for this renewal of mediation? It is true that mediation has always existed as a way of resolving disputes. But the context has changed. Nowadays, mediation is a response to an unprecedented crisis in the judicial system.

Mediation is often presented as an alternative to the judiciary and as an answer to the crisis in the judicial system, of which the most visible causes are overworked courts, long delays before cases come to court, complexity, formalities and the high cost of procedures. But, the crisis of the judiciary is just one facet of a generalized crisis in our system of social regulation. We too often forget that, in the past, most disputes were resolved within the family, neighbourhood or school. However, those traditional places of regulation are also going through a crisis, which is why the judiciary and, above all, the police are more and more being called upon to resolve minor disputes.

To address the crisis in the mechanisms of social regulation, the authorities in various countries, especially the USA, have sought to develop alternatives to the judiciary model, such as mediation, conciliation and arbitration. Since forms of legal mediation like victim–offender or family mediation have gone through their most important development in the past few years, I would like to devote special attention to social or community mediation programmes, for they conform to another logic of mediation. These experiments reveal the emergence of a new mode of social regulation (or model of action) that rules relations between individuals and, more broadly, between the state and civil society.

REGULATION AND SOCIALIZATION AT THE NEIGHBOURHOOD
LEVEL

Over the last few years, events at Vénissieux and Vaulx-en-Velin in
France and at Los Angeles in the USA have highlighted the deficiencies
of social regulations in the neighbourhoods of big cities and showed how
the slightest dispute can degenerate into a riot.

The Crisis in the System of Social Regulation

Though we cannot claim that the nature of disputes has changed, the multiplication of quasi riots over the past two decades reveals a new form of
dispute. In our societies, conflicts linked with material reproduction, such
as labour disputes, appear to have lost their centrality. Whereas new conflicts have appeared 'in the fields of cultural reproduction' (Habermas,
1981: 390), social integration and socialization, they create new problems
for quality of life, equal rights, the individual, personal achievement and
social identity (Habermas, 1981: 432). These types of dispute suggest
some form of resistance both to attempts to colonize everyday life
(Habermas, 1981) and to the consequences of a way of life that is getting
more collective and more complex (in the realms of neighbourhood,
family, intercommunity, consumer and environmental disputes). Their
regulation requires new modes of conflict resolution that are more consensual, for they are based on conciliation and communication rather than
on sanction or compensation. The point is no longer to settle a problem by
proclaiming who is right and who is wrong, 'but to resolve a problem that
is raised among the persons who are to carry on living side by side'
(Vescovi, 1983: 17).

It is in the underprivileged suburbs of the big cities that we can best
evaluate the failure of the welfare state's continuing rationalization of
conflict regulation procedures. This is done through the proliferation of
specialists like social workers, special education workers and youth
leaders in social centres, the police and the judiciary (Bonafe-Schmitt et
al., 1992: 72). Superimposing institutions that worked in the same district
for most of the time without any coordination did not prevent social
explosions. This leads us to understand that social disorganization is not
resolved efficiently by increasing the strength of social workers,
magistrates and policemen.

To remedy this situation in France, the state, in collaboration with local communities, launched various urban policies (*politiques de la ville*) through successive neighbourhood social development procedures (*développement social des quartiers*) and city contracts (*contrats villes*). But, in practice, these procedures did not lead to any fundamental change in the action logic of the different institutions. Partnership remains marginal and is usually more idle talk than actual application. In the social sphere, it is necessary to put an end to 'social Taylorism' and to rethink modes of social regulation in neighbourhoods. Indeed, it is important to remember that family, church, school or neighbourhood resolved most disputes in the past. But, the infiltration of the welfare state through all the pores of social life has led to a questioning of these intermediary structures between state and civil society. This explains why the police, judiciary and social workers are now the only interlocutors in most of the disputes that used to be resolved within the family or neighbourhood.

The Creation of Proximity Structures

Social mediation is based on the idea that the neighbourhood needs to be recognized as a relevant place of conflict institutionalization, which implies the creation of proximity structures. This is why special attention has been paid to the localization of mediation places in social mediation programmes. Mostly they take place in first-floor apartment blocks in the heart of the neighbourhood so that they are easily noticeable and accessible to residents.

The specificity of social mediation programmes is that they are based on the implication that the residents are the mediators. This distinguishes mediation from some other experiments such as the *Maison de Justice* (House of Justice) in France (Cf. Dourlens and Vidal-Naquet 1993 and Wyvekens 1995). Advocates of mediation aim not only to resolve disputes, but also to encourage communication and create socialization places. For this reason, special attention is paid to the choice of mediators, who are selected to accord with the socio-demographic composition of the neighbourhood. The reason for the great diversity of this representation is that the mediators are considered less as the defenders of their communities than as a link between them. On this issue, French social mediation programmes differ from US community mediation programmes. They reflect the differences in integration patterns based on the French 'republican or universalistic' model as against the Anglo-Saxon 'community or differential' model.

A Socialization Place

Social mediation programmes are not restricted to the mere institution-alization of modes of dispute resolution in the neighbourhoods; their point is also to encourage socialization by sending for some residents to be mediators. The point of the structure is not to do justice, but to give rise to actions that aim to rebuild some forms of sociability from the dispute regulation and at reconstituting socialization places. The affirmation of this principle implies that mediators need to be residents in the neighbour-hood and that any potential psychological or legal qualification must not be a primary criterion in the selection of mediators. This absence of pro-fessional references does not mean that mediators have not been trained in mediation, for the process of mediation cannot be improvised and requires the attainment of some skills.

By appealing to the active participation of the disputants, persons in charge of social mediation programmes pursue the objective of creating a place of dispute institutionalization and regulation calling for legitimacy that may be termed 'social legitimacy'. This legitimacy is based on the ability of mediation structures to be recognized by the residents of these neighbourhoods as relevant places of dispute resolution, thus contributing to the reconstitution of social relations in these degraded neighbourhoods. This form of legitimacy cannot be enacted; it is rather gained through practical experience, the passing months and the trust the disputants have put in them when they referred directly to the neighbourhood mediation instance before any preliminary referral to the judiciary.

THE DIFFERENT KINDS OF LOGIC OF SOCIAL MEDIATION

Social mediation is a plural phenomenon because, as a mode of social regulation, it is underlain by different kinds of logic that have led us to distinguish forms of mediation linked with dispute resolution from those linked with communication.

Mediation Activities Linked with Dispute Resolution Activities

Social mediation experiments adhere to a logic that is different from the logic of judiciary mediation. Their purpose is to create new regulation places in the neighbourhood by sending for the residents to take part in the resolution of disputes. The aim is not the creation of a parallel judiciary system, but rather to settle socialization places.

Paralegal Neighbourhood Mediation: A Logic of Integration

The archetype of this mediation programme was given to us by the Valence experiment in 1985, followed by the one in Ulis in 1989. These generated a model of neighbourhood dispute resolution in which municipalities and public prosecutors' offices joined forces to combat feelings of insecurity and to rebuild social relations in the wider neighbourhood. A particular feature of these experiments is that they were set up jointly by municipalities and public prosecutors' offices and that neighbourhood residents were asked to perform the role of mediators.

The programme in Valence was an excellent illustration of the logic of social integration, for its aim was to re-establish 'social peace' in degraded neighbourhoods by trying, through mediation, to resolve those everyday family, neighbour or ethnic disputes that undermine social relations.

To bring this mediation programme into operation, magistrates used the structures of the Communal Council for the Prevention of Delinquency (*Conseil communal de Prévention de la Délinquance* or CCPD) to mobilize all the institutions that had been selected to intervene in the neighbourhood. Another manifestation of the logic of social integration was in the choice of criteria for selecting the mediators, who were recruited from among the neighbourhood's residents. However, the decision to use non-professionals did not mean that the mediators were left to themselves. On the contrary, a tight link was forged between the mediation service and the judiciary. The mediators received their cases from public prosecutors' offices and the results of their mediations were checked, but not controlled, by magistrates.

This type of mediation has limited application, for now, more than ten years after the Valence experiment began, it has been adopted in only a limited number of cities. Some of the earliest programmes were carried out in the Essonne district (*département*), as in Ulis and Gif sur Yvette.

Social or Neighbourhood Mediation: A Logic of Reappropriation

As far as we know, the first neighbourhood mediation took place in the

'Themis/Boutique de Droit' (law shop) experiment in Lyons. It brought lawyers and neighbourhood residents together at the very first referral by the disputants, who lived or worked in the same neighbourhood, in this case Perrache/Lyon (Bonafe-Schmitt et al., 1992: 145). For many years, this programme served as an example for similar mediation structures in other cities such as Nantes, Vénissieux, Décines, Saint Priest and Villefontaine.

These neighbourhood mediation programmes are distinguishable from the Valence one in that they try to develop an element of voluntarism in the residents' direct referral to these structures. It is usually on the CCPD's initiative that mediation programmes centred on direct referral by residents are set up for cases that have not arisen through a complaint to the police, as in the Saint Priest CCPD programme. Most cases, however, are tinged with both civil and penal aspects, such as neighbourhood disputes linked with noise nuisance, different lifestyles and conflicts between youths and adults.

Such mediation programmes not only establish mediation structures in the neighbourhood but they recruit mediators who live in the neighbourhood and who are trained in this type of intervention. The success of this kind of mediation structure depends on the residents recognizing the legitimacy of their interventions, which in turn implies being well integrated into the neighbourhood. Training neighbourhood mediators also has a socializing function in that it encourages the community to favour this form of dispute resolution and creates new solidarities.

Despite the support of the *Delegation interministérielle à la Ville* (urban ministry), neighbourhood mediation programmes did not develop to the same extent as community mediation programmes did in the USA. There are fewer than 15 of them in France, whereas there are more than 400 in the USA. The USA's faster pace of community mediation development compared with France can partly be explained by the different principles that give rise to the mediation programmes in these two countries.

Mediations Linked to Communication Activities

Mediation cannot be restricted to dispute resolution; it also extends to so-called 'communication activities'. This category includes all forms of intervention by a third party that has a lot to do with mediation but are not primarily dedicated to dispute resolution.

Public Interventions

The development of mediation techniques to improve communications between communities and public utilities is usually at the city's initiative. Some municipalities engage 'intercultural mediators', recruited from the foreign-origin communities, to improve modes of communication and promote better integration. The terminological choice is not neutral, for the designation 'intercultural mediator' actually hides the existence of real 'community mediators'. Indeed, they are mostly recruited from their community of origin and given the role of intermediary precisely to promote better integration in these populations.

Many of the mediators trying to improve communications between communities and the public utilities are recruited from among so-called *personnes-relais* (relay people), or more often *femmes-relais* (relay women). A recent survey underlined the ambiguity of their function – they have no clearly defined role and do not have the advantage of any particular status, yet are given the title of mediator and allowed to follow a proper training (Delcroix et al., 1995).

In the field of education, some people who are not on the Ministry of Education staff intervene as mediators. Depending on the programme, they are called either *parents-relais* or intercommunity mediators. Their functions are established by city initiatives or by organizations that are associated with or work in the field of immigration. The mission assigned to these mediators is to facilitate communication between schools and families of foreign origin and to help teachers organize extra-curricular activities. This strand of mediation is close to that of the school mediators set up by the Ministry of Education on 25 April 1996 to facilitate a dialogue between teachers and parents of children from another culture and speaking a foreign language.

Over the past three or four years, on the initiative of either the state or individual cities, 'cultural' or 'library' mediators have been introduced alongside the intercultural ones. There is an instrumental logic to the creation of these new functions, for, in the case of the Lyons municipal library, they both help libraries handle 'difficult publics' and direct them towards participating in the fight against social exclusion.

Community Interventions

In the cultural field, some non-profit-making organizations have become involved in a number of initiatives to fight social exclusion. One such example is ATD Quart Monde, which set up book mediators (*mediateurs du livres*) in underprivileged neighbourhoods by using residents to fulfil the functions of cultural activity leaders (Kupier, 1996). The logic behind these experiments is that excluded people should reappropriate their own cultural activities.

On the legal level, non-profit-making organizations such as law shops (*boutiques de droit*) give legal advice and serve as 'legal mediation places'. Unlike other professional lawyers, those in the *boutiques de droit* merely give legal advice and leave it up to the users to decide whether or not to proceed. They also fulfil a mediation role by giving the user's enquiry a legal interpretation, or by decoding complex language used by public or private organizations to make the communication easier.

MEDIATION: A NEW PATTERN OF SOCIAL REGULATION

Mediation is not limited to mere communication or methods of dispute resolution; it carries a new regulation pattern and a new mode of action that promise to restore relations between the state and civil society.

Mediation: A New Pattern of Action

An analysis of the mediation phenomenon cannot be restricted to mere methods of dispute resolution used by welfare states to spread their social control, or to the new appearance of participants on the dispute resolution market. Mediation is also a new social movement, a new form of common action, implying a restoration of relations between the state and civil society through the creation of 'intermediary places of social regulation' (Laville, 1994: 46). To this extent, the process of mediation carries another conception of the actor and the action in the sense that the mediators are 'meaning actors' (*acteur de sens*) (Laville, 1994: 47), willing to participate in the reconstitution of new 'intermediary structures' between the state and citizens. The point is to create new socialization and regulation places, new 'existential communities' (*communautées existentielles*) (White, 1994: 46) that would be founded on forms of solidarity that would appeal to a communicational rather than an instrumental rationality.

We are prudent in our use of the notion of community, especially nowadays that traditional communities have been 'dismantled, disrupted and disorganized by the consequences of the modern rationality', and when others are rising from 'religious fundamentalism, ethnic chauvinism, cults or other non rational phenomenon' (White, 1994: 47). However, we hypothesize that the mediation process is likely to produce a new form of common action (Giraud, 1993) that would allow the constitution of new forms of solidarity, a new common identity through the existence of these existential communities.

Even if social mediation programmes rest on new forms of actions and activities that are not directed by interests or power relations, this has not stopped the authorities considering these new functions as opportunities to create new jobs. Thus, mediation creates proximity jobs, sometimes called *petits boulots* (low-income jobs), which should be useful in the fight against the rise in unemployement.

Mediation: A New Pattern of Social Regulation

Social mediation programmes rest on the idea that an approach in term of conflict is ill adapted to the resolution of certain types of conflicts, such as neighbourhood disputes. For this type of case, it is advisable to privilege a mode of dispute resolution that uses a 'negociatory' or 'therapeutic' approach (Silbey and Sarat, 1989: 479). Mediation is the only type of intervention that is able to rebuilt future relations between the parties by considering their problems as primary rather than abstract notions.

But, the development of mediation comes up against a tendency towards the judicialization of social relations or 'colonization of everyday life', to quote Habermas. According to him, for some disputes it would be proper to adopt procedures that aim to achieve a consensus, namely procedures that consider the parties as major participants able to represent their own interests and manage their affairs by themselves. The elaboration of a rationale built on consensus should not be confused with the search for a 'lax consensus', but rather for a 'dissensus' in order to reach an agreement (Debarbieux, 1995: 142). In constructing this agreement, it is necessary to look for points of disagreement as well as of agreement, for the problem is not to reduce disagreements but to be able to live with them, to find a *modus vivendi*. By implicating the parties more in the dispute resolution, mediation allows them not only to overcome their disagreements, but also to build new relations, thus further reinforcing the normative character of the decisions made. This quest for a new consensus built on negotiated rules often, especially in big cities, makes the reconstruction of torn social relations possible. In large cities, where former community pressures no longer function, the negotiations or mediation favour the reconstitution of new socialization and regulation places.

SOCIAL MEDIATION: A COUNTERCULTURE

Nowadays, the changes should not be overestimated, for the emergence of this alternative pattern of dispute regulation has its own difficulties. This should lead us to interpret the changes, not in terms of rupture, but in terms of transformation and adaptation to the present system.

The Culture of 'Resorting to Force' Relations

If it is impossible to negate the importance of force, violence and power in social relations, it is, however, fitting to question the theories that 'end up analysing all social relations as resorting to force relations' (Boltanski, 1990). In the light of these ideas, it is fitting to re-examine the notions of compromise and agreement, which result not from a conflict logic but from a logic of cooperation, in which the mutual interests of the parties involved in the negotiation process are respected.

The culture of 'resorting to force' relations is one reason why only 50 to 70 per cent of disputants, depending on the mediation office, agree to engage in mediation at all (Bonafe-Schmitt et al., 1992: 145). Of these parties, despite the mediators' efforts, only between 70 and 90 per cent reach agreement. All this tends to show the strength of resistance to the development of a consensual mode of dispute resolution.

The analysis in terms of an evolution from a model of dispute to a more consensual one has been sharply criticized by numerous US authors. They denounce the 'ideology of harmony' on the grounds that it does not consider the inequality of power in US society. According to them, the ideology of harmony rests on dispute denial, for its subject is not to prevent the causes of the disputes but to prevent their expression (Abel, 1981; Nader, n.d.). They emphasize that the followers of this ideology encourage the parties to see only alienation, hostility and excessive cost in judicial proceedings, and a process that encourages civic and community responsibility in mediation. They reject the view that mediation transforms conflicts into communication problems and disputes about rights into relational or affective differences. Speaking more broadly, the ideology of harmony seems to carry a particular model of society that is based on the belief that everyone shares the same goals and values, which as a consequence would favour better pacification of populations through the extension of social control.

The Lack of Cases

All things considered, quantitatively speaking social mediation is a marginal phenomenon given that the number of recorded cases dealt with by the different mediation offices varies between 30 and 100 a year. This number is very low compared with the number of cases registered for the different jurisdictions' proceedings.

Qualitatively speaking, disputes dealt with by social mediators usually have something to do with neighbourhood troubles. The great majority of these troubles are over noise nuisance, relationship problems and conflicts related to ownership. Without drawing up a dispute typology, under noise nuisances are household appliances such as washing machines, drills, stereos and lawn mowers; under relationship problems are conjugal quarrels, repeated parties, discussions late at night and disturbances by animals (dogs barking or roosters crowing). Relationship troubles can sometimes degenerate into insults between neighbours, menaces and racist remarks or 'rumours'. Under conflicts related to ownership are boundary disputes (overhanging tree branches, objections about property limits), as well as questions of rights, such as car parking rights.

The disputes are often of an everyday kind and do not usually warrant police intervention, still less judicial proceedings. Yet, these are precisely the types of issues which, because they are subject to repetition − neighbourhood disputes, minor damage to goods, altercations with gangs of youths − create a feeling of insecurity.

CONCLUSION

Mediation is a complex and highly diverse phenomenon. Mediation programmes are not intended to solve judiciary dysfunction but to propose another model of dispute resolution based on decentralization, deprofessionalization and delegalization. For the next few years we cannot expect a fast development of social mediation, for, with the predominance of the all-powerful conflictive mode and the tendency to judicialize conflict, this mode of dispute resolution belongs to a 'counterculture'.

Despite these difficulties, the development of mediation still reveals an evolution in our societies towards more pluralism in systems of social regulation. This is especially true of social mediation, which raises questions about everything automatically being done through the state (*tout par l'état*). Indeed, it is designed less to introduce new professional regulations than to build new mediation places, new intermediary structures between the state and citizens. From a wider point of view, this pattern of mediation should allow the reconstitution of socialization places. This would foreshadow new modes of regulation that reveal not only changes in the distribution and organization of power, but also a redefinition of relations between so-called civil society and the state, and more particularly, a redefinition of the legitimacy of the power of dispute resolution.

Notes

1. This chapter is extracted from several pieces of research engaged in over the past few years, namely Bonafe-Schmitt, 1992; Bonafe-Schmitt, et al., 1992; and Bonafe-Schmitt, et al., 1995.

References

Abel, R. (1981) 'Conservative Conflict and the Reproduction of Capitalism: The Role of Informal Justice', *International Journal of the Sociology of Law*, 9 (September) 245–67.

Agozino, B. (1997) 'Changes in the Social Construct of Criminality among Immigrants in the United Kingdom', in S. Palidda (ed.) *Délit d'Immigration: Immigrant Delinquency* (Commission Européenne, COST A2).

Amsterdam in Cijfers (1996) *Amsterdam in Cijfers: Jaarboek 1996* (Amsterdam: Amsterdam Municipal Council Bureau for Research and Statistics).

Amsterdam Municipal Council (1996) *De Economie in de Regio Amsterdam 1996* (Amsterdam: Amsterdam Municipal Council, Department of Economic Affairs/Research).

Amsterdam Work Monitor (1996) *Amsterdamse Werkmonitor: De Stand van Zaken van het Werkgelegenheidsbeleid* (Amsterdam: Amsterdam Municipal Council, Department of Social and Cultural Affairs/Department of Economic Affairs) fourth quarter.

Anderson, B. (1983) *Imagined Communities: Reflections on the Origin and Spread of Nationalism* (London: Verso).

Anthias, F. and N. Yuval-Davis, (1992) *Racialized Boundaries* (London: Routledge).

Anwar, M. (1994) *Race and Elections: The Participation of Ethnic Minorities in Politics* (Coventry: University of Warwick, Monographs in Ethnic Relations) 9.

Asad, T. (1990) 'Multiculturalism and British Identity in the Wake of the Rushdie Affair', *Politics and Society*, 18 (4) 455–80

ASLK (1997) *Waarden van de Onroerende Goederen* (Brussels: ASLK).

ATIAD (1996) *Türkisches Unternehmertum in Deutschland: Die unsichtbare Kraft, Bestandsaufnahme 1996 und Perspektiven für das Jahr 2010* (Düsseldorf: ATIAD).

Atkinson, J. M. (1978) *Discovering Suicide: Studies in the Social Organization of Sudden Death* (London: Macmillian Press).

Ausländerbeauftragte des Landes Bremen (1995) Vor allem zuständig für deutsche Sauberkeit: Ausländische Beschäftigte im Öffentlichen Dienst (Bremen: Ausländerbeauftragte des Landes).

Ausländerbeauftragter des Senats der Freien und Hansestadt Hamburg 1995, Zweiter Bericht an den Senat Zur Arbeit des Ausländerbeauftragten in den Jahren 1993 bis 1995, November 1995

Austin, R. (1994) '"An honest living": Street Vendors, Municipal Regulation, and the Black Public Sphereí, *Yale Law Journal*, 103 (8) 2157–78.

AUT-AUT (1996) *Special issue* (275).

Bachrach P. and M. Baratz (1980) 'Two faces of Power', in H. Hahan and C. Levine, *Urban Politics* (London: Longman).

Bagley, C. (1973) *The Dutch Plural Society: A Comparative Study in Race Relations* (Oxford: Oxford University Press).

Baldwin-Edwards M. and M. A. Schain (eds) (1994) *The Politics of Immigration in Western Europe* (Newbury Park: Frank Cass and Company).

Barrett, S. and C. Fudge (1981) 'Reconstructing the field of analysis', in S. Barrett and C. Fudge (eds) *Policy and Action* (London: Methuen) 249–78.

Barth F. (1969a) 'Introduction', in F. Barth (ed.) *Ethnic Groups and Boundaries: The Social Organization of Culture Difference* (Oslo and London: Scandinavian University Books).

— (ed.) (1969b) *Ethnic Groups and Boundaries: The Social Organisation of Cultural Difference* (London: Allen & Unwin).

Barthes, R. (1957) *Mythologies* (Paris: Seuil).

Basch, L., N. Glick Schiller and C. Szanton Blanc (1994) *Nations Unbound: Transnational Projects, Postcolonial Predicaments, and Deterritorialized Nation-States* (Langhorne, PA: Gordon & Breach).

Bauman, Z. (1989) *Modernity and the Holocaust* (Cambridge: Polity).

— (1990) 'Modernity and Ambivalence', *Theory, Culture and Society*, 7 (2/3) 143–69.

— (1991) *Modernity and Ambivalence* (Cambridge: Polity).

— (1992) *Mortality, Immortality and Other Life Strategies* (Cambridge: Polity).

Bayer, A. E. (1965) *Surinaamse Arbeiders in Nederland* (Assen: Van Gorcum and Comp–Dr H. J. Prakke and H. M. G. Prakke).

Beauftragte der Bundesregierung für die Belange der Ausländer (1995) *Daten und Fakten zur Ausländersituation* (Bonn) December.

Bell, D. (1973) *The Coming of Post-Industrial Society: A Venture in Social Forecasting* (New York: Basic Books).

Benton, G. and H. Vermeulen (eds) (1987) *De Chinezen* (Muiderberg: Coutinho, Migranten in de Nederlandse samenleving nr. 4).

Berdowski, Z. (ed.) (1994) *Etnische Groepen in Amsterdam*. *Jaarbericht 1994* (Amsterdam: Amsterdam Municipal Council, Bureau for Research and Statistics).

Berg, H., T. Wijsenbeek and E. Fischer (eds) (1994) *Venter, Fabriqueur, Fabrikant: Joodse Ondernemers en Ondernemingen in Nederland 1976–1940* (Amsterdam: Jewish Historical Museum).

Bericht der Beauftragten der Bundesregierung für die Belange der Ausländer über die Lage der Ausländer in der Bundesrepublik Deutschland (1994) Bonn.

Bhabha, H. K. (1994) *The Location of Culture* (London: Routledge).

Bhatt, C. (1997) *Liberation and Purity* (London: UCL Press).

Bigo, D. (1996) *Police en Réseaux: L'expérience européenne* (Paris: Presses de la Fondation Nationale des Sciences Politiques).

Blom, E. and T. Romeijn (1981) 'De kracht van traditie: Hoe Chinezen succesvol opereren in het restaurantwezen', *Sociologische Gids*, 28 (3) May/June, 228–38.

Blumstein, A., J. Cohen, S. E. Martin and M. H. Tonry (1983) *Research on Sentencing: The Search for Reform* (Washington: National Academy Press).

Body-Gendrot, S. (1995) *Ville et Violence* (Paris: PUF) 2nd edn.

— (1996a) *Réagir dans les Quartiers en Crise: La Politique des Empowerment Zones* (Paris: La Documentation française).

— (1996b) 'Paris, a 'Soft' Global City?' *New Community* (October) 595–606.

— (1997) 'Marginalization and Political Responses in the French Context', in P. Hamel (ed.) *Urban Fields–Global Spaces* (London: Sage).

— (1998) 'Now You See, Now You Don't: Comments on Paul Gilroy's', *Ethnic and Racial Studies*, September, 848–58.

Bolkestein, F. (1997) *Moslims in de Polder* (Amsterdam: Uitgevrij Contact).

Boltanski, L. (1990) *L'Amour et la Justice comme Compétence: Trois essais de sociologie de l'action* (Paris: Editions Metaillé).

Bonacich, E. (1972) 'A Theory of Ethnic Antagonism: The Split Labor Market', *American Sociological Review*, 37, October, 547–9.

Bonafe-Schmitt, J.-P. (1992) *La Médiation: une justice douce* (Paris: Syros-alternative).

Bonafe-Schmitt, J.-P., N. Schmutz and R. Bonafe-Schmitt (1992) *Médiation et Régulation sociale: approche comparative, France–USA–Grande-Bretagne* (Lyons: PPSH).

Bonafe-Schmitt, J.-P., D. Jullion, N. Schmutz and R. Bonafe-Schmitt (1995) 'La Médiation pénale: approche comparative France–Etats-Unis (Lyons: PPSH).

Borgogno, V. (1990) 'Le discours populaire sur l'immigration: un racisme pratique', *Peuples méditerranéens* (51) April–June.

Bouamama, S. (1989) 'Elections municipales et immigration: essai de bilan', *Migrations-Société*, 1 (3) 25–45.

—— (1994) *Dix ans de marche des Beurs: Chronique d'un mouvement avorté* (Paris: Desclée de Brouwer).

Bovenkerk, F. and C. Fijnaut (1996) 'Georganiseerde criminaliteit in Nederland. Over allochtone en buitenlandse criminele groepen', *Inzake Opsporing. Enquêtecommissie opsporingsmethoden. Bijlage VIII, Deel I, Onderzoeksgroep Fijnaut. Autochtone, allochtone en buitenlandse criminele groepen* (Enquête Opsporingsmethoden, TK 1995–1996, 24 072) no. 17.

Bovenkerk, F. and L. Ruland (1992) 'Artisan Entrepreneurs: Two Centuries of Italian Immigration to the Netherlands', *International Migration Review*, 26/3 (Fall) 927–39.

Bovenkerk, F., A. Eijken and W. Bovenkerk-Teerink (1983) *Italiaans ijs: De opmerkelijke historie van de Italiaanse ijsbereiders in Nederland* (Meppel/Amsterdam: Boom).

Bovenkerk, F., B. den Brok and L. Ruland (1991) 'Meer, minder of gelijk? Over de arbeidskansen van hoog opgeleide leden van etnische groepen', *Sociologische Gids*, 38/3 (May/June) 174–86.

Brah, A. (1996) *Cartographies of Diaspora: Contesting Identities* (London: Routledge).

Brion, F. (1997) 'Chiffrer, Déchiffrer: Incarcération des étrangers et construction sociale de la criminalité des immigrés en Belgique', in S. Palidda (ed.) *Délit d'Immigration: Immigrant Delinquency* (European Commission, COST A2).

Bui-Trong, L. (1996) 'Incivilités et violences juvéniles', *Les Cahiers dynamiques* (4) January.

Economic Research Bureau (1994) *De Economische Betekenis van Minderheden voor de Arbeidsmarkt* (Hoofdorp: Economic Research Bureau).

Burgess, E. (1928) 'Residential Segregation in American Cities', *Annals of American Academy of Political and Social Science*, CXL, November, 105–15.

Burgers, J. and G. Engbersen (1996) 'Globalisation, Migration and Undocumented Immigrants', *New Community*, 22 (4) 619–36.

Burgers, J., P. Reinsch, E. Snel and H. Tak (1996) *Burgers als ieder ander: Een advies inzake lokaal beleid en minderheden* (Utrecht: AWSB research papers).

Canada, G. (1995) *Fist, Knife, Stick, Gun* (Boston: Beacon Press).

Canetti, E. (1992) *Crowds and Power* (London: Penguin) first edn 1960.

Castel, R. (1994) *Les métamorphoses de la question sociale* (Paris: Fayard).

— (1995) *Les Métamorphoses de la Question sociale* (Paris: Fayard).

Castles, S. and Miller, M. (1993) *The Age of Migration* (London: Macmillan).

Cesarani, D. and M. Fulbrook (1996) *Citizenship, Nationality and Migration in Europe* (London: Routledge).

Cesari, J. (ed) (1996) *Réseaux transnationaux entre L'Europe et le Maghreb* (Brussels) 2 vols.

— (1997a) *Etre musulman en France aujourd'hui* (Paris: Hachette).

— (1997b) *Faut-il avoir peur de l'Islam?* (Paris: Presses de Sciences Politiques).

Ceyhan, A. (1997) '"Migrants as a Threat": A Comparative Analysis of Securitarian Rhetoric: The European Union (France) and the United States (California)', Paper presented at the panel 'Orientation Towards Immigrants in Europe II' at the ESCA 5th Biennial International Conference (Seattle, 29 May–1 June 1997).

Chevalier, L. (1976) *Classi lavoratrici e classi pericolose: Parigi nella rivoluzione industriale* (Bari: Laterza).

Choenni, A. (1997) *Veelsoortig Assortiment: Allochtoon Ondernemerschap in Amsterdam als Incorporatietraject 1965–1995* (Amsterdam: Proefschrift Universiteit van Amsterdam).

Christopher, W. (1991) *Report of the Independent Commission on the Los Angeles Police Dept.*

Cicourel, A. V. (1968) *The Organization of Juvenile Justice* (New York: John Wiley & Sons).

— (1973) *Cognitive Sociology* (Glencoe: Free Press).

Cohen, R. (1997) *Global Diasporas: An Introduction* (London: UCL Press).

Coing, H. (1966) *Renovation urbaine et changement social* (Paris: ed. Ouvrières).

Coleman, J. S. (1990) *Foundations of Social Theory* (Cambridge, MA: The Belknap Press of Harvard University Press).

Commission de la nationalité (1988) *Entre Français aujourd'hui et demain: Rapport de la Commission de la Nationalité* (Paris: UGE-LA Documentation Français) 2 volumes.

Courbage, Y. and P. Fargues (1992) *Chrétiens et Juifs dans l'Islam arabe et turc* (Paris: Fayard).

Crowley, J. (1992) 'Le rôle de la Commission for Racial Equality dans la représentation des minorités ethniques britanniques', *Revue européenne des migrations internationales*, 6 (3) 45–61.

— (1997) *'Communautés de souffrance': le racisme comme principe d'identité* (Paris: FNSP/Ceri), working paper.

Dassetto F. (1991) *Immigrés et communes, équilibres difficiles: le cas de Saint-Josse-ten-Noode*, Sybidi Papers no. 12, Academia, Louvain-la-Neuve.

de Certeau, M. (1986) 'Economies ethniques: pour une école de la diversité', *Annales ESC*, 4.

de Corte, S. and W. de Lannoy (1994) 'De migraties van Marokkanen en Turken binnen het Brusselse Gewest in de periode 1988–1992', in E. van Hecke and M. Goossens (eds) *Liber Amicorum Herman Van der Haegen*, Acta Geographica Lovaniensia (34) 61–7.

de Graaf, H. (1986) *Plaatselijke Organisaties van Turken en Marokkanen* (The Hague: NIMAWO) 2nd edn.

de Graaf, H., R. Penninx and F. Stoové (1988) 'Minorities Policies, Social Services, and Ethnic Organisations in the Netherlands', in S. Jenkins (ed.) *Ethnic Associations and the Welfare State* (New York: Columbia University Press).

de Jong, W. (1989) 'The Developement of Inter-Ethnic Relations in an Old District of Rotterdam between 1970 and 1985', *Ethnic and Racial Studies*, 12 (2) 257–78.

de Rudder, V. (with the collaboration of M. Guillon) (1987) *Autochtones et Immigrés en Quartier populaire: D'Aligre à l'îlot Châlon* (Paris: CIEMI/L'Harmattan).

— (1991) 'Le racisme dans les relations interethniques', *L'homme et la société* (102) 75–91.

Debarbieux, E. (1995) 'Pratique de Recherche sur la Violence à l'école par une médiation sociologique', *Skholé* (2).

Defert, D. (1991) ' "Popular Life" and Insurance Technology', in Graham Burchell, Colin Gordon and Peter Miller (eds) *The Foucault Effect: Studies in Governmentality* (London: Harvester Wheatsheaf) 211–33.

Delcroix, C. et al. (1995) *Synthèse de la Recherche nationale portant sur Rôles et Perspectives des Femmes-relais en France* (Paris: ADRI).

den Boer, M. (1994) 'The Quest for European Policing: Rhetoric and Justification in a Disorderly Debate', in M. Anderson and M. den Boer (eds) *Policing Across National Boundaries* (London: Pinter) 174–96.

Deslé, E. (1990) 'Bouwen en wonen te Brussel (1945–1958): de mocizame uitbouw van de keynesiaanse welvaartstaat en de rol van de mediterrane gastarbeiders', *Belgisch Tijdschrift voor de Nieuwste Geschiedenis*, (21) 413–82.

Donzelot, J. (1993) 'The Promotion of the Social', in M. Gane and T. Johnson (eds) *Focault's New Domains* (London: Routledge) 106–38.

Dourlens, C. and P. Vidal-Naquet (1993) *L'Autorité comme Prestation: La justice et la police dans la politique de la Ville* (Paris: CERPE).

Dray, J. (1992) *Rapport 2832 sur les violences urbaines* (Assemblée Nationale).

Dumm, T. (1996) *Michel Foucault and the Politics of Freedom* (London: Sage).

Durkheim, É. (1965) *The Elementary Forms of Religious Life*, 1st edn 1912, translated by J. W. Swain (New York: The Free Press).

Elias, N. and J. L. Scotson (1965) *The Established and the Outsiders: A Sociological Enquiry into a Community Problem* (London: Frank Cass).

Engelbrektsson, U.-B. (1978) *The Force of Tradition: Turkish Migrants at Home and Abroad* (Göteborg: Acta Universitatis Gothoburgensis).

Ewald, François (1996) *Histoire de l'État providence* (Paris: Grasset).

Fagan J., and D. Wilkinson (forthcoming) 'The Functions of Adolescent Violence', in D. Elliott and B. Hamburg (eds) *Violence in Schools* (Cambridge: Cambridge University Press).

Faist, T. (1995) *Social Citizenship for Whom? Young Turks in Germany and Mexican Americans in the United States* (Aldershot: Avebury).

— (1997) 'From Common Questions to Common Concepts', in T. Hammar, G. Brochmann, K. Tamas and T. Faist (eds) *Migration, Immobility and Development: Multidisciplinary Perspectives* (Oxford: Berg) 247–76

— (1998) 'International Migration and Transnationalization', *Archives Européennes de Sociologie* (Autumn).

Fayman, S. and P. Simon (1991) *Les Activités économiques du Bas-Belleville* (Paris: Report to Urban Development Agency, Ministry of Sport, Housing and Fisheries).

Feirabend, J. and J. Rath (1996) 'Making a Place for Islam in Politics: Local Authorities Dealing with Islamic Associations', in P. S. van Koningsveld and W. A. R. Shadid, *Islam, Hinduism and Politics in Europe* (Kampen: Kok Pharos).

236   *References*

Field, S. (1984) *The Attitudes of Ethnic Minorities* (London: HMSO).
— (1991) *Trends in Crime and their Interpretation: A Study of Recorded Crime in Post-War England and Wales* (London: HMSO).
Foucault, M. (1975) *Surveiller et Punir* (Paris: Gallimard).
— (1976) *Histoire de la sexualité. 1. La volonté de savoir* (Paris: Gallimard).
— (1989) *Résumé des Cours: 1970–1982* (Paris: Julliard).
— (1991) 'Governmentality', in G. Burchell, C. Gordon and P. Miller (eds) *The Foucault Effect: Studies in Governmentality* (London: Harvester Wheatsheaf) 87–104.
— (1997) *Il faut défendre la société: Cours au Collège de France (1975–1976)* (Paris: Gallimard Seuil).
Friedrichs, J. (1997a) 'Context Effects of Poverty Neighbourhoods on Residents', in H. Vestergaard (ed.) *Housing in Europe* (Hørsholm: Danish Building Research Institute) 141–60.
Gans, H. J. (1962) *The Urban Villagers: Group and Class in the Life of Italian-Americans* (New York: Free Press Glencoe).
— (1979) 'Symbolic Ethnicity: The Future of Ethnic Groups and Cultures in America', *Ethnic and Racial Studies*, 2, (1) 1–20.
Garfinkel, H. and H. Sacks (1970) 'On Formal Structures of Practical Actions', in J. McKinney and E. A. Tiryakian, *Theoretical Sociology. Perspective and Developments* (New York: Appleton Century Crofts).
Gaskell, G. and P. Smith (1981) 'Are Young Blacks Really Alienated', *New Society*.
— (1985) 'Young Black's Hostility to the Police: An Investigation into its Causes', *New Community*, 12 (1) 66–74.
Geddes, A. (1993) 'Asian and Afro-Caribbean Representation in Elected Governments in England and Wales', *New Community*, 20 (1) 43–58.
Geisser, V. (1997) *Ethnicité républicaine: Les élites d'origine maghrébine dans le système politique français* (Paris: Presses de la Fondation Nationale des Sciences Politiques).
Gerster, F. (1996) 'Zuwanderung und Arbeitsmarkt', in Forschungsinstitut der Friedrich-Ebert-Stiftung (ed.) *Integration und Konflikt: Kommunale Handlungsfelder der Zuwanderungspolitik* (Bonn: Forschungsinstitut der Friedrich-Ebert-Stiftung) 19–34.
Giesen, B. (1991) *Die Entdinglichung des Sozialen: Eine evolutionstheoretische Perspektive auf die Postmoderne* (Frankfurt/M).
Gilroy, P. (ed.) (1982) *The Myth of Black Criminality* (London: Merlin).

— (1983) 'Police and Thieves' in Centre of Contemporary Cultural Studies (ed.) *The Empire Strikes Back: Race and Racism in Britain* (London: Hutchinson).

— (1990) 'The End of Anti-Racism', in W. Ball and J. Solomos (eds) *Race and Local Politics* (London: Macmillan) 191–209.

— (1991) 'It Ain't Where You're From, It's Where You're At. . . The Dialectics of Diasporic Identification', *Third Text* (13) 3–16.

Giraud, C. (1993) *L'Action commune* (Paris: L'Harmattan).

Gitlin, T. (1996) *The Twilight of Common Dreams* (New York: Metropolitan Books).

Goetz, E. G. (1996) 'The US War on Drugs as Urban Policy', *International Journal of Urban and Regional Research*, 20 (3) September, 539–49.

Goldberg, A. (1992) 'Selbständigkeit als Integrationsfortschritt?' *Zeitschrift für Türkeistudien* (7) 75–92.

Goossens L. (1983) 'Het sociaal huisvestingsbeleid in België sinds 1830', in Koning Boudewijn Stichting (ed.) *Sociaal Woonbeleid* (Brussels: Koning Boudewijn Stichting) 12–31.

— (1988) 'Belgium', in H. Kroes, F. Ymkers and A. Mulder (eds) *Between Owner-Occupation and Rented Sector: Housing in Ten European Countries* (Brussels: de Bilt) 215–41.

Gordon, C. (1991) 'Governmental Rationality: An Introduction', in G. Burchell, C. Gordon and P. Miller (eds) *The Foucault Effect: Studies in Governmentality* (London: Harvester Wheatsheaf) 1–51.

Gordon, D. (1988) 'The Global Economy: New Edifice or Crumbling Foundations?' *New Left Review*, 168, 24–65.

Gordon, D. M., R. Edwards and M. Reich (1982) *Segmented Work, Divided Workers: The Historical Transformation of Labour in the United States* (Cambridge: Cambridge University Press).

Gouldner, A. W. (1960) 'The Norm of Reciprocity: A Preliminary Statement', *American Sociological Review*, 25 (2) 161–78.

Grant, D. M., M. L. Oliver and A. D. James (1996) 'African Americans: Social and Economic Bifurcation', in R. Waldinger and M. Bozorgmehr (eds) *Ethnic Los Angeles* (New York: Russell Sage Foundation) 379–412.

Green, N. (1986) *The Pletzl of Paris: Jewish Immigrant Workers in the Belle Epoque* (New York: Holmes and Meier).

Grewal, S. et al (1989) *Charting the Journey* (London: Sheba).

Grossberg, L., C. Nelson and C. Treichler (eds) (1992) *Cultural Studies* (London: Routledge).

238 References

Guillon M. (1996) 'Inertie et localisation des immigrés dans l'espace parisien', *Espace, Populations, Sociétés* (1) 55–64.

Gurr, T. (1995) 'Foreword', in J. I. Ross (ed.) *Violence in Canada* (Oxford: Oxford University Press) viii–xvii.

Habermas, J. (1981) *Théorie de l'agir communicationnel: Tome 2, Pour une critique de la raison fonctionnaliste* (Paris: Fayard).

—— (1990) 'La crise de l'Etat-Providence et l'épuisement des énergies utopiques', in *Ecrits politiques* (Paris: Editions du Cerf) French translation.

Hagan, J. (1994) *Crime and Disrepute* (Thousand Oaks, California: Pine Oaks Press).

Hagan, J. and R. D. Peterson (eds) (1995) *Crime and Inequality* (Stanford: Stanford University Press).

Hall, R. (1978) *Black Separatism in the United States* (Hanover: University Press of New England).

—— (1988) 'New Ethnicities', in K. Mercer (ed.) *Black Film British Cinema: ICA Documents 7* (London: British Film Institute).

Hall, S. (1991) 'Old and New Identities, Old and New Ethnicities', in A. D. King (ed.) *Culture, Globalization and the World System* (London: Macmillan).

Hall, S. and Held, D. (1989) 'Citizens and Citizenship', in S. Hall and M. Jacques (eds) *New Times: The Changing Face of Politics in the 1990s* (London: Verso).

Hall, S., C. Critcher, T. Jefferson, J. Clarke and B. Roberts (1978) *Policing the Crisis: Mugging, the State and Law and Order* (London: Macmillan).

Hammar, T. (1990) *Democracy and the Nation-State*, Aldershot: Avebury

Hannerz, U. (1969) *Soulside: Inquiriers into Ghetto Culture and Community* (New York and London: Columbia University Press).

Hargreaves, A. G. (1996) 'The French Media and the "Banlieues"', *New Community*, 22 (4) 607–18.

Harvey, D. (1973) *Social Justice and the City* (Oxford: Basil Blackwell).

—— (1987) 'Flexible Accumulation through Urbanization: Reflexions on Post-modernism in the American City', *Antipode* (19) 260–80.

Häußermann, H. and W. Siebel (1993) 'Die Politik der Festivalisierung und die Festivalisierung der Politik: Große Ereignisse in der Stadtpolitik', in H. Häußermann and W. Siebel (eds) *Festivalisierung der Stadtpolitik. Stadtentwicklung durch große Projekte* (Berlin: Leviathan Soderheft).

Haut conseil à l'intégration (1991) *Pour un modèle français d'integration* (Paris: La Documentation Française).

Henkes, B. (1995) *Heimat in Holland: Duitse Dienstmeisjes, 1920–1950* (Amsterdam: Babylon–De Geus).

Heritage, J. (1984) *Garfinkel and Ethnomethodology* (Cambridge: Polity Press).

Hervieu-Leger, D. (1993) *La religion pour mémoire* (Paris: Editions du Cerf).

Hobsbawn, E. (1966) *Les primitifs de la révolte* (Paris: Fayard).

Holdaway, S. (1996) *The Racialisation of British Policing* (Basingstoke: Macmillan).

— (1997) 'Constructing and Sustaining "Race" within the Police Workforce', *The British Journal of Sociology*, 48 (1) 19–34.

Holdaway, S. and A.-M. Barron (1997) *Resigners? The Experience of Black and Asian Police Officers* (Basingstoke: Macmillan).

Hoolt, J. and D. Scholten (1996) *Etnische Groepen in Amsterdam: Jaarbericht 1996* (Amsterdam: Bureau for Strategic Minorities Policy).

Huysmans, J. (1995) 'Migrants as a Security Problem: Dangers of "Securitizing" Societal Issues', in Robert Miles and Dietrich Thränhardt (eds) *Migration and European Integration: The Dynamics of Inclusion and Exclusion* (London: Pinter) 53–72.

— (1997) 'European Identity and Migration Policies: Socio-economic and Security Questions in a Process of Europeanisation', *Political Science Working Papers No. 9* (Budapest: Central European University).

Ireland, P. (1994) *The Policy Challenge of Ethnic Diversity* (Cambridge, MA: Harvard University Press).

Jacquemet G. (1984) *Belleville au XIXème Siécle: Du faubourg à la ville* (Paris: Editions EHESS).

James, W. (1992) 'Migration, Racism and Identity: The Caribbean Experience in Britain', *New Left Review* (193) 15–55.

James, W. and C. Harris (eds) (1993) *Inside Babylon: The Caribbean Diaspora in Britain* (London: Verso).

Jargowsky, P. (1996) *Poverty and Place: Ghettos, Barrios and the American City* (New York: Russell Sage Foundation).

Jenkins, R. (1994) 'Rethinking Ethnicity: Identity, Categorization and Power', *Ethnic and Racial Studies*, 17 (2) 197–223.

Jenkins, S. et al. (ed.) (1988) *Ethnic Associations and the Welfare State: Services to Immigrants in Five Countries* (New York: Columbia University Press).

Joint Consultative Committee (1990) Operational Policing Review (Surbiton: Joint Consultative Committee).

Junger-Tas, J. (1997) 'Ethnic Minorities and Criminal Justice in the Netherlands', in M. Tonry (ed.) *Ethnicity, Crime and Immigration: Comparative and Cross-National Perspectives* (Chicago: University of Chicago Press).

Kappler, A. and S. Reichart (eds) (1996) *Facts about Germany*, (Frankfurt: Societäts-Verlag).

Kasarda, J. D., J. Friedrichs and K. Ehlers (1992) 'Urban Industrial Restructuring and Minority Problems in the US and West Germany', in M. Cross (ed.) *Ethnic Minorities and Economic Change in Europe and North America* (Cambridge: Cambridge University Press) 250–75.

Kehla, J., G. Engbersen and E. Snel (1997) *'Pier 80': Een Onderzoek naar Informaliteit op de Markt* (The Hague: Ministry of Social Affairs and Employment/VUGA Onderzoek in Opdracht van de Commissie Onderzoek Sociale Zekerheid).

Kelfaoui, S. (1996) 'Un "vote maghrébin" en France?' *Hérodote* (80) 130–55.

Kepel, G. (1984) *Les Banlieues de l'Islam* (Paris: Seuil).

Kerner Report (1968) *Advisory Committee on Civil Disorders* (London: Government Printing Office).

Kertzer, D. I. (1988) *Rituals, Politics and Power* (New Haven: Yale University Press).

Kesteloot, C. (1985) 'L'évolution du mode d'occupation des logements à Bruxelles, 1970–1981', *Revue Belge de Géographie*, 109 (4) 227–34.

—— (1995) 'The Creation of Socio-spatial Marginalisation in Brussels: A Tale of Flexibility, Geographical Competition and Guestworkers' Neighbourhoods', in C. Hadjimichalis and D. Sadler (eds) *Europe at the Margins: New Mosaics of Inequality* (Chichester: John Wiley) 69–85.

—— (1998) 'The Geography of Deprivation in Brussels and Local Development Strategies', in S. Musterd and W. Ostendorf (eds) *Urban Segregation and the Welfare State: Inequality and Exclusion in Wetsern Cities* (London: Routledge) 126–47.

Kesteloot, C., H. Vandenbroecke, H. van der Haegen, D. Vanneste and E. van Hecke (eds) (1996) *Atlas van Achtergestelde Buurten in Vlaanderen en Brussel* (Brussels: Ministerie van de Vlaamse Gemeenschap).

Kesteloot C., P. de Decker and A. Manço (1997) 'Turks and Housing in Belgium, with Special Reference to Brussels, Ghent and Visé', in S. Özüekren and R. van Kempen (eds) *Turks in European Cities: Housing and Urban Segregation* (Utrecht: European Research Centre on Migration and Ethnic Relations, Utrecht University) 67–97.

Kloosterman, R. C. (1994) 'Amsterdamned: The rise of Unemployment in Amsterdam in the 1980s', *Urban Studies*, 31 (8) 1325–44.

— (1996a) 'Mixed Experiences: Postindustrial Transition and Ethnic Minorities on the Amsterdam Labour Market', *New Community,* 22 (4) 637–53.

— (1996b) 'Double Dutch: Trends of Polarisation in Amsterdam and Rotterdam after 1980', *Regional Studies,* 30 (5) 367–76.

— (1998) 'Immigrant Entrepreneurship and the Welfare Stateí, in J. Rath (ed.) *Immigrant Businesses on the Urban Economic Fringe: A Case for Interdisciplinary Analysis* (Houndmills, Basingstoke, Hampshire: Macmillan Press).

Kloosterman, R. C., J. P. van der Leun and J. Rath (1997a) *De Economische Potenties van het Immigrantenondernemerschap in Amsterdam* (Amsterdam: Amsterdam Municipal Council and Department of Economics, University of Amsterdam).

— (1997b) *Over Grenzen. Immigranten en de Informele Economie* (Amsterdam: Het Spinhuis).

Kockelkorn, H. (1994) 'Allerbeste werkers: Joodse ondernemers in de grafische industrie', in H. Berg,. Wijsenbeek and E. Fischer (eds) *Venter, Fabriqueur, Fabrikant. Joodse Ondernemers en Ondernemingen in Nederland 1976–1940* (Amsterdam: Jewish Historical Museum) 130–45.

Koot, W. and P. Uniken Venema (1985) 'Etnisering en etnische belangenbehartiging: Een nieuw stijgingskanaal', *Migrantenstudies,* 1 (1) 4–16.

Kulbach, R. (1996) 'Ideen für eine integrative Stadtpolitik', in Forschungsinstitut der Friedrich-Ebert-Stiftung (ed.) *Integration und Konflikt. Kommunale Handlungsfelder der Zuwanderungspolitik* (Bonn) 35–48.

Kupers, R. H. (1995) *Albert Cuyp Wereldbazaar: Mogelijkheden om de Albert Cuyp en Omgeving Aantrekkelijker te Maken voor Allochtone Bezoekers en Toeristen* (MA thesis, Amsterdam: University of Amsterdam, Institute for Urban Planning and Demography)

Kupier, A. (1996) 'Les Médiateurs du Livre: analyse des activités', *Bulletin d'Informations de l'Association des Bibliothécaires de France* (170):

Kymlicka, W. (1995) *Multicultural Citizenship* (Oxford: Oxford University Press).

Laé, J. F. (1989) *Travailler au noir* (Paris: Métailier).

Laville, J.-L. (1994) 'Economie solidaire et Crise de l'Etat en Europe', *Lien Social et Politiques-RIAC* (32).

Layton Henry, Z. (1990) *The Political Rights of Migrant Workers in Western Europe* (London: Sage).

242   *References*

— (1992) *The Politics of Immigration* (Oxford: Blackwell).

Le Galès, P. and A. Bagnasco (eds) (1997) *Villes en Europe* (Paris: La Découverte).

Leman, J. (1997) 'Undocumented Migrants in Brussels: diversity and the anthropology of illegality', *New Community*, 25 (1) 25–41.

Lesthaeghe R. (1995) 'La Deuxième Transition démographique dans les Pays occidentaux: une Interprétation', *Actes de la Chair Quetelet* (Paris: L'Harmattan) 133–80.

Levi-Strauss, C. (1958) *Anthropologie structurale* (Paris: Plon).

Lewis, B. (1986) *Juifs en Terre d'Islam* (Paris: Calmann-Lévy).

Leydesdorff, S. (1987) *Wij Hebben als Mens Geleefd: Het Joodse Proletariaat van Amsterdam 1900–1940* (Amsterdam: Meulenhoff).

Lieberson, S. (1980) *A Piece of the Pie: Blacks and White Immigrants since 1880* (Berkeley: University of California Press)

Light, I. (1998) 'Globalization and Migration Networks', in J. Rath (ed.) *Immigrant Businesses on the Urban Economic Fringe* (Houndmills, Basingstoke, Hampshire: Macmillan Press).

Lindo, F. (1994) 'Het Stille Succes: De sociale stijging van Zuidewispese arbeidsmigranten in Nederland', in H. Vermeulen and R. Penninx (eds) *Het Democratisch Ongedudl: De Emancipatie en Integratie van Zes Doelgroepen van het Minderhedenbeleid* (Amsterdam: Het Spinhuis).

Live, Y. S. (1993) 'Les Asiatiques: immigrations et représentations', *Hommes et migrations* (1168).

Lowi T. (1977) *American Government, Incomplete Conquest* (Hillsdale, Illinois: Dryden Press).

Lucassen, J. (1997) 'Gilden und Wanderung: die Niederlande', in K. Schulz (ed.) *Verflechtungen des Europäischen Handwerks vom 14. bis zum 16. Jahrhundert* (Munich: Schriften des Historisches Kolles, Oldenbourg).

Lucassen, L. and R. Penninx (1994) *Nieuwkomers, Nakomelingen, Nederlanders. Immigranten in Nederland 1550–1993* (Amsterdam: Het Spinhuis).

Ma Mung, E. (1996) 'Non-lieu et utopie: la diaspora chinoise et le territoire', in George Prévélakis (ed.) *The Networks of Diasporas* (Paris: L'Harmattan) 205–14.

Ma Mung, E. and G. Simon (1990) *Commerçants maghrébins et asiatiques en France: Agglomération parisienne et villes de l'Est* (Paris: Masson).

McGregor, S. and A. Lipow (1995) *The Other City* (Humanities Press).

Maneri, M. (1997) 'Immigrati e classi pericolose: Lo statuto dell' "extracomunitario" nella stampa quotidiana', in M. Delle Donne (ed.) *Immigrazione-Integrazione: Stereotipi e Pregiudizi nelle Relazioni Etniche* (Rome: Edizioni Lavoro).

Manning, P. K. (1977) *Police at Work* (Cambridge: MIT Press).

Marshall, T. H. (1950) *Citizenship and Social Class* (Cambridge: Cambridge University Press).

Marshall-Goldschvartz, A. J. (1973) *The Import of Labour: The Case of The Netherlands* (Rotterdam: Rotterdam University Press).

Martens, P. L. (1997) 'Immigrants, Crime and Criminal Justice in Sweden', in M. Tonry (ed.) *Ethnicity, Crime and Immigration: Comparative and Cross-National Perspectives* (Chicago and London: The University of Chicago Press).

Martiniello, M. (1992) *Leadership et pouvoir dans les communautés d'origine immigrée* (Paris: CIEMI/L'Harmattan).

— (1993) 'Pour une sociologie politique de la situation post-migratoire en Belgique', in M. Martiniello and M. Poncelet (eds) *Migrations et minorités ethniques dans l'espace européen* (Brussels: De Boeck Université) 167–86.

— (1994) 'Citizenship of the European Union: A Critical View', in Rainer Bauböck (ed.) *From Aliens to Citizens: Redefining the Status of Citizens in Europe* (Aldershot: Avebury).

— (1996a) 'La Citoyenneté multiculturelle de l'Union européenne: Une Utopie postnationale', in M. Telo and P. Magnette (eds) *Repenser l'Europe* (Brussels: Éditions de l'Université de Bruxelles) 127–38.

— (1996b) *L'ethnicité dans les Sciences sociales contemporaines* (Paris: PUF)

— (1997) *Sortir des ghettos culturels* (Paris: Presses de Sciences Politiques, La Bibliothèque du Citoyen).

Mason, D. (1992) *Some Problems with the Concepts of Race and Racism* (Leicester: University of Leicester, Department of Sociology).

— (1994) 'On the Dangers of Disconnecting Race and Racism', *Sociology*, 28 (4) 845–58.

Medam A. (1995) *Blues Marseille* (Marseilles: Editions Jeanne Laffitte).

Meert, H. (1998) 'De geografie van het overleven: bestaansonzekere huishoudens en hun strategieën in een stedelijke en rurale context', unpublished Ph.D. thesis, Katholieke Universiteit Leuven, Leuven.

Meert, H., P. Mistiaen and C. Kesteloot (1997) 'The Geography of Survival in Different Urban Settings', *Tijdschrift voor Sociale en Economische Geografie*, 2 (88/2) 169–81.

Mehan, H. and H. Wood (1975) *The Reality of Ethnometodhology* (New York: Wiley).

Memmi, A. (1974) *Juifs et Arabes* (Paris: Idées/Gallimard).

Merriman, J. M. (1994) *Aux marges de la ville: Faubourgs et banlieues en France 1815–1870* (Paris: Seuil).

Michel, P. (1996) *Politique et Religion: la grande mutation* (Paris: Albin Michel).

Miellet, R. L. (1987) 'Immigratie van katholieke Westfalers en de modernisering van de Nederlandse detailhandel', *Tijdschrift voor Geschiedenis* (100) 374–93.

Miles, R. (1982) *Racism and Migrant Labour* (London: Routledge & Kegan Paul).

Miles, R. (1989) *Racism* (London: Routledge).

Miller, M. (1981) *Foreign Workers in Western Europe: An Emerging Political Force* (New York: Praeger).

Mingione, E. (1991) *Fragmented Societies: A Sociology of Work Beyond the Market Paradigm* (Oxford: Basil Blackwell).

Ministerium für Arbeit, Gesundheit und Soziales des Landes Nordrhein-Westfalen (1994) *Landessozialbericht. Band 9: Ausländerinnen und Ausländer in Nordrhein-Westfalen. Die Lebenslage der Menschen aus den ehemaligen Anwerbeländern und die Handlungsmöglichkeiten der Politik* (Düsseldorf: Ministerium für Arbeit, Gesundheit und Soziales des Landes Nordrhein-Westfalen).

Minow, M. (1997) *Not Only for Myself: Identity, Politics and Law* (New York: The New Press).

Mistiaen P., H. Meert and C. Kesteloot (1995) 'Polarisation socio-spatiale et stratégies de survie dans deux quartiers bruxellois', *Espace-Populations-Sociétés* (3) 277–90.

Moch, L. (1992) *Moving Europeans: Migration in Western Europe Since 1650* (Bloomington: Indiana University Press).

Model, S. (1993) 'The Ethnic Niche and the Structure of Opportunity: Immigrants and Minorities in New York City', in M. Katz (ed.) *The 'Underclass' Debate: Views from History* (Princeton, NJ: Princeton University Press).

Modood, T. et al. (1997) *Ethnic Minorities in Britain: Diversity and Disadvantage* (London: Policy Studies Institute).

Mollenkopf, J. (1997a) *Hollow in the Middle: The Rise and Fall of New York City's Middle Class* (New York: Report to the New York City Council) December.

—— (1997b) 'Changing Patterns of Inequalities in New York City' (paper presented at the International Sociological Association meeting in Berlin).

Mollenkopf, J. and M. Castells (1991) *Dual City: Restructuring New York* (New York: Russell Sage Foundation).

Moore, J. (1997) *Positive Action in Action: Equal Opportunities and Declining Opportunities in Merseyside* (Aldershot: Ashgate Press).

Morokvasic, M., A. Phizacklea and H. Rudolph (1986) 'Small Firms and Minority Groups: Contradictory Trends in the French, German and British Clothing Industries', *International Sociology*, 1 (4) December, 397–419.

Moynihan, D. (1965) *The Negro Family: The Case for National Action* (Washington: United States Department of Labor).

Nader, L. (n.d.) 'The ADR Explosion: The Implication of Rhetoric in Legal Reform', typescript.

National Commission on Law Observance and Enforcement (1931) *Crime and the Foreign Born* (Washington: US Government Printing Office).

Neveu, C. (1993) *Communauté, nationalité et citoyenneté: De l'autre côté du miroir: les Bangladeshis de Londres* (Paris: Karthala).

Ni Brolchain, M. (1990) 'The Ethnicity Question for the 1991 Census: Background and Issues, *Ethnic and Racial Studies*, 13 (4) 542–67.

Noorman, J. (1994) 'Städtische Minderheitenpolitik in Frankfurt/M: Lösungsansatz für institutionell bedingte Kooperations-und Leistungsdefizite', in M. M. Jansen and S. Baringhorst (eds) *Politik der Multikultur: Vergleichende Perspektiven zu Einwanderung und Integration*, (Baden-Baden).

Obadia, A. (ed.) (1997) *Entreprendre la ville* (La Tour d'Aigues: Editions de l'Aube)

OECD (1995) *Labour Force Statistics 1973–1993* (Paris: OECD).

Olzak, S. (1983) 'Contemporary Ethnic Mobilization', *Annual Review of Sociology* (9) 355–74.

Olzak, S and J. Nagel (1986) *Competitive Ethnic Relations* (New York: Academic Press).

Ory, P. (1994) 'Paris, lieu de création et de légitimation internationales', in A. Marès and P. Milza (eds) *Le Paris des étrangers depuis 1945* (Paris: Publications de la Sorbonne).

Palidda, S. (1994) 'Polizia e domanda di sicurezza a Milano', in M. Pavarini (ed.) *I nuovi confini della penalità* (Parma: Pratiche Editrice).

—— (1995) 'Devianza e criminalità', in Fondazione Cariplo-ISMu, *Primo rapporto sulle migrazioni 1995* (Milan: Franco Angeli).

—— (ed.) (1997) *Délit d'Immigration: Immigrant Delinquency* (European Commission, COST A2).

Panafit, L. (1997) 'Les Problématiques de l'Institutionalisation de l'Islam en Belgique (1965–1996)', in F. Dassetto (ed.) (1997) *Facettes de l'Islam belge* (Brussels: Academia-Bruylant) 254–69.

Parekh, B. (1991) 'British Citizenship and Cultural Difference', in G. Andrews (ed.) *Citizenship* (London: Lawrence & Wishart).

Park, R. E. (1925) 'The City: Suggestions for the Investigation of Human Behavior in the Urban Environment', in R. E. Park, E. Burgess and M. McKenzie, *The City* (Chicago: University of Chicago Press).

Pastore, M. (1995) 'Produzione normativa e costruzione sociale della devianza e criminalità tra gli immigrati', *Quaderni ISMU* (9/95).

Penninx, R. (1979) 'Naar een algemeen etnisch minderhedenbeleid? Schets van de sociale positie in Nederland van Molukkers, Surinaamse en Antilliaanse Nederlanders en mediterrane werknemers en een inventarisatie van het Nederlandse overheidsbeleid: Voorstudie', in WRR, *Etnische Minderheden* (The Hague: Government Publishing Office, Rapporten aan de Regering 17) 1–174.

Penninx, R. and L. van Velzen (1977) *Internationale arbeidsmigratie: Uitstoting uit 'thuislanden' en maatschappelijke integratie in 'gastlanden' van buitenlandse arbeiders* (Nijmegen: SUN, Sunschrift 124).

Péraldi, M. et al. (1995) 'Le marché des pauvres, espace commercial et espace public', *Revue Européenne des Migrations Internationales*, 11 (1) 77–98.

Perez Commissaire (1995) *La Cité interdite* (Paris: unpublished report).

Pessar, P. R. (ed.) (1997) *Caribbean Circuits: New Directions in the Study of Caribbean Migration* (New York: Center for Migration Studies).

Pfohl, S. (1985) *Images of Deviance and Social Control: A Sociological History* (New York: McGraw Hill).

Piore, M. (1979) *Birds of Passage: Migrant Labour and Industrial Societies* (Cambridge: Cambridge University Press).

Polanyi, K. (1944) *The Great Transformation* (New York: Rinehart).

Portes, A. (1981) 'Modes of Structural Incorporation and Present Theories of Labor Immigration', in M. Kritz, C. Keeley and S. M. Tomasi (eds) *Global Trends in Migraiton: Theory and Research on International Population Movements* (New York: Center for Migration Studies) pp. 279–97.

—— (ed.) (1995) *The Economic Sociology of Immigration: Essays on Networks, Ethnicity and Entrepreneurship* (New York: Russell Sage Foundation).

Portes, A. and J. Sensenbrenner (1993) 'Embeddedness and Immigration: Notes on the Social Determinants of Economic Actioní, *American Journal of Sociology*, 98 (6) 1320–50.

Préteceille, E. (1998) *Division sociale et Services urbains*, vol. 1. *Inégalités et contrastes sociaux en Ile de France* (Paris: Iresco).

Puskeppeleit, J. and D. Thränhardt (1990) *Vom Betreuen Ausländer zum gleichberechtigten Bürger: Perspektiven der Beratung und Sozialarbeit, der Selbsthilfe und Artikulation und der Organisation und Integration der eingewanderten Ausländer aus den Anwerbestaaten in der Bundesrepublik* (Freiburg).

Pryce, K. (1979) *Endless Pressure* (Harmondsworth: Penguin).

Raes, S. (1996) 'De Nederlandse kledingindustrie en het mediterrane gebied: Migrerende bedrijven en migranten ondernemers', *Sharqiyy, t*, 8 (2) 143–65.

Rath, J. (1988) 'Political Action of Immigrants in the Netherlands. Class or Ethnicity?', *European Journal of Political Research*, 16 (6) November, 623–44 (Special issue on 'Immigration and Politics' edited by Z. Layton-Henry).

——(1991) *Minorisering: de Sociale Constructie van Etnische Minderheden* (Ph.D. thesis, University of Utrecht).

——(1993) 'Les Immigrés aux Pays-Bas', in O. le Cour Grandmaison and C. Withol de Wenden, *Les Étrangers dans la Cité: Expériences européennes* (Paris: La Découverte) 138–48.

——(ed.) (1998a) *Immigrant Businesses on the Urban Economic Fringe: A Case for Interdisciplinary Analysis* (Basingstoke: Macmillan Press).

——(1998b) 'The Informal Economy as Bastard Sphere of Social Integration', in E. Eichenhofer and P. Marschalck (eds) *Migration und Illegalität* (Osnabrück: Universitätsverlag Rasch).

Rath, J. and R. Kloosterman (eds) (1998) *Rijp en Groen: Het Zelfstandig Ondernemerschap van Immigranten in Nederland* (Amsterdam: Het Spinhuis).

Rath, J., R. Penninx, K. Groenendijk and A. Meyer (1996) *Nederland en zijn Islam. Een Ontzuilende Samenleving Reageert op het Ontstaan van een Geloofsgemeenschap* (Amsterdam: Het Spinhuis).

Rattansi, A. (1992) 'Changing the Subject? Racism, Culture and Education', in J. Donald and A. Rattansi (eds) *'Race', Culture and Difference* (London: Sage).

Raulin A. (1986) 'Mise en scène des commerces maghrébins parisiens', *Terrain* (7).

——(1988) 'Espaces marchands et Concentrations urbaines minoritaires: La petite Asie de Paris', *Cahiers Internationaux de Sociologie* (85).

Rekers, A. M. (1993) 'A Tale of Two Cities: A Comparison of Turkish Enterprises in Amsterdam and Rotterdam', in D. Crommentuyn-

Ondaatje (ed.) *Nethur School Proceedings 1992* (Utrecht: Nethur) 45–66.

Rex, J. (1973) *Race, Colonialism and the City* (London: Routledge & Kegan Paul).

—— (1985) *The Concept of a Multicultural Society* (Warwick: Occasional Papers in Ethnic Relations N°3, Centre for Research in Ethnic Relations).

—— (1991) *Ethnic Identity and Ethnic Mobilisation in Britain* (Warwick: Monographs in Ethnic Relations N°5, Centre for Research in Ethnic Relations).

—— (1994) 'Ethnic Mobilisation in Britain', *Revue Européenne des Migrations Internationales*, 10 (1) 7–31.

Rex, J., D. Joly and C. Wilpert (1987) *Immigrant Associations in Europe* (Aldershot: Gower).

Rey, H. (1996) *La Peur des Banlieues* (Paris: Presses de Sciences Politiques).

Roberts, B. (1994) 'Informal Economy and Family Strategies', *International Journal of Urban and Regional Research*, 18 (1) 6–23, special edited by B. Roberts.

Roland, C. (1962) *Du ghetto à l'occident, deux générations de Yiddisches en France* (Paris: Ed. de Minuit).

Room, G. (ed.) (1995) *Beyond the Threshold* (Bristol: The Policy Press).

Rouse, Roger (1991) 'Mexican Migration and the Social Space of Postmodernism', *Diaspora*, 1 (1) 8–23.

Rutherford, J. (ed.) (1990) *Identity: Community, Culture, Difference* (London: Lawrence & Wishart).

Sachs, B. (1997) 'Je suis un jeune qui habite Montreuil', *Informations sociales*, 62, 4–15.

Sacks, H. (1972) 'Notes on Police Assessment of Moral Character', in Turner (eds) *Studies in Social interaction* (New York: The Free Press) 280–93.

Safran, W. (1991) 'Diasporas in Modern Societies: Myths of Homeland and Return', *Diaspora*, 1 (1) 83–95.

Saggar, S. (ed.) (1998) *Race and British Electoral Politics* (London: UCL Press).

Saïdi, A. and J. Aghion (1987) 'L'Islam à Liège', *Tribune Immigrée*, (21) 88–9.

Saint-Blancat, C. (1995) 'Une Diaspora musulmane en Europe?' *Archives de Sciences sociales des Religions*, 92 (October–December) 9–24.

Sampson, R., S. Raudenbush and F. Earls (1997) 'Neighborhoods and

Violent Crime: A Multilevel Study of Collective Efficacy', *Science*, 277, 918–24

Sanguinetti, A. (1991) (ed.) *Le livre blanc sur les droits de l'homme au Maroc* (Paris: EDI/Ligue des droits de l'homme).

Sassen, S. (1988) The Mobility of Labour and Capital: A Study in International Investment and Labor *Flow* (Cambridge/New York: Cambridge University Press).

—— (1991) *The Global City: New York, London, Tokyo* (Princeton, NJ: Princeton University Press).

Sayad, A. (1977) 'Les trois âges de l'émigration algérienne en France', *Actes de la Recherche en Sciences Sociales*, (15).

—— (1991) *L'Immigration ou les Paradoxes de l'Altérité* (Bruxelles: De Boeck).

—— (1997) 'L'Immigration et la "pensée d'État": Reflexions sur la double peine', in S. Palidda (ed.) *Délit d'immigration: Immigrant delinquency* (European Commision, COST A2).

Scarman, Lord (1981) *The Brixton Disorders* (London: HMSO).

Schain, M. (1994) 'Ordinary Politics: Immigrants, Direct Action and the Political Process in France', *French Politics and Society*, 12 (2 and 3), Spring/Summer, 65–83.

Schmitt, H. (1996) 'Aufgaben und Funktionen des Ausländerbeauftragten', in Forschungsinstitut der Friedrich-Ebert-Stiftung (ed.) *Integration und Konflikt: Kommunale Handlungsfelder der Zuwanderungspolitik* (Bonn) 85–92.

Schoeneberg, U. (1983) 'Participation in Ethnic Associations: The Case of Immigrants in West Germany', *International Migration Review*, XIX (3) 416–35.

Schrover, M. (1994) -"Gij zult het bokje niet koken in de melk zijner moeder": Joodse ondernemers in de voedingsen genotmiddelenindustrie', in H. Berg, T. Wijsenbeek and E. Fischer (eds) *Venter, Fabriqueur, Fabrikant: Joodse Ondernemers en Ondernemingen in Nederland 1976–1940* (Amsterdam: Jewish Historical Museum) 160–90.

—— (1996) 'Omlopers in Keulse potten en pottentrienen uit het Westerwald', in M. Hart, J. Lucassen and H. Schmal (eds) *Nieuwe Nederlanders. Vestiging van Migranten door de Eeuwen Heen* (Amsterdam: Stichting Beheer /Instituut voor Maatschappijwetenschappen) 101–20.

Schulze, G. (1994) 'Jenseits der Erlebnisgesellschaft: Zur Neudefinition von Solidaritaet', *Gewerkschaftliche Monatshefte*, (6) 337–43.

Schuster, J. (1998) *Poortwachters over Immigranten*, Ph.D. thesis, Utrecht University.

Schutz, A. (1967) *Collected Papers 1: The Problem of Social Reality* (The Hague: Martinus Nijhoff).

Segre, S. (1993) 'Immigrazione extracomunitaria e delinquenza giovanile: Un'analisi sociologica', *Studi Emigrazione* (111) 384–415.

Shaw, C. and H. McKay (1942) *Juvenile Delinquency and Urban Areas* (Chicago: University of Chicago Press).

Shaw, M. and D. Riley (1985) *Parental Supervision and Juvenile Delinquency* (London: HMSO).

Shearing, C. and R. Ericson (1991) 'Culture as Figurative Action', *The British Journal of Sociology*, 42 (4) 481–506.

Sheffer, G. (1996) 'Wither the Study of Ethnic Diasporas? Some Theoretical, Definitional, Analytical and Comparative Considerations', in George Prévélakis (ed.) *The Networks of Diasporas* (Paris: L'Harmattan) 37–46

Silbey, S. and A. Sarat (1989) 'Dispute Processing in Law and Legal Scholarship: From Institutional Critique to the Reconstruction of the Juridical Subject', *Denver University Law Review*, 66 (3).

Simmel, G. (1971) *On Individuality and Social Forms: Selected Writings*, edited by Donald N. Levine (Chicago: University of Chicago Press).

——(1955) *Conflict and the Web of Group-Affiliations*, 1st edn 1922, translated by K. H. Wolff and R. Bendix (Glencoe: The Free Press).

Simon, P. (1993) 'Les quartiers d'immigration: "ports de première entrée" ou espaces de sédentarisation? L'exemple de Belleville', *Espace, Populations, Sociétés* (2) 379–88.

Simon, P. and C. Tapia (1998) *Juifs tunisiens à Belleville: chronique d'une intégration* (Paris: Autrement).

Skogan, W. G. (1990a) *Disorder and Decline* (Berkeley: University of California Press).

——(1990b) *The Police and Public in England and Wales* (London: HMSO).

Smeets, H. M. A. G. (1993) *Etnische Minderheden bij de Overheid. Faalen Slaagfactoren bij Positieve-Actiebeleid* (Rotterdam: ISEO, Erasmus University of Rotterdam).

Smith, D. J. (1997) 'Ethnic Origins, Crime and Criminal Justice in England and Wales', in M. Tonry (ed.) *Crime and Justice* (Chicago: University of Chicago Press) 101–82.

Smith, M. P. and J. R. Feagin (eds) (1995) *The Bubbling Couldron: Race, Ethnicity and the Urban Crisis* (Minneapolis: University of Minnesota Press).

——(eds) *The Bubbling Cauldron* (Minneapolis: University of Minnesota Press).

Solomos, J. and L. Back (1995) *Race, Politics and Social Change* (London: Routledge).

Stack C. (1977) *All Our Kin: Strategies for Survival in a Black Community* (New York: Harper & Row).

Staring, R. (1998) 'International Migration, Undocumented Immigrants And Immigrant Entrepreneurship', in J. Rath (ed.) *Immigrant Businesses on the Urban Economic Fringe: A Case for Interdisciplinary Analysis* (Houndmills, Basingstoke, Hampshire: Macmillan Press).

Steinberg, S. (1995) *Turning Back: The Retreat from Social Justice in American Thought and Policy* (Boston: Beacon Press).

Strudel, S. (1996) *Votes Juifs: Itinéraires migratoires, religieux et politiques* (Paris: Presses de Sciences Politiques).

Sudnow, D. (1965) 'Normal Crimes', *Social Problems* (12) 255–62, 264–72.

Suttles G. (1968) *The Social Order of the Slum* (Chicago: University of Chicago Press).

Szakolczai, A. (1992) 'On the Exercise of Power in Modern Societies, East and West', *EUI Working Papers in Political and Social Sciences. No. 92/22* (Florence: European University Institute).

Taboada-Leonetti, I. (1989) 'Cohabitation pluri-ethnique dans la ville: stratégies d'insertion locale et phénomènes identitaires', *Revue Européenne des Migrations Internationales*, 5 (2) 51–69.

Tarrius, A. (1995) *Arabes de France dans l'économie mondiale souterraine* (La Tour d'Aigues: Editions de l'Aube).

Taylor, R. (1996) 'Political science encounters "race" and "ethnicity"', *Ethnic and Racial Studies*, 19 (4) 884–95.

Taylor, S. (1982) *Durkheim and the Study of Suicide* (New York: St Martin's Press).

The, A. M. (1989) 'Indochinese artsenfamilies in Nederland', *Migrantenstudies*, 5 (2) 18–31.

Thompson, B. (1983) 'Social Ties and Ethnic Settlement Patterns', in W. C. Mc Cready (ed.) *Culture, Ethnicity and Identity: Current Issues in Research* (Chicago: Academic Press).

Thränhardt, D. (1987) 'Einwanderer in bundesdeutschen Kommunen', in H. E. Fuchs and H. Wollmann (eds) *Hilfen für ausländische Kinder und Jugendliche. Wege aus dem gesellschaftlichen Abseits?* (Basel) 98–115.

Tillie, J. (1994) *Kleurrijk kiezen: Opkomst en stemgedrag van migranten tijdens de gemeenteraadsverkiezingen van 2 maert 1994* (Utrecht: Nederlands Centrum Buitenlanders).

Tonry, M. (1997) 'Ethnicity, Crime and Immigration', in M. Tonry (ed.)

Ethnicity, Crime and Immigration: Comparative and Cross-National Perspectives (Chicago and London: The University of Chicago Press) 1–30.

Toubon, J-C. and K. Messamah (1991) *Centralité immigrée: Le quartier de la Goutte d'Or* (Paris: L'Harmattan/CIEMI).

Tribalat, M. (1995) *Faire France* (Paris: Découverte).

Tribalat, M. et al. (1995) *Enquête Mobilité géographique et Insertion sociale: Rapport final* (Paris: INED).

Valensi L. (1986) 'La Tour de Babel: Groupes et Relations ethniques au Moyen-Orient et en Afrique du Nord', *Annales ESC* (4).

van Amersfoort, J. M. M. (1973) 'De Surinamers', in J. M. M. van Amersfoort (ed.) *Allochtonen in Nederland: Beschouwingen over de gerepatrieerden, Molukkers, Surinamers, Antillianen, buitenlandse werknemers, Chinezen, vluchtelingen, buitenlandse studenten in onze samenleving*, 1st edn 1971 (The Hague: Government Publishing Office) 145–77.

van den Eende, M. and A. Martens (1994) *De Noordwijk, de Herhuisvesting van de Uitgewezenen* (Berchem: EPO).

van der Valk, I. (1996) *Van Migratie naar Burgerschap: Twintig Jaar Komitee Marokkaanse Arbeiders in Nederland* (Amsterdam: Instituut voor Publiek en Politiek).

van der Wee, H. (1987) *Prosperity and Upheaval: The World Economy 1945–1980* (Berkeley: University of California Press) 518ff.

van Dijk, T. A. (1991) *Racism and the Press* (London: Routledge).

van Heek, F. (1936) *Chineesche Immigranten in Nederland* (Amsterdam: J. Emmering's Uitgevers Mij).

Vandermotten, C. (1994) 'Le Plan Régional de Développement de la Région de Bruxelles-capitale', in C. Vandermotten (ed.) *Planification et Stratégies de Développement dans les Capitales européennes* (Brussels: Edition de l'Université de Bruxelles) 195–206.

Veenman, J. (1994) *Participatie in perspectief: Ontwikkelingen in de sociaal-economische positie van zes allochtone groepen in Nederland* (Houten/Zaventem/Lelystad: Bohn Stafleu Van Loghum/Koninklijke Vermande).

Vermeulen, H., M. van Attekum, F. Lindo and T. Pennings (1985) *De Grieken* (Muiderberg: Coutinho, nr. 3).

Vescovi, E. (1983) 'Le Règlement des Conflits hors des Tribunaux', in H. Kotz and R. Ottenhof, *Les Conciliateurs–La Conciliation: une étude compartative* (Paris: Economica).

von Beyme, K. (1994) 'Politikverdrossenheit und Politikwissenschaft', in Claus Leggewie (ed.) *Wozu Politikwissenschaft? Über das Neue in der Politik* (Darnstadt) 49–60.

Wacquant L. J. D. (1994) 'Protection, discipline et honneur: une salle de boxe dans le ghetto américain', (unpublished paper) July.

Waddington, P. A. J. (1984) 'Black Crime, the 'Racist' Police and Fashionable Compassion', in D. Anderson (ed.) *The Kindness That Kills* (London: Society for Promoting Christian Knowledge).

— (1986) 'Mugging as a Moral Panic', *British Journal of Sociology*, 37 (2) 37–46.

Wæver, O. (1995) 'Securitization and Desecuritization', in Ronnie Lipschutz (ed.) *On Security* (New York: Columbia University Press) 46–86.

Waldinger, R. (1995) 'The "Other Side" of Embeddedness. A Case-Study of the Interplay of Economy and Ethnicityí, *Ethnic and Racial Studies* (18) 555–79.

— (1996) *Still the Promised City? African-Americans and New Immigrants in Postindustrial New York* (Cambridge, MA: Harvard University Press).

Waldinger, R. and M. Bozorgmehr (eds) (1996) *Ethnic Los Angeles* (New York: Russell Sage Foundation).

Webber, M. (1963) 'Order in Diversity: Community without Propinquity', in Wingo Lowdon (ed.) *Cities and Space: The Future Uses of Urban Land* (Baltimore: Johns Hopkins Press) 23–54,

Werbner, P. (1990) *The Migration Process: Capital, Gifts and Offerings among British Pakistanis* (Oxford, Berg).

— (1991) 'Black and Ethnic Leadership in Britain: A Theoretical Overview', in P. Werbner and M. Anwar (eds.) *Black and Ethnic Leaderships: The Cultural Dimension of Political Action* (London: Routledge).

White, D. (1994) 'La Gestion communautaire de l'Exclusion', *Lien Social et Politiques-RIAC* (32).

Wieder, D. L. (1974) *Language and Social Reality: The Case of Telling the Convict Code* (Paris: Mouton).

Wilson, K. and A. Portes (1980) 'Immigrant Enclaves: An Analysis of the Labor Market Experience of Cubans in Miami', *American Journal of Sociology* (86) 295–319.

Wilson, W. J. (1996) *When Work Disappears: The World of the New Urban Poor* (New York: Alfred A. Knopf Incorporated).

Winant, H. (1995) 'Dictatorship, Democracy and Difference: The Historical Construction of Racial Identity', in M. P. Smith and J. Faegin (eds) *The Bubbling Cauldron* (Minneapolis: University of Minnesota Press).

Withol de Wenden, C. (1977) 'La représentation des immigrés en Europe', *Recherches sur les migrations* (5–6) 1–23.

254 *References*

— (1978) *Les Immigrés dans la Cité* (Paris: La Documentation française).

— (1988) *Les Immigrés et la Politique* (Paris: Presses de la Fondation Nationale des Sciences Politiques).

Withol de Wenden, C. and A. Hargreaves (1993) 'The Political Participation of Ethnic Minorities in Europe: A Framework for Analysis', *New Community* (guest editor's introduction) 20 (1) 1–8.

Wrench, J. and J. Solomos (eds) (1993) *Racism and Migration in Western Europe* (Oxford: Berg).

Wyvekens, A. (1995) 'L'Analyse des activité des Maisons de Justice et du Droit du Tribunal de Grande Instance de Lyon' (ERPC, Université de Montpellier I).

Young, I. M. (1990) *Justice and the Politics of Difference* (Princeton: Princeton University Press).

Zentrum für Türkeistudien (1989) *Türkische Unternehmensgründungen – Von der Nische zum Markt? Ergebnisse einer Untersuchung bei türkischen Selbständigen in Dortmund, Duisburg und Essen* (Opladen: Westdeutscher Verlag).

Zolberg, A. R. (1995) 'Response: Working-Class Dissolution', *International Labor and Working-Class History*, 47 (Spring) 28–38.

Index

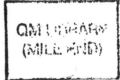